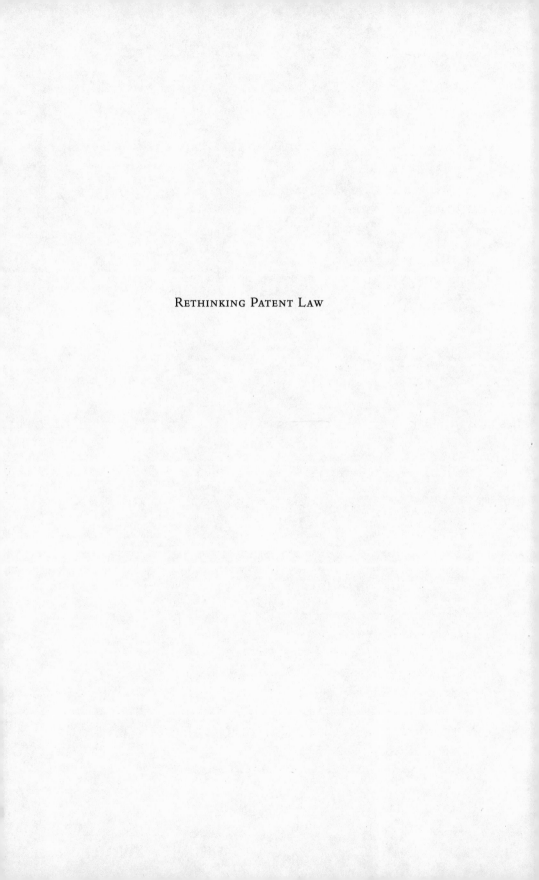

RETHINKING PATENT LAW

# Rethinking Patent Law

## Robin Feldman

HARVARD UNIVERSITY PRESS

Cambridge, Massachusetts, and London, England 2012

*Library of Congress Cataloging-in-Publication Data*

Feldman, Robin.
Rethinking patent law / Robin Feldman.
p. cm.
Includes bibliographical references and index.
ISBN 978-0-674-06468-3 (alk. paper)
1. Patent laws and legislation—United States.   I.  Title.
KF3114.F38 2012
346.7304'86—dc23      2011041720

*This book is dedicated to my husband, Boris, and our children,*
*Natalie, Talya, Eli, Sam, and Adam*

# Contents

# Introduction

Patent law has all too often languished in the back rooms of academia. Viewed as unimportant by some and impenetrable by others, patent law rarely receives the type of attention lavished on perennial favorites such as constitutional law, international human rights law, or even, in the modern world of music downloading and Internet videos, copyright law. A confluence of recent events, however, is bringing patent law into the limelight, highlighting contradictions that have remained hidden for some time in the obscurity of patent law's arcane code and its isolated brethren. Gone are the days when the Supreme Court took few, if any, patent cases. In recent years the Court has accepted numerous patent cases, generally overturning the logic of the court below.[1] High-profile patent cases have drawn the attention of the public and media as well. For example, much of the nation was transfixed as a highly technical patent case threatened to shut down the popular Blackberry telephone and Internet device. Those poor souls addicted to what is colloquially known as the "CrackBerry" waited with great trepidation to see whether the device they depended on so desperately would go dark.

In a similar vein, newspapers have carried numerous articles commenting on the modern phenomenon of the "patent troll," an enterprise that produces no products but simply buys or develops patents with the intent of going after successful companies whose products may infringe something in the troll's portfolio.

The public spectacle has continued with cases like *Association for Molecular Pathology v. United States Patent & Trademark Office,* concerning patent rights related to testing for a genetic predisposition to certain types of breast cancer.[2] A group of parties challenged the patents, claiming that patents on genes and related inventions should be declared invalid. Publicity in the case featured civil rights advocates arguing that "too much patent protection can, in fact, trample our civil liberties" and poor women explaining that they were unable to afford the expensive test.[3] The lower court decision, which is currently on appeal, threatens to unwind thirty years of patent law related to genetic inventions.

Even the pope wants to talk about patents. In a recent encyclical letter, Pope Benedict XVI took a firm stand against strong patent protection, chiding wealthy nations for rigid and excessive zeal in the assertion of rights, particularly in the field of health care.[4] One knows that an area of legal doctrine has truly arrived when it attracts papal attention.

The modern spotlight on patents is generating increasing interest in this once-forgotten field. This remarkable moment in history provides an opportunity to consider significant shifts in our understanding of patents.

This book argues that we should begin this exploration of patent law by fundamentally rethinking our image of patents in the following manner. It is axiomatic in patent law that the patent defines the rights that have been granted. Patents are frequently described as setting out the "metes and bounds" of the inventor's rights, analogous to the way in which boundary lines delineate the extent of a piece of land. This image of patents infuses patent law and drives both patent doctrine and theoretical debates. The notion that a patent defines the rights is so deeply ingrained in patent law that it would be unthinkable to suggest anything different. That, however, is exactly what I intend to do.

This book suggests that the entire conceptualization of patents as establishing the boundaries of the rights granted is simply wrong. Rather than delineating a patent holder's rights, a patent creates no more than an opportunity to bargain. It is an invitation to enter into the process of negotiating a definition of rights. One can think of this conceptualization as the bargain aspect of patents.

In my view, the bargain aspect is true both as a matter of how patents actually work in the modern world and as a matter of necessity. In other words, not only does the modern American patent system operate this way, but it would also be quite difficult for the system to operate in any other way.[5] Among other reasons, patents cannot possibly delineate the boundary of an inventor's rights because those rights will be established in relation to products that have yet to be created at the time of the patent grant. One cannot create definitive measurements at a time when the tools of measurement do not yet exist.[6]

With ordinary property, we may wrangle over its value, and we may wrangle over rights in relation to it. Nevertheless, we do have some sense of what the "it" is. With patents, the contours are established individually— each time and for each patent. Moreover, they are established in the face of rapidly changing knowledge and meaning. Words, which by nature are subject to great swings of interpretation, are chosen to describe an invention that by definition did not exist before and that will be compared against things that may not exist when the words are chosen. Taken together, this set of circumstances ensures that a patent could never grant a definitive and clearly bounded set of rights. Rather, a patent grants some form of an opportunity—a seat at the bargaining table, with certain rules in place. The contours of what the patent holder ultimately receives will be determined by certain factors, including the nature of those against whom the bargaining proceeds and the serendipitous element of what products emerge during the term of the patent.

One might imagine that problems of rapidly changing knowledge and meaning are modern problems. After all, modern fields such as genetics and nanotechnology are moving at a breathtaking pace, constantly pressing the bounds of what we thought we knew and understood. Perhaps a few modern fields are causing all of the problems.

One must remember, however, that what is understandable and recognizable to us today seemed bold and new to our predecessors. Consider one of the seminal American patent cases, decided in 1853. The case concerned that wonderful newfangled mode of communication, the telegraph, and its strange companion alphabet of dots and dashes.[7] In defining the reach of the patent, the Supreme Court had to contemplate the definition of this method of information transfer, known by its inventor as "electro-magnetism." What fell within the invention, and what fell outside of it? What part should be considered unpatentable scientific principles, and what part should be considered a patentable application of those principles? Such questions are no different from what a modern genetics case must grapple with. In short, those things that are new have the potential to challenge our ability to define them, no matter what period of history one examines.

As a result, from a theoretical perspective, it is unlikely that patents could define the extent of the rights granted. From a practical perspective as well, the modern American patent system does not operate as if the patent defines the rights. For example, those who draft patents try to place a series of tools within the language that they can choose among, long after the patent has been issued. At the time of application, and even when the patent issues, there is no way to know what technologies will develop, what markets will develop, and how a particular patent will be useful. In addition, patent language is malleable, particularly in the face of evolving technology. One cannot know how a patent will be interpreted by the courts. Patent holders must have a library of possible terms they can choose among as markets, licensing negotiations, and court cases advance.

In addition, the practical footprint of a patent holder's rights generally develops during licensing interactions, and these involve much more than simply presenting one's patent and pointing to the language of the claim. The reach of a particular patent's language may depend on factors related to the size of the company, its position relative to others with whom it must negotiate, and the company's other assets. For example, the ideal way to assert one's patent is against someone who holds no counterweapons. If you make telephones but also hold a patent on coffee machines, you can approach coffee manufacturers without worrying about what patents they will throw back at you. The same is true if you have a small amount of revenue. Low revenue can make you a less appealing target for a patent countercharge, given that infringement damages would be minimal. Interactions like these are anticipated and planned for from the first moment of a patent application.

Patent holders also use contracts to try to construe claims in different fashions. For example, contract drafters can choose to draft a license that either permits a particular set of uses or grants rights to anything under the patent. If one chooses to license for particular uses, one is in essence contractually construing the claims. Consider an analogy from copyright regarding outrage over the Google Books settlement.[8] The settlement resolved a dispute between Google and organizations representing authors and publishers over Google's project to electronically scan all existing books. Part of the concern was that the complicated settlement agreement, once in place, would establish rules that would govern the market interaction and might prove difficult to dislodge, regardless of what alternative legal interpretations might have been available.

All of this must be understood in the context that the extent of the rights cannot truly be known until the day that the patent expires. Only then are we likely to know how the various broader and narrower claims stood up when tested and how the market that might provide licensing targets developed.

One could argue that the image of the patent system presented in this chapter reflects nothing more than flaws in the system. Perhaps the bargaining flows from our legal system's inability to develop clear rules, particularly those related to interpretation of patent claims.[9] Perhaps certain structural elements in our court system are less than optimal,[10] or perhaps the way we grant and prosecute patents is flawed.[11]

All of these concerns may be accurate, and they would certainly affect the level of bargaining. In fact, if the bargain aspect provides an accurate portrayal, we may want to rein in elements that fail to cabin the bargaining in an optimal fashion. Nevertheless, the fundamental nature of the patent system is such that no matter how brilliantly we design and apply the rules, the patent cannot definitively identify the rights granted. There simply is not enough information at the time of the patent grant.

Illuminating the bargain aspect has the potential to alter more than just our theoretic conception of the patent system. If the nature of the patent system is substantially different from that which was previously assumed, one should consider whether that difference is a good thing and how government can structure its response to these new perspectives. Imagine that the government is selling property but the boundaries are not set from the start. We cannot walk the property or know what we are handing over. Under those circumstances, we have a greater responsibility—and a much more difficult task—than if we are simply transferring a piece of land. When the game is more complicated, it places a greater burden on the system to ensure that the game operates fairly and efficiently.

This is not to suggest that patents are entirely unbounded or that the grant of a patent sets off a complete free-for-all. There must be some structure, and that structure exists in relation to the invention. Words may be flexible, but they are not infinitely malleable, at least not in a system that applies some semblance of consistency in its rules of interpretation.

Similarly, I do not want to suggest that we are or should be granting patents as an act of faith, confident that a court or the Almighty will construct something appropriate for us in the end. That would be reminiscent of the classic folktale in which a child prays by reciting the alphabet, knowing that heaven will combine the letters into the appropriate words.[12] I would not wish to suggest that our modern patent system operates in this fashion. Properly construed, patent rules do and should set boundaries to restrain the reach of an individual patent holder and to identify the level of contribution an inventor must make before acquiring any rights at all. Disclosure rules in their proper application should prevent an inventor from giving us the alphabet and assuring us that we can compose Shakespeare.[13] Nor should we allow inventors to stretch their grasp to things that are only somewhat similar to the invention. As one scientist wonderfully explained, one should not allow an inventor to say, "Sure, I gave you the Constitution. I just had a few words mixed around, but I got essentially what America is about."[14]

No patent is infinitely expandable. Nevertheless, the range of possible rights that could result from any individual patent is quite broad, and the players in the patent world seem to operate with an innate understanding of that. Although no one has yet articulated it as such, the organic beast that is the patent world operates with an instinctive understanding of the game.[15]

The fact that the patent world operates with this innate understanding should provide some comfort and reassurance to those concerned about the reliance interests that might be inherent in a system in which the articulated message presupposes that the patent defines the rights granted. Although the image of the bargain aspect clashes with the accepted scholarly narrative of patents, it corresponds to a vision that would ring true to those in the patent world.

In choosing the term "bargain aspect," I am paying homage to the philosopher Wittgenstein and his notion of aspect seeing. Wittgenstein used the term "aspect seeing" to describe how it is possible to see something new in an object when the object remains unchanged.[16] The classic example of the phenomenon is Wittgenstein's shadow drawing of a duck that can also be seen as a rabbit.[17]

As a philosophy scholar explained, "One may walk by one's old friend, but once the old friend is recognized, one cannot 'unsee' the old face in the new."[18]

Scholars over the last century have suggested a variety of theories of patent law, each with its own insight into the nature of the system. In writing this book, I am hopeful that it will illuminate a different aspect of patenting so that readers looking at patents in the future will never quite see them in the same way again.

The following chapters describe the bargain aspect of patents and explore its implications for patent law. Chapter 1 describes the scholarly narrative, including the gospel that the patent defines the rights granted. The chapter then describes the bargain aspect of patents, presenting a theoretic analysis of the patent system to explain why patents cannot have definitive metes and bounds. Chapter 2 presents a descriptive analysis of how patents operate as an opportunity to bargain rather than a grant of rights. Chapter 3 describes the general implications of the bargain aspect for the types of questions that courts explore.

The next three chapters apply insights from the bargain aspect of patents to some of the most challenging questions in modern patent law. Chapter 4 asks whether software, genes, and business methods are proper subjects for

*Figure 1:* Source: Ludwig Wittgenstein, *Philosophical Investigations* (Oxford, 1958), p. 194.

patents and explores the issue of where processes of nature end and processes of human inventions begin. Chapter 5 examines the proper relationship between patent, antitrust, regulation, and contract law and provides examples, including pharmaceutical patents. Chapter 6 explores whether the footprint of a patent should reach beyond the state of the art at the time of the invention and focuses on inventions in the biomedical industry. These are the types of fundamental issues we have an opportunity to reconsider at this extraordinary time.

# I

## The Bargain Aspect of Patents

> It is a bedrock principle of patent law that the claims of a patent
> define the invention to which the patentee is entitled. . . . Because
> the patentee is required to define precisely what the invention is,
> the [Supreme] Court explained it is unjust to the public, as well as
> an invasion of law, to construe it in a manner different from the
> plain import of its terms.[1]

These words, uttered *en banc* by the Federal Circuit in 2005, would not
seem the least bit surprising to anyone versed in patent law and commentary. It is almost a throwaway line, a way of starting at basic principles with
which we can all agree. The implication is not just that the words of the patent provide some form of limitation in a boundless universe of possibilities
but rather that the patent is definitive and that the boundaries are specific
and definite. The court's job when confronted with a patent is to figure out
precisely what was granted.

Patent commentary follows the same theme. It is rich with imagery anal-
ogizing a patent to a piece of land. In fact, the imagery is so commonplace that
examples are almost endless.[2] The claims are commonly described as setting

the metes and bounds of the invention, similar to the way in which property lines delineate a piece of land. For example, the seminal article on patent scope describes the claims portion of a patent in the following manner: "Analogous to the metes and bounds of a real property deed, they distinguish the inventor's intellectual property from the surrounding terrain."[3] Similarly, a basic background text on patent law sketches the analogy in great detail, including drawings of land boundaries to help explain how patent law works.[4] "[L]and is described by 'metes and bounds' defining the boundaries of the land. For example, a building plot may be legally described as follows: A building lot bounded on the north by K Street, on the east by 13th street, on the west by 14th Street and on the south by I Street. . . . Like the certificate of title to a car or the deed to a piece of land, a patent contains an identifying description of the patented invention describing the metes and bounds of the invention."[5]

Thus, the claims portion of a patent is commonly viewed as delineating the boundaries of the rights. This element of a patent is considered an es-

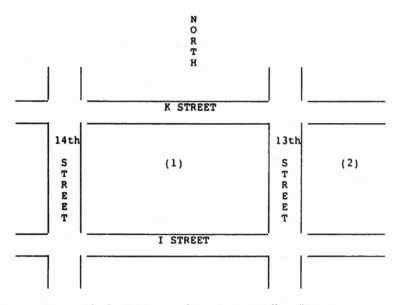

*Figure 2:* Source: Charles E. Lipsey and Amy L. Tsui Collins, "Patent Infringement in the Field of Biotechnology," in Gale R. Peterson, ed., *Understanding Biotechnology Law: Protection, Licensing, and Intellectual Property Policies* (New York, 1993), p. 241.

sential part of the way that a patent functions and a necessity for giving others notice of the extent of rights that the government has given to the patent holder.[6]

As a side note, the analogy to land that I am discussing here is distinct from other comparisons made between patent law and property law. For example, many authorities describe patents as a form of property, which would make them subject to property rules rather than liability rules.[7] Modern debates in this arena relate to whether the patent holder's right to exclude should be absolute or whether compulsory licensing might be appropriate.[8] For my purposes here, I am describing the legal imagery that envisions patents as having formal and definitive boundaries, analogous to property lines for a piece of land.

Even those who view the notion of locking up any ideas at all as arbitrary do not view the boundaries of an individual invention as such. Consider the legendary patent scholar, William Robinson. In his classic treatise on patent law from 1890, Robinson describes the patent system as an arbitrary intrusion into the natural law of invention in which all citizens receive and profit from each other's new ideas as they are revealed.[9] Despite this assessment, he holds fast to the notion that the boundaries of an invention are distinct and that this distinctiveness is of critical importance to the patent system:

> The one unchangeable factor in all legal questions relating to inventions is the invention itself. An invention is either a physical operation or a physical instrument, and as such its essential characteristics are determined by the laws of nature. No human legislation, no judicial interpretation, can increase, modify, or diminish its necessary attributes, and no legal doctrine concerning it can be correct which is based upon a partial or erroneous view of those inherent qualities that differentiate it from all other actual or possible inventions.[10]

Even for Robinson, the contours of the invention definitively establish the boundaries, and those boundaries establish the rights granted by the patent.

Robinson eloquently argues for the existence of an innate definition of an invention that creates the patent right. Nevertheless, few modern scholars would suggest that we are able to identify the essential nature of an invention as clearly as Robinson's words might indicate. Rather, modern scholarship is awash with complaints about our inability to know how a patent will be interpreted and whether a patent or a particular claim will be upheld.[11] As one scholarly piece has noted, "Claim construction is sufficiently uncertain that many parties don't settle a case until after the court has construed the claims, because there is no baseline for agreement on what the patent might possibly cover."[12] In another example, one prominent practitioner and commentator discussing a divided Federal Circuit opinion lamented the current state of American patent law, arguing that it is "difficult if not impossible to avoid panel splits as manifested in *Kinetic Concepts*. . . . Indeed, it is possible that both constructions are acceptable."[13]

Our struggles are generally attributed to weaknesses in the current state of the doctrines,[14] such as insufficient or excessive powers of review,[15] inadequate approaches to disclosure, or insufficient interpretation rules.[16] The Patent and Trademark Office receives its own generous share of the criticism. It is portrayed either as incompetent at screening out improper claims or, more sympathetically, as simply understaffed.[17]

The aspect of patents that I describe in this chapter suggests that such problems do not merely reflect flaws in the system; they are the system.[18] We can certainly exacerbate the effects of how the system works in the rules that we choose. Nevertheless, by necessity, a patent does not grant a definitive set of rights. Rather, it is an invitation to bargain over the definition of those rights.

This is not to suggest that the presence of uncertainty in the patent system is necessarily inefficient. Some scholars have suggested that uncertainty at points in the patent system may enhance efficiency by directing the resources of the patent system at those patents that matter in the moments that matter.[19] In this vein, Mark Lemley and Carl Shapiro argue that uncertainty is inherent in the patent system as an efficiency accommodation to the fact that a massive number of patents are filed each year, few of which have commercial value, and that third parties cannot meaningfully participate in the patent granting process.[20] Other scholarship suggests that the wide range of potential outcomes in patent cases exists because patent doctrines are drafted in a way that allows substantial discretion on the part of judges and patent examiners, again viewing that discretion as a positive attribute of the system.[21]

The bargain aspect, however, focuses on another element of the system. It suggests that the presence of uncertainty and malleability in the system is inevitable. Recognizing and managing that uncertainty, as well as the bargaining it engenders, is the challenge for the legal system.

## Theoretic Analysis: The Nature of Patents

As described earlier, common wisdom holds that a patent grants a definitive set of rights. This section suggests, however, that given the nature of patents, it is simply not possible for a patent grant to create anything more than a starting place. The result flows from a confluence of three problems that can be described in terms of the lack of a shared conception, the limitations of language, and the effects of time. All of these problems can be traced to what I would call the paradox of newness, which can be explained in the following manner.

By definition, patents should be granted only on those things that have never existed before. Under patent law, a device or a method must be novel, and even those inventions that consist of a combination of existing elements must be able to demonstrate that the combination is new and nonobvious.

With the creation of new things, the relevant society lacks a shared understanding of what those things are and how they might be differentiated from other things. This uncertainty is exacerbated by the limitations of language, particularly language that is being used to describe things that did not exist when the language developed and that will also be used as a measure against future inventions that do not exist at the moment that even the limited language is chosen.

Finally, although the patenting process begins with an invention, the full dimensions of that invention will not be understood until later developments in the relevant arts. Those developments are likely to occur long after the patent has been granted. The following sections describe each of these three problems in detail.

### THE LACK OF A SHARED CONCEPTION

A wealth of scholarship in the field of philosophy is devoted to the problem of trying to define the world around us. As human beings, we struggle with attempts to identify and create categories for the content of our experiences, whether those experiences involve a concrete item like a rock or an abstract concept like the truth.[22] In trying to understand what "gold" is, for example, a philosopher might try to assign a categorization based on what could be discovered about its natural properties.[23] From that perspective, "gold" would be a yellow metal, for example, but not a deity.

Within these attempts to understand the world around us, we must have certain concepts to which we are committed. Do we believe that God exists? Do we believe that water exists? Without a shared commitment to the existence of at least some concepts, members of a society are unlikely to be able to engage in much of a meaningful dialogue or to analyze those things around them in useful fashion.

This does not mean that our commitment to the existence of something and our shared concept of that thing can answer all questions about its identity or about the many implications that flow from its identity. Nevertheless, theoretical discussions about those things to which we are committed will be quite different from discussions related to things that are new or even things that have yet to be discovered. To put it simply, a discussion about the implications of medium-sized dry goods will be quite different from a discussion about the implications of the Higgs boson, something for which we have seen no evidence other than in mathematical equations.[24] Patents are likely to fall between the two. The requirements of the patent application provide some evidence to work with beyond mathematical equations. Nevertheless, patented inventions fall closer to the Higgs boson end of the spectrum. Their newness deprives us of an opportunity to have developed a shared conception to which we as a society are committed. That definitional commitment can develop only over time as the contours of the boundaries are fully explored.

Compare the grant of a patent to the grant of a license for hunting bears. As a society, we may not have an exhaustive and exclusive definition of the features that define a bear. Nevertheless, we have some conception of the notion of a bear, to which we are committed. Our attempts to define bears for the purposes of the license grant will be fundamentally different from an attempt to define, for example, dark matter, something that may or may not exist but about which we have some clues. We may argue about the definition of bears at the margin, and those arguments may even lead to a redefinition of the nature of a bear. Nevertheless, we have some commitment to the core concept of what a bear is. That level of commitment to a core concept is unlikely to be true for cases in which we are attempting to define what is new and unfamiliar to us.

Of course, with patents, the shared conception need not exist for society at large. Patents are designed to speak to those skilled in the relevant art, and it is persons of ordinary skill in the art who would need to have the shared concept. Nevertheless, for an invention to be patentable, it must be nonobvious to this all-important group. Thus, even from the perspective of narrow and dedicated experts, a patent must teach something that is unfamiliar and for which new constructs and understandings will develop over time, even for those dedicated to the relevant field.

The same is true for a comparison of patent rights to rights in relation to land. With land, new types of rights may emerge—water rights, air rights, subsistence rights—and these rights again have the potential to redefine the nature of property. Once those rights emerge, however, the contours are identified for a class of rights. With patents, the contours of each individual patent must be determined anew because there must be something new in each patent.

## The Limitations of Language

Moses then turned and found himself in [a] house of study. He sat down at the back of eight rows of scholars and listened carefully as they argued points of Law. The argument was abstruse, and despite occasional references to the Torah of Moses, Moses failed to make head or tail of it. . . . He crept from the study house disconsolate. Why was Moses so disturbed by this incident? A fundamental point had been made clear to him. It was not until he sat in the study house that he realized the paradox of truth enshrined in language, the glittering nature of the human mind . . . reflects back from each sacred word, six hundred thousand facets.[25]

The lack of a shared conception is exacerbated by problems related to language. Such is the paradox of "truth enshrined in language," described in the preceding quote. Even if there is an essential truth to any invention, a shared conception upon which we would all agree, that conception must be represented by words in the patent. The nature of language is such that once the truth is enshrined in it, the words chosen are subject to twisting and turning in a myriad of directions.

As one scholarly article explains, "Even after claim construction, the meaning of the claims remains uncertain, not only because of the very real prospect of reversal on appeal but because lawyers immediately begin fighting about the meaning of the words used to construe the words of the claims."[26]

With regard to philosophy, the philologist Max Müller said of the problem that "[N]othing is more certain than that two people hardly ever take the same word in the same sense, and that just the most important words are often used in entirely different sense by different philosophers. Hence all our misunderstandings, all our quarrellings, all our so-called systems of philosophy, everyone differing from the other, and yet all starting from the same given facts, all collected by the same eyes and the same minds!"[27] Commentators have made similar observations in other fields.[28]

Within law itself, indefiniteness of language is not a problem unique to patent law. The frustrations of interpreting language are shared by those engaged in the fields of contract law and legislation, as well as by any lawyer or scholar who has ever tried to glean precedent from a case.[29] Nevertheless, in the realm of patent law, the indefiniteness of language presents particular challenges.

First, the entire concept of patenting revolves around the idea of granting rights for introducing something that has not existed before and is not obvious based on those things that do exist. Thus, in describing an invention in a patent, one must often use existing language to describe something that by definition has never existed. Whatever language society has chosen to represent those things that exist around us must be pressed into the service of describing something that did not exist when the language and its concepts developed.

It is, of course, possible that language concepts exist when the invention does not. The human mind can conceive of and describe many concepts long before those concepts can be translated into reality. In those circumstances, the language constructs may be in place already, and the inventor can turn to them.

In addition, many inventions flow from combining existing elements in a new way to achieve a new result[30] or from translating concepts from one arena to another.[31] In that case, inventors may be able to draw on language libraries developed in other contexts. For example, society understood the concept of flight in birds long before the Wright brothers invented flying machines. The Wright brothers would have had a wealth of words related to flight to draw upon in describing their invention.

Nevertheless, no matter how creative the human mind and its linguistic developments may be in the abstract, the translation of that abstract into a particular successful practice can easily wander into new and unexpected territory. The new territory can create linguistic challenges even for those inventions that rely heavily on concepts for which language exists.[32]

There certainly may be minor, technical inventions whose innovations are just barely differentiated enough from the prior art to warrant patenting but not so different that existing language tools are insufficient. For much of patenting, however, applying old language to new concepts will create challenges that prevent certainty at the time of the grant.

In addition, in understanding the challenges of linguistic uncertainty for patent law, one must think not only of the invention that is patented but also of other products and inventions that will be created in the future. When a court engages in an infringement analysis, the process involves comparing an accused product to the words of the patent grant as those words have been interpreted. Thus, even if we have linguistic devices for describing a patented invention, we may be using that language as the basis for a comparison of the invention to something that did not exist at the time the language developed. Once again, the patent system is relying on language to serve as the basis for understanding something that did not exist when the language developed. This additional challenge makes the indefiniteness of language much more problematic in patent law than in contract law, for example.[33]

At this point I suspect that some patent mavens will object. In determining the meaning of words in a patent, courts are supposed to think only of the invention and not of the product that might be infringing. In other words, before a court gets to the part of the case that asks whether a product is infringing, it is supposed to decide what the patent terms mean and to do so without considering the accused product.

Although such is the procedure in theory, it is a little like asking the court not to think about the elephant in the room.

One might imagine that such mental compartmentalization would be difficult for most ordinary mortals, and judges are no exception. Even if courts were able to accomplish this superhuman task, the contours of the accused product would still play a significant role in defining the boundaries of the patent grant. On the most basic level, that product and its characteristics will frame the questions that are asked about the words of the patent in the first place. In addition, regardless of the construction chosen, the words of the claim will eventually be compared to the accused product to determine infringement, and that comparison will determine the boundaries of the rights. Those boundaries are impossible to anticipate without full knowledge of what products will develop to which the patent must be compared.

Thus, however one chooses to describe and distinguish the invention, that description will be repeatedly compared to products and inventions that did not exist at the time of the patent grant. It is this question-and-answer process that will ultimately result in a bounded set of rights. The bounded set of rights, however, cannot be known until the end of the patent term, when all potential products have appeared and all questions have been asked. Although one can try to predict what type of questions might arise in a comparison to unknown future developments, it is no more than a prediction.

One should note, by the way, that the end of the patent term does not necessarily signal an end to the process of defining the patent. Future inventors will have to argue that their inventions fall outside of the expired patent in order to demonstrate that their work is different from prior art. This continuing exploration of the definition of the patent is no longer relevant to the holder of the expired patent, given that any rights related to that patent have expired. Nevertheless, the process of defining the reach of a patent may extend beyond its life. Thus, even when a patent expires, it continues to cast a ghostly shadow across the landscape.

## The Weakness of Fixation in Time

The grant of a patent is a one-time event. It occurs at a single, fixed moment in time with the sealing of a document that is presumed to contain the description of the invention and the rights granted. At that moment, however, none of the parties has the information that would be necessary to know the contours of those rights. In fact, that information is unknowable at the time of the patent grant. The full dimensions of the invention will not be understood until later developments unfold. It is impossible to definitively identify the boundaries of the rights conferred at the time of the grant.

Perhaps the simplest way to think of this is the following. Meaning is contextual. One cannot develop a complete understanding of the meaning of something without the full context of all those things that might or might not be included in the meaning.

If, at the time of the patent grant, one could anticipate everything that would be developed during the twenty-year term of the patent, one might have some hope of creating a definition of the invention and identifying the boundaries of that definition. No one, however, will have all of that information until the end of the twenty years. The boundaries of the invention, its definition, will be developed as the new products emerge that will give us an opportunity to shape the definition. These will give us an opportunity to ask, "Is the invention A or is it B?"

The nature of the questions and, to some extent, the resulting definition will be determined by the serendipity of the products that emerge. Certain developments will lead us to flesh out a particular contour of the definition that otherwise would remain unexplored. It does not matter whether we say the reference point for the definition is the words we have chosen for claims or the nature of the invention itself.[34] At the moment of the patent grant, insufficient information exists to understand the shape of the rights.

The importance of future developments to the definition of a patent holder's rights cannot be overestimated. Edmund Kitch offered a wonderful example of this in his classic article on the prospect theory of patents:

> [A]n inventor who is the first to combine an internal combustion engine with a drive train, wheels, and a steering mechanism may claim the combination (as Selden did in his controversial patent) although the particular combination is so slow and unreliable under actual conditions of use that horse-drawn vehicles are commercially superior. Subsequent inventors of superior automobiles will infringe that claim even if their contributions to

the design of automobiles are what, in fact, made them commercially practicable.[35]

At the time of the patent grant, no one can predict what products will emerge, what commercial applications will develop, and what areas of the patent contours will be explored as a result of these developments.

The problem is amplified by the unpredictability of scientific discovery. Developments in the world of science and technology can unfold in radically unpredictable ways,[36] making it impossible to anticipate and resolve the rights questions that will emerge over the life of the patent.[37]

Given the extent of those things that cannot be known, patent holders in combination with future inventors and the courts will develop a definition of the invention during the patent term. This process creates the bargaining of the patent system, as patent holders and others vie with each other in the development of the definition of the rights.[38]

Patent doctrines themselves recognize the open-ended nature of the patent grant. Consider the concept of undue experimentation. A patent holder is permitted to claim a broad range of embodiments of an invention—well beyond anything that the patent holder has actually attempted or demonstrated.[39] That reach is limited, however, by the requirement that those skilled in the art must be able to carry out the invention from the information disclosed in the patent without undue experimentation.[40]

The concept of "undue experimentation" is an interesting one. It necessarily suggests that one who tries to follow the information disclosed in a patent may, indeed, have to engage in some form of experimentation. Thus, the doctrine is an implicit recognition of the considerable lack of information available at the time of the grant.

I should note at this point that the challenge of developing the definition of rights for a patent is distinct from the valuation challenges that affect all types of property. At any fixed moment in time, those who hold rights in any type of property cannot necessarily predict what its ultimate valuation will be. An unprepossessing scrap of land may turn out to be the key tract for the development of a shopping mall, making its value much greater than anyone would have predicted. This can certainly leave plenty of room for market actors to negotiate the use of that property and its valuation. Such valuation variations, however, are distinct from the type of bargaining contemplated with the bargain aspect. With the tract of land described earlier, we may argue about the value of the property, but we have some sense of where one tract of land stops and the neighboring tract begins. With patent rights, it is the definition of land itself that is at issue every time in every case.

For example, consider the invention of a device for making biodegradable grocery bags. The patent may contain several claims, including one that lists the use of any organic wood residue and another that lists a particular type of wood.

Over time, however, it may become clear that certain wood residues will not work without the type of alteration or adaptation that would be considered "undue experimentation."[41] Thus, the broader claims are less likely to survive a challenge. On the simplest level, the definition of the patent rights is narrower than it appeared at the time of the grant. On a deeper level, the parties will factor that weakness into their navigation of the boundaries of the invention. From either perspective, one's understanding of the invention and its limitations developed only over time as further work in the field and in the application of the invention unfolded.[42]

Consider Rob Merges and Richard Nelson's early discussion of the onco-mouse patent.[43] Scientists at Harvard University created and patented a strain of mice genetically engineered to be particularly susceptible to cancer. Invention of the mouse was considered a dramatic breakthrough in cancer research because the mouse allowed scientists to more quickly and easily evaluate the effects of cancer causes and treatments.[44] The university received a patent on a variety of things including the mouse as a product and the process of creating the mouse.[45] In addition, however, the university received a patent on using that process in higher-order, nonhuman mammals.[46]

At the time of the patent, the inventors had not applied the process broadly to all higher-order, nonhuman animals. Suppose it turned out that applying the process to nonrodents required significant additional work or even a scientific breakthrough to be successful. At that point, claims relating to mammals other than rodents would have been very weak and likely to be invalidated. This information would emerge, however, only as the invention was more fully applied over time.[47]

One could argue that this is merely an example of the fact that our patent system allows overbroad claiming. Perhaps in order to obtain the broader claim, the inventors should have demonstrated successful application of the process to at least a few examples of the group.[48]

Although the patent system might require that an inventor provide some examples of the group in order to claim the group, uncertainty would still exist. It would be impractical for the patent system to require inventors to have investigated every example of a claimed group. For example, suppose the inventors of the oncomouse had applied the process to a substantial enough portion of the group mammals to convince those skilled in the art that the process was broadly applicable to the entire group. If, however, subsequent developments revealed that a small number of mammals were not subject to easy application of the process, again, the broader claim (or at least claims with language that related to anything including the recalcitrant mammals) would be at risk.

Courts have been known to creatively read a claim to discover that the inventor never intended to claim anything related to the part of the category that is now suspect, but such a reading requires ignoring the rules of patent construction, not to mention rules of common sense.[49]

We could choose to completely forbid claims related to groups, but that is likely to be unworkable.[50] Patent holders have to be able to draw claims broadly enough that others cannot make minor variations. Would we say, for example, that an inventor could not list wood or metal or lubricant as an ingredient because each of these words represents a group, and groups are forbidden in claiming unless the inventor can demonstrate having tested every item in the group?

In reality, our modern patent system is quite generous in allowing broad claims to large groups. Such an approach leaves much information unknown and unknowable at the time of the patent. The root of the problem, however, is not in our approach to claiming. No realistic approach to claiming could eliminate it.

One could argue that bargaining within the patent system is merely an artifact of the modern claiming system and the way in which we ask inventors to define their creations. In fact, some scholars attribute problems in delineating the boundaries of an invention to the necessity of identifying categories and the impossibility of defining categories in a bounded fashion.[51] They argue that the problem can be traced to the development of the modern peripheral claiming system, which requires claims that define the outer limits of what the inventor is entitled to.[52] According to this argument, it is peripheral claiming, with its task of defining the outer limits of an invention that leads us to the current state of affairs in which we are ironically unable to delineate the boundaries of an invention.

The problem of newness, however, applies regardless of whether the patent system requires a type of claim that must describe the boundaries of the territory covered by an invention or the type of claim that must describe the core of the inventive principle. In all of these approaches to describing and defining an invention, the patent system still faces the lack of shared conception for new creations, the indefiniteness of language, particularly language that must relate to things that are new, and the inability to describe the boundaries of something without the knowledge of things that have yet to be developed. These types of problems make it theoretically impossible for a patent to definitively identify the rights that have been granted, no matter what claiming approach we choose.

## PATENTS AS NEGATIVE RIGHTS

The nature of patent rights as negative rather than affirmative rights may also contribute to the creation of a bargaining interaction. Despite popular misconceptions or at least very sloppy language,[53] a patent does not grant the right to *do* anything. It grants no more than the right to exclude others from making, using, or selling the invention.

To actually do something with the invention, the patent holder may have to navigate among many others who have the ability to block the manufacture, sale, or use of a product. At the most obvious level, such parties may include the various regulatory agencies that must evaluate and approve products. This is particularly important for inventions in the life sciences field, where patent rights can be useless without FDA approval.

From the perspective of the bargain aspect of patents, those able to block a potential application of an invention may include other rights holders. Although a patent holder has the right to exclude others from making, using, or selling things within the sphere of an invention, the patent holder may not be standing alone in that sphere. Others may have the right to exclude from that sphere as well. This information often comes as a surprise to those outside the patent fraternity. Nevertheless, the overlapping nature of patent rights is essential to the fabric of our patent system.

Consider an inventor who obtains a patent on a new chemical substance that is useful for dyeing candy a bright shade of blue.[54] Having identified one use for the product created, the patent holder may be able to claim rights in that new substance for all uses.[55] Suppose a later inventor, John, discovers that the substance is also useful for treating spinal-cord injuries. John can receive a use patent that covers the application of the already existing substance for the purpose of treating spinal-cord injuries.[56]

At this point, the original patent holder has the right to exclude anyone from any use of the chemical, while John has the right to exclude anyone from using the chemical to treat spinal-cord injuries. Neither one can operate in the commercial space related to treating spinal-cord injuries without permission from the other. Thus, both patent holders must navigate around and negotiate with the other to capitalize on their patents.

Suppose, instead, that the original inventor had received a patent on producing the chemical rather than a patent on the chemical itself. Perhaps the chemical itself was not sufficiently new, and the novelty lay in the method of producing it. Now suppose a later inventor makes the method better, using essentially the patented method but creating an improvement. The later inventor can get an improvement patent. At this point, both inventors hold rights in the space covered by the most commercially desirable use of the chemical, and neither can operate there without the approval of the other.[57] Again, both parties must grapple with the existence of the other in order to capitalize on their right to exclude.

Blue dye related to spinal-cord injuries sounds awfully far fetched. Lest readers believe that the hypothetical is the product of an overactive academic imagination, however, the hypothetical is based on recent discoveries at the University of Rochester.[58]

The point of the hypothetical is simply that although a patent holder stands in a circle of rights, others may be standing in parts of the same circle as well.[59] The potential for multilayered rights in the same inventive space enhances the bargaining nature of patents. The frequent navigation and negotiation create opportunities for parties to bargain over the contours and definitions of their various rights, particularly given that they are bargaining around the definition of things that, by necessity, have never existed before.

One could certainly design a patent system that avoided having overtly overlapping rights. The law could specify that only one patent holder could hold rights in a particular space, although that would be a drastic departure from the U.S. patent system. Even that alteration, however, would not result in a clear delineation of patent rights at the time of the grant. The problem of newness would remain.

## Factors of the Legal System That Are Magnified with Patents

The discussion in the chapter so far has focused on problems particular to the patent system itself. In understanding patents, however, one must also consider factors that affect the legal system as a whole.

### RIGHTS MUST BE ACTUALIZED

For example, all rights must be actualized. A right is worth very little unless someone has the capacity and willingness to assert it. In the process of actualization of those rights, some slippage is bound to occur. At the very least, the margins of the rights will be altered as rights holders factor the costs of exploring and defending their rights into the decision of what to pursue.[60] After all, parties who wish to assert those rights must bear the costs of determining the boundaries and pursuing enforcement. When costs exceed benefits, parties may choose to forgo assertion of an area of the right, effectively narrowing the right through abdication.

This observation is particularly applicable to rights systems that involve private enforcement. In the absence of public officers charged with enforcement, the rights holder bears all of the costs associated with asserting rights. The patent system is such a system of private enforcement, in which a patent holder must search out transgressors and pursue them for infringement.[61] Patent holders thus would be expected to factor in the full costs of this exploration and enforcement when deciding whether to pursue their rights, a consideration that could lead to much more limited rights than the rights of those who can share the costs of enforcement with a public enforcement agency.

In addition, the characteristics of the patent system magnify the effects of this phenomenon.[62] Uncertainty increases the risks and the costs associated with asserting one's rights. Thus, the unknowables inherent in the patent system add to the projected costs that a rational patent rights holder would calculate, affecting the choices those rights holders make about what rights to assert.

## COASIAN PRIVATE BARGAINING

Patent law certainly is not the only area of law subject to private bargaining. Application of Coase's famous work gives some hint of the extent of bargaining that can take place among the parties in any dispute. In his seminal article of 1960, Ronald Coase laid the foundation for much of law and economics by arguing that, absent significant transaction costs, it does not matter which of two parties is assigned legal liability in a private dispute.[63] Regardless of the initial assignment of liability, the parties will bargain to an efficient outcome. As John Donohue has noted, an important lesson from Coase's work is that in examining the effects of legal regimes, one must remember the ability of affected parties to reorder the apparently fixed environment through private bargaining.[64]

If parties can alter the outcome of a fixed legal regime through private bargaining, imagine the extent and impact of the bargaining when the legal environment is not the least bit fixed. Imagine further the complexity of the bargaining among multiple parties who may have both overlapping and conflicting interests.

Patent law also is not the only area of law in which a document that appears to fix the rights of particular parties may, in fact, be subject to the development of those rights over time. Consider a comparison to contract law. Under classical contract theory, parties are presumed to have reached a meeting of the minds on these issues in the contract, and no contract could exist without such a shared understanding.[65] Relational contract theory, which emerged in the late twentieth century, suggests that contracting is not always a matter of discrete moments in which agreements are fully fixed. Rather, parties to a contract may be engaged in long-term, durable relationships, in which the terms of the agreement should be understood in context and parts of the agreement may be left open over time.[66]

Even relational contract theory, however, suggests that contracts are a mixture of the fixed and the fluid.[67] With most contracts, at least some elements will involve the discrete and the particular—those things in which a meeting of the minds has occurred and some reasonable semblance of a resolution has been reached at the time of the contract.

In contrast, the unexpected and the unknown are the essence of the patent system. They are the basis upon which all parties must proceed after the grant of the patent. At the time of the patent grant, no one can know what the minds will have to meet about. Among other things, the inventor requesting the patent and the sovereign granting it cannot know what products will be developed against which the patent will be read.

## Are All Legal Rights Subject to Bargaining?

Patent is not the only area of law in which players must adapt to changing circumstances over time. One could compare patents to any form of legal precedent, whether that precedent is a case, a piece of legislation, or a constitutional provision. Law constantly evolves, and no legal framework can ever hope to definitively resolve the issues that will emerge.

As I have explained in the past, doctrinal structures are not enduring in law.[68] Those wishing to escape the confines of any doctrinal structure will seek out the interstices, the open spaces within whatever has been decided, rendering that structure insufficient for resolving the question. Of course, evolution in the legal system is subject to fidelity to precedent and the need to convince others that we are being faithful to that precedent. Nevertheless, our all-too-human nature, combined with the relentless march of social and technological change in society, ensures that precedent must constantly be applied to that which did not exist or was uncontemplated at the time of the precedent.[69]

One might reasonably wonder whether the experience of patent law reflects the nature of all rights. Is it possible that the entire legal system operates such that rights are nothing more than a starting place from which to bargain?

There are at least three possible answers to this question. First, perhaps patent law is truly anomalous. Although the challenges of judicial interpretation may be similar for patent law and constitutional law,[70] for example, the context in which those rights play out are quite different. Patent rights are designed for commercial exploitation. The realization of those rights involves a process of extensive commercial interaction, as patent holders use their "right to exclude" to navigate economic opportunities. Regardless of whether patent holders choose to manufacture products that embody the invention, license someone else to manufacture them, block the creation of products, or engage in a combination of these activities, they will use their right to exclude in order to ensure economic returns from the choices they make.

Although some commercial rights may operate in a similar fashion, other legal rights are not necessarily subject to this form of economic realization. If voting rights, for example, could be sold, traded, or otherwise commodified, the process of developing their boundaries might look quite different from what we are accustomed to seeing in the realm of voting rights and more like that of patents.

Other unusual factors also contribute to the operation of patent rights as a system of bargaining. Innovation in science occurs swiftly. This creates a rapid-fire succession of unexplored questions. Moreover, patent rights last only twenty years, which encourages patent holders to identify and move quickly on questions related to the boundaries of those rights. After all, one has only a limited period of time to capitalize on any potential returns from the patent. The hyperintense and accelerated time frame of patent rights makes them much more susceptible to the type of strategic behavior that creates a bargaining system for the contours of the rights.

Very few types of individual claims or societal grants could exhibit the unique combination of uncertainty, intensity, and commercialization evident with patent rights. Most other legal rights, therefore, remain safe from the discomforting observations suggested here.

A second possible answer could be that all rights are like patent law. Rights may be granted by legislation or constitution, or they may emerge in some natural form. In either case, however, legal rights provide no more than a starting place—an opportunity for relevant parties to negotiate over the territory the rights holder will ultimately receive. Delineation of the contours of those rights will take place over time as new issues, new challenges, and new facts emerge.

Most legal issues are to some extent uncertain. Courts would have very little to do if the full contours of legal rights were clear from the outset of all interactions. Nevertheless, I suspect that many scholars will balk at the notion that rights are either no more than a starting place or something to be bargained over. It comes perilously close to suggesting that rights have little meaning, or perhaps only meaning at the core. I share that discomfort.

My instinct is that the truth may be closer to a third possibility. Perhaps all rights are essentially the same, whether they are public rights or private rights, patent rights or voting rights. If any one of them unfolded in an intense, rapid-fire environment that is subject to explicit and extensive trading, one would see similar characteristics and effects. Most rights, however, will not be subject to such a volcanic environment and thus will not develop in an analogous fashion. Nevertheless, the experience of seeing one type of right in such an environment may provide some insight into the development of rights as a whole. The topic for the moment is patent rights, however, and the broader exploration will have to wait for another day.

## Of Bears, Fishing, Gambling, and Other Analogies

The current conceptualization of a patent as analogous to the grant of a plot of land fails from a theoretical perspective. Regardless of how brilliantly we craft legal doctrines or how scrupulously we apply them, the definition of an invention cannot be captured in a single, freeze-frame moment at the start of the patent term. The problems of newness ensure the impossibility of such an endeavor. The definition of a patent, by necessity, will develop over time as information forms, new products emerge, and the relevant parties circle each other in an attempt to find the most advantageous position.

If this is the nature of patents, then how can one characterize such a beast? What is a more useful conceptualization of patents than comparison to a plot of land? In approaching the question, I am mindful of the notion that all conceptualizing is to some extent tainted.[71] Law is certainly no better than the human beings who craft and implement it, which makes it remarkably flawed. Nevertheless, one should still attempt to find some measure of order in the Titan's chaos. An imperfect attempt is better than none at all.[72]

One might begin by considering the other imagery that has been offered to represent patents in the past. Each image has useful insights to offer, although no single image is complete without the bargain aspect.

The most fully explored patent image of the twentieth century was Edmund Kitch's suggestion that the patent system should be compared to the mineral rights system of the Gold Rush in the American West.[73] During the Gold Rush, those who identified surface mineralization could file a claim and be granted the right to develop the claim site.[74] Kitch argued that this system allowed an efficient coordination of effort, in which a single agent could determine the optimal level of investment and ensure coordination among all agents necessary to develop the rights.

Comparing patents to the mineral claims system, Kitch argued that patents allow a single agent to coordinate efficient development and commercialization of an invention. Following this observation, Kitch argued that the patent system should grant broad patents at an early stage in order to enhance the coordination. Kitch's theory of patents is known as the "prospect theory," in reference to gold prospectors who worked their mineral claims. It was an attempt to dispute the traditional "reward theory" of patents, in which a patent is viewed as society's reward for creating and revealing an invention.

The reward theory certainly has significant shortcomings as either a theoretic or descriptive account of the patent system. In particular, the vast majority of patents provide no monetary return to the patent holder. Some patents have little or no commercial value, and society may not be able to utilize or appreciate the value of an invention until long after the patent has expired. In addition, if one set out to reward those things that are of greatest value to society, one might choose to reward basic research in theoretical science rather than the latest gadget combining an iPod with a pedometer. Most important, Kitch's observation, that the patent grant arrives well before society knows whether the invention will be of value, argues strongly against the notion of a patent as a reward for the inventor's contribution to society.[75]

Kitch's comparison of patents to mineral claims, however, has been beaten into the ground. As John Duffy has noted, while Kitch's theory has been hailed as "one of the most significant efforts to integrate intellectual property with property rights theory," it has generated criticism that the theory is "without foundation" and is "little influenced by any concern for reality."[76] In fact, the design of the mineral claims system was quite different from that of the patent system. A mineral claim could extend only a fixed distance from the find, and the boundaries had to be clearly marked. In addition, a miner had to actively work a claim before property rights would vest. Rules such as these limited the number and dimension of the claims and avoided overlap. These limitations helped ensure that claims were fully exploited and avoided inefficient claim thickets, thereby mitigating concerns about over- or underdevelopment.[77]

In contrast, the patent system has no such limitations. No modern theorists would ever suggest that the boundaries of an individual patent are clearly marked, at least not in today's legal environment, and patent holders are under no obligation to exploit their inventions. These differences alone guarantee that the patent system cannot operate as effectively as the mineral claims system, regardless of what one thinks the limitations of that system might have been.

As a number of Kitch's critics have also pointed out, prospect theory suffers from its failure to acknowledge the distortive effects of transaction costs. If transaction costs are low, a single inventor might indeed be able to determine the optimal level of investment and ensure coordination among all of the agents necessary to develop the rights. The single, coordinating inventor would have every incentive to license the invention to other inventors or contract with them to produce follow-on inventions in order to fully develop technology in the field and earn as much profit as possible. In the real world, however, transaction costs are high, and the type of coordination Kitch envisioned would not be easy or inexpensive. Thus, the firm that controls an entire field would not be able to efficiently and effectively coordinate licensing for products and follow-on innovation. The result of granting a broad pioneering license to a single inventor would be stunted technological progress.

Finally, in responding to the prospect theory, scholars have noted that the patent system does not appear to operate in the manner suggested by prospect theory. For example, the PTO and the courts have generally resisted granting broad pioneering patents.[78] Moreover, even as a broad analogy, the analogy of patents to mineral claims falls short. With something tangible, like minerals in the ground, there is a finite amount to be rationed among potential claimants. Even if the parties do not know the extent of the gold in the ground at the time of the claim, an amount exists at that moment. At the extreme, one knows that the maximum possible amount would be if the entire ground were solid gold.

Of course, finding the boundaries of mineral rights and consequently the boundaries of minerals can be more complex than it might appear. One need only remember the movie *There Will Be Blood* for a fictionalized example. In one graphic and bloody scene, a man discovers to his despair that having sold his soul in order to broker a deal for oil rights, the oil has already been removed by drainage onto another property. The rights are worthless.

Despite inevitable challenges and complexities, the physical nature of minerals creates some form of natural boundaries. In contrast, inventions have no such natural boundaries. Intellectual property is neither tangible nor necessarily of finite nature, except perhaps for its duration. Those things that will be invented and to which the idea will be applied will define the universe of potential boundaries. Setting the rules for efficient division of the unbounded is likely to involve challenges far beyond those faced when setting the rules for efficient division of the bounded, regardless of the meandering path that the bounded may take.

The same problem would affect variations on the mineral rights analogy in which a patent could be compared to fishing rights, for example. Fishing rights may be less bounded than mineral rights, given that fish spawn and tides shift. Nevertheless, one still can more easily extrapolate the potential edges of the boundaries with rights related to tangible items like fish than rights related to innovations.[79]

On the topic of hunting and fishing, one could try to analogize a patent to a hunting license, and there are some appealing comparisons, whether one is talking about hunting for big game or for a parking space. One of my favorite examples comes from the parking information materials at Stanford University. Those materials at one time noted that a parking permit is no more than a "hunting license." It allows one to look for a parking space and grants the right to claim it if one is found, but it offers no guarantee that a space exists or that you will find one. Having tried to park on the campus many times, I always find myself in agreement with the description.

The average patent holder might feel some affinity for the description as well, at least from the standpoint of chasing any returns from a patent.[80] A patent is no guarantee that a patent holder will be able to capitalize on an invention, and the vast majority of patents yield no monetary returns.[81] Thus, patent holders may feel that a patent gives them the right to pursue some form of return for their investment without the guarantee that any exists or that they will find it.

The comparison does not work well, however, beyond the notion of chasing returns. The legal system has a clear method of identifying parking spaces, and woe to the undergraduate who tries to convince a traffic judge that space under a tree constitutes parking.

Whether one is hunting parking spaces or bears, the relevant society has some shared notion of the essential elements that define the quarry, although room for disagreement may exist at the margins. The problem for patents is that society has a limited understanding of what it is granting, and insufficient information exists for developing that understanding at the time of the grant. In the end, hunting analogies are as unsatisfactory as fishing analogies.

In contemplating hunting analogies, one should note that the courts have used the notion of a "hunting license" as a pejorative to indicate what a patent is *not*. "[A] patent is not a hunting license. It is not a reward for the search, but compensation for its successful conclusion," noted the Supreme Court in 1966.[82]

Other scholars have argued over whether patents are best analogized to a track meet or a treasure hunt. In a track meet, all of the racers start at the same moment, while in a treasure hunt, those who drag themselves out of bed early—that is, commit resources earlier in the process—can improve their chances.[83] Others compare the granting of patents to auctions rather than a treasure hunt.[84]

Still others compare patents to options on the theory that, with both, the holder of the right can choose to exercise it, which will require an additional dedication of resources, or allow it to expire unused. In particular, Shaun Martin and Frank Partnoy compare patents to a form of call options in which the rights holder has the choice of monetizing the right by commercially developing it, suing others, or threatening suit.[85] They argue that the current system improperly favors exercising the option in the form of litigation over development. In their fascinating analysis of litigation choices, the authors capture some of the strategic elements of modern patent practice.

Each of these analogies offers useful insights into the patent system. Nevertheless, they all assume that a patent grants some form of definitive right. Whether it is the treasure to be found, the option to be exercised, or

the auction item secured through a successful bid, all of these conceptual-
izations implicitly and explicitly involve receiving a definitive set of rights
identified in the patent grant.[86] The image is incomplete without an appreciation of the bargain aspect of patents, and I contend that this image must
be a part of any conceptualization of patents.

Specifically, to the extent that things are new, that newness will prevent
the creation of definitive boundaries. Instead, patent holders, in combination with future inventors and the courts, will develop a definition of the
invention during the patent term. This give-and-take creates the bargaining
of the patent system as patent holders and other relevant parties grapple
over the development of the definition of the rights. Thus, any imagery of
patents must include the notion a patent is no more than an opportunity to
bargain. It is an invitation to enter into the process of negotiating a definition of rights during the life of the patent, a seat at the negotiating table with
certain rules in place. Such is the nature of patents, and no conceptualization is complete without the bargain aspect.

## Who Are the Bargainers?

In understanding the bargaining inherent in the patent system, it is helpful
to have some sense of the identity of the various bargainers. These are the
parties who will shape the definition of the rights granted with any individual patent.

Although we are talking about the definition of "rights" granted with a
patent, it is important to remember that a patent grants only negative rights.
After all, it grants no more than the right to exclude others from making,
using, and selling the invention. Thus, when we talk of patent "rights," we
are talking about restricting non-patent holders from engaging in activities
covered by the patent.

Consider the hypothetical patent for the biodegradable grocery bag
mentioned earlier. If the question is, who is being excluded by the patent,
one could approach this question in the abstract by thinking about society's
collective and undivided interest in engaging in the activity covered by the
patent. It is certainly possible to imagine an organized society in which no
activity of any kind can be undertaken without some form of permission
granted by the sovereign entity. In fact, given the range of regulation in

modern American society, covering everything from pharmaceutical production to sidewalk sales, some might argue that our society actually operates in that way. In general, however, individuals in most organized societies, both now and historically, would have been free as an initial matter to engage in bag making for themselves or their neighbors. The ability to engage in that activity remains in the hands of all citizens until the sovereign, in the form of the PTO, distributes those previously undivided interests to an inventor.

One could offer the metaphysical quibble that there really was no freedom to make the biodegradable bag before the inventor came along. The bag did not exist. How could one be free to engage in a nonexistent activity? The simple answer is the following. Prior to the patent grant, all members of society would have been free to invent the bag and then use it. After the patent grant, individuals are not allowed to use the bag even if they discover it on their own. Independent creation may be a defense to copyright infringement, but it is no defense to patent infringement.[87]

In addition, even an individual's explorations and experimentation in an area may end up infringing a patent. Although U.S. patent law has a common law exception for experimental use, that exception has been interpreted so narrowly that it is difficult to imagine any circumstances in which it would operate.[88]

By starting with an organized society, I am avoiding exploration of the rights of individuals in a state of nature or in a loosely connected setting. As interesting as that might be, I am inclined to see it as beyond the limits of usefulness for this book. For those interested in this form of more abstract exploration of intellectual property rights, see *Coming to the Community*.[89]

In the context of an organized society, however, the grant of a patent is viewed as an exchange between society and the inventor. In return for creating and revealing a substantial invention, society grants the inventor the right to exclude others from that invention for a limited time.

Historically, the grant of the patent has not always followed the path of exchange for invention. For a period of time in British history, patents became a grant of royal privilege to engage in an enterprise, conferred not for the introduction of something new but merely for the good fortune of being well connected to the Crown.[90] In such a system, a patent looks somewhat like a gift from the sovereign consisting of society's previously undivided

interests. In the case of such a gift from the Crown, perhaps the most important bargaining was that inherent in gaining enough influence in the royal
court to be granted the privilege.

The U.S. legal system, however, treats a patent as an exchange for the
introduction of something new to society. The traditional view of a patent
as an exchange for invention includes an image of bargaining in the context
of negotiations between the inventor and the sovereign over the grant of the
patent itself. The give-and-take of the patent application process is well known
to anyone in the patent system. The applicant and the government, in the
form of the PTO, enter into a series of negotiations over whether a patent
will be issued and what the final language will be. The process normally
includes rounds of responses, adjustments, rejections, and revisions as the
applicant tries to obtain the broadest language possible and examiners try
to limit that reach in light of prior art or discontinuities between the breadth
of what the applicant has claimed and the narrowness of what the applicant
has disclosed.[91]

In the common conceptualization of patents, however, any bargaining
would necessarily stop at the critical moment when the patent is issued. In
theory, activity shifts at that point to the proper interpretation of the rights
that have been granted.

If the nature of patents is such that the extent of the rights cannot be
determined at the time of the grant, however, the image of the bargaining
parties as just the inventor and the sovereign is far too limited. The range of
parties who will have an opportunity to participate in shaping the rights
will be extensive, and many of the parties have the potential to shift roles
along the way. The group will include future innovators, whose creations
will form the questions that help define the boundaries of the rights. The
group will also include potential licensees, who will bargain over the definition of the rights as they navigate the choice of licensing, inventing around
the patent, or attacking the validity of the patent.

To add another layer, recall that in our patent system, the sovereign distributes certain rights, but these rights are not exclusive. The inventor may
hold nothing more than rights that overlap with the rights of those who create improvements or other uses, a circumstance that invites extensive bargaining with other patent holders not just over markets but also over the
definition of the patented territory itself.

In addition to these garden-variety bargainers, the modern patent landscape includes participants of a more exotic nature. In recent years public-interest organizations have joined the fray, searching out prior art that will invalidate patent claims.[92] Their efforts are a response to concerns that many weak patents have been issued and that weak patents clog the system. Loosely following the open-source efforts in software, such organizations hope to harness the power of the public to search out and attack prominent patents. Although some organizations rely on altruism or perhaps the reputational thrill of unseating a powerful player, other organizations offer patent bounties. For example, the group Article One offered a $50,000 reward for helping to invalidate certain Rambus patents.[93]

The groups have two outlets for their information. First, any member of the public may file a request for reexamination of a patent within two years of its issuance by presenting relevant prior art that the examiner did not consider. The motives of those filing for the reexamination are irrelevant. The Hatfields are free to file against the McCoys, and competitors can certainly file for reexamination of patents issued to their rivals, although there may be advantages to choosing litigation over reexamination.[94]

A second outlet for the patent hunting groups is the courtroom. Ordinarily, no public-interest group, let alone the public at large, would have standing to challenge the validity of a patent in court. Invalidity is a defense to patent infringement, and one must be at some risk of an infringement charge to raise the defense.[95] Some groups, however, are offering their hunting services and information to those who are defending against a charge of patent infringement.[96]

These groups intend to use the resources of interested members of the public to augment governmental resources and shift the balance of power away from large patent holders and holders of overly broad, nonmeritorious patents.[97] In other words, although the government may have distributed some of the interests that were previously held by the public, the public is not necessarily silent and may continue to find ways to negotiate over those grants.

It is possible that such efforts will not always be warmly welcomed. A different approach to perceived patent abuses has drawn a defamation lawsuit against a self-described patent troll tracker.[98] Such a response, however, merely highlights the range of bargaining tactics available to those at the table.

An interesting new addition to the patent landscape is the emergence of companies that buy, sell, broker, license, and auction patents.[99] These companies have the potential to provide greater liquidity for patents and to speed up the process of determining their value.[100] Non-practicing entities, that is, those who hold patents on inventions but do not make products themselves, are well known in the patent landscape. They may choose to license their inventions or to pursue companies they believe are infringing their patents.

Non-practicing entities have engendered much public criticism and controversy. They have drawn the epithet "patent troll" in reference to the children's fairy tale about the frightening creature who sits under a bridge, popping up out of nowhere to confront poor passersby and demand payment of a fee before they are allowed to cross the bridge.[101] From a more appealing perspective, others have noted that the ultimate non-practicing entities are universities who receive patents from their basic research and generally just license their invention to outside producers.[102] From either perspective, entities created so specifically for the purpose of developing a patent market are an important phenomenon that is likely to add to the cacophony of voices at the table.

Throughout this process, one also should not forget the sovereign's continued participation. As described earlier, rights are of little use unless they can be actualized. To the extent that actualization involves the courts, a judge's interpretation of the rights will significantly affect their contours. Where the definition of the rights cannot be developed at the time of the patent grant, the role of the courts is particularly important.[103]

On one level, the approach has the flavor of one-sided decision making rather than bargaining. The sovereign in the form of the courts rather than the PTO adjusts the level of rights that will be available going forward. On a more subtle level, however, a court case offers its own bargaining forum. The opposing parties vie for differing definitions of the rights and may be joined by amici, the solicitor general, academics, and others.

Of course, the fact that rights must be actualized affects numerous rights, not just patent rights. At the simplest level, if actualization requires court action, the fact that the court is interpreting the rights may create opportunities for the court to affect the contours of those rights. This is true regardless of whether one views the source of a right as legislation, a constitution, the product of free-will agreement, or some natural entity. Whatever the origin, the process of interpreting those rights in the courts will ultimately affect the shape of those rights. Where rights are uncertain, tradable, and rapidly evolving, however, one particularly takes note of the bargaining that occurs in the courtroom.

Throughout all of the bargaining that a patent holder faces during the life of the patent, it is important to note that only some of the process will involve the sovereign's active participation. Although judicial proceedings, agency reexaminations, and even legislative changes will involve the sovereign's participation in one of its various forms, much of the process will take place outside the sovereign's purview. For some crucial junctures, such as the exchange of exploratory letters, licensing negotiations, and internal decisions of what to defend and what to abandon, the sovereign may not participate at all. For other interactions, such as those related to settlements and to the timing, order, and choice of filing lawsuits, the sovereign may participate to a limited degree.

For example, when a patent holder chooses to file different lawsuits against different individuals based on different patents covering the same product, judges are certainly involved in each suit, but they may not have grounds to affect those litigation choices, even if opposing parties object.

In short, in an organized society, one can think of the ability to engage in the activity covered by the patent as an interest held in undivided form by all members of the society. When the sovereign distributes those interests to an individual inventor, the remaining members of the society have the potential to become competing inventors, licensees, overlapping rights holders, or even outside challengers. All of these parties in interest, along with the sovereign itself, will vie with each other over the contours of the rights. These are the bargainers.

# 2

## How Modern Patents Operate

Chapter 1 explains that, from a theoretical perspective, the traditional conceptualization of patents as defining the boundaries of rights granted is insufficient. Given the problems associated with the newness of an invention, one cannot possibly delineate the contours of the rights at the moment the grant is conferred.

This chapter presents a descriptive analysis of modern patents. It demonstrates that the patent system operates as a complex set of bargaining interactions in which the rights associated with any individual patent are developed. Within this system, the moment of the patent grant is not a definitive grant of rights; it is no more than the start of the bargaining.

### Stocking the Library

Preparations for the bargain are evident from the moment the patent drafting process begins. Those who draft patents try to create a library of terms that can be called upon, depending on how the bargaining unfolds. One can think of this as having a vast room full of books to pull off the shelf, depending on one's needs at a particular time. Having a broad array provides flexibility for the patent holder during the application process and for the life of the patent.

The process of applying for and negotiating a patent, known as patent prosecution, involves extended rounds of questions, responses, revisions, continuations, rejections, and revivals until the patent is granted with its final language. For example, more than 80% of modern patent applications are rejected after the initial examination, although the rejection is not final.[1] These nonfinal first rejections invite the patent applicant to respond to the examiner's arguments.

Even patent applications that are issued a second, "final" rejection stand a good chance of being issued as a patent at some point. More than half of the patent applications that receive a so-called final rejection will eventually issue as patents either through a Request for Continued Examination or by an appeal to the Board of Patent Appeals.

Thus, much of the process at the Patent and Trademark Office (PTO) looks like an extended bargaining session, with the inventor and the PTO as the bargaining parties. Looking at the negotiation in very broad terms, inventors generally try to obtain the most expansive language possible, while the PTO works to scale back the language in light of prior art or limitations on what the patent holder has actually created. As an inventor, I might want to argue, for example, that the product I created using mouse DNA should provide enough basis for me to claim products using similar DNA from any mammal. The PTO, however, may be reluctant to grant so broadly on the grounds that, given the state of the art, the transition from creating the product with mouse DNA to creating a product with human DNA would require too much experimentation. The claim is thus outside the realm of my actual invention.[2]

Certain doctrines and procedures during patent prosecution increase the likelihood of bargaining both at the patent office and beyond. For example, patent interpretation doctrine requires that patent examiners give claims language its broadest possible interpretation.[3] In addition, the patent applicant is not supposed to expand the application language beyond what is supported by the initial disclosure,[4] but examiners frequently demand that an applicant narrow the language. Both doctrines encourage patent applicants to begin by reaching broadly, leaving room to back away from certain sections or interpretations of the language either at later stages in the patent prosecution, in licensing negotiations, or at the courthouse.

### The Structure of Modern Claims Practice

The structure of modern claims further enhances bargaining. A patent is generally conceptualized as having two parts, the specification and the claims.[5] The specification must enable a person of ordinary skill in the art to make and use the invention without further experimentation. More specifically, the specification will generally include a title; a background of the invention, in which the patent application may describe problems in the art that the invention solves; a brief summary of the invention; and a detailed description that is complete enough to allow a person of ordinary skill in the art to make and use the invention.[6] In addition, the specification must also set forth the "best mode," which is the preferred embodiment known to the inventor.[7] The claims come after the detailed description of the invention and are intended to define the invention by setting forth the boundaries of the patentee's rights.[8]

Consider a very simple example. Customers at coffeehouses can pick up an insulated sleeve to slip over the cup and protect their fingers from the heat of the beverage. The sleeves are patented products.[9]

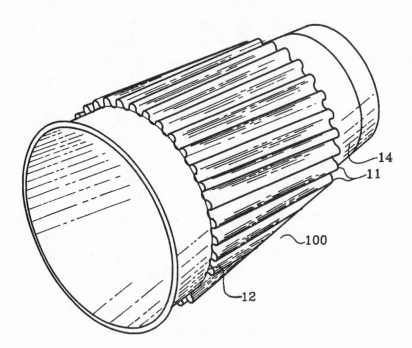

*Figure 3:* U.S. Patent No. 5,205,473.

One of the relevant patents explains that hot-beverage containers traditionally have been constructed out of either wax-coated paper or polystyrene. Each of those materials has drawbacks. Polystyrene is an excellent insulator, but it is neither recyclable nor biodegradable, and incineration releases toxic fumes. Wax-coated paper is more easily recyclable and degradable but provides low insulation.

Although the specification covers four pages, not including the thirteen drawings, the key description of the invention is the following:

> This invention provides corrugated beverage container holders . . . which are environmentally friendly and which provide adequate insulation properties approaching those of polystyrene. The corrugated tubes of these products preferably contain longitudinally extending flutes and include a generally tapered or conical structure, typical of beverage containers. The corrugation can be made of cellulosic materials, including craft paper, sulfite paper, or recycled paper.

There are eighteen claims in the patent, including the following:

1. A recyclable, insulating beverage container holder, comprising a corrugated tubular member comprising cellulosic material and at least a first opening therein for receiving and retaining a beverage container, said corrugated tubular member comprising fluting means for containing insulating air; said fluting means comprising fluting adhesively attached to a liner with a recyclable adhesive. . . .
5. The holder [mentioned in claim 1], wherein a surface of said liner is coated with a water-resisting agent.
6. The holder [mentioned in claim 1], wherein said fluting comprises sinuous fluting.

In other words, the claims here cover the invention created with a range of materials and made in various forms, including a water-resistant, foldable, and wavelike shape.

Given the structure of modern claiming, patent applicants can offer a variety of possible dependent and independent claims in the hopes of reaching out in as many different directions and as far as possible.[10] If the PTO or a later court invalidates one of the claims for any reason, the patent holder can fall back on the remaining ones. Thus, the structure of the claims in modern practice fits a bargaining strategy in which many weapons are placed in the arsenal that can be called upon, traded away, or later relinquished.

### BARGAINING AT THE PTO AS INFORMATION EMERGES

The traditional view of patenting may anticipate a certain amount of bargaining during the patent prosecution process as the inventor and the PTO argue over the level of information that was available in the prior art and the nature of the inventor's contribution. Nevertheless, it does not capture the wild scramble of patenting. The traditional view is still grounded in the notion that the invention, as described in the application, exists in some finite fashion and that the PTO's job is to properly identify and cabin the definition of what has been created. Again, this fixed-frame view of patenting and inventing bears little resemblance to modern patent practice. Rather, inventors carefully choose the library of terms and information disclosed in the initial application to make room for as much continued development as possible. Not only do patent applicants monitor the market and other inventors—adjusting the language to try to cover emerging products—but they also continue their own work. If the language in the specification is broad enough, one can find ways to amend the patent during the prosecution process as one continues to learn more. Thus, the process of invention, intertwined with the process of defining that invention, continues throughout the patent application process.

This is particularly true with life science inventions, whether related to biotechnology or pharmacology. In the early stages of drug development, the only available data may be those that emerge from working with cultured cells or mice. At that point, it is not possible to know which of the variants will actually make tumors shrink in human subjects or cure diabetes, for example. It may be several years after conception before the inventor knows the best embodiment, the most viable embodiment, or the most commercially reasonable embodiment. An inventor cannot afford to wait. A delay of several years could run afoul of the rules that encourage prompt patenting of inventions and could risk the possibility that others will patent first. Thus, a patent applicant must try to think of as many embodiments as possible, knowing that the focus can change during the application process and beyond.

The risk that others may patent first is particularly great when many researchers are working in the same field. One former in-house lawyer for a pharmaceutical company noted that in his work at the company, he had drafted and submitted patents on various newly discovered genes. In drafting the applications, he had done his best to think up various prophetic embodiments for using the gene to treat a range of diseases. A prophetic example describes an embodiment of the invention that is based on predicted results rather than actual work that the inventors have done or results they have achieved.[11] A couple of times the lawyer noticed that another company had filed a patent application on the same gene and used similar prophetic embodiments a few weeks before, presumably having applied similar guesswork. Everyone is moving fast and shooting from the hip, hoping to sort things out along the way.

Bioscience is not the only area in which work continues as the patent application progresses and beyond. Rather, the approach is shared throughout many areas of innovation. In electrical engineering, for example, practitioners note that some patents related to semiconductor chips and programs may be filed with little more than an outline. The inventor may have filled in the outline by the time the patent issues, but that is more a function of industry characteristics than of any patenting requirements. Innovations occur so rapidly in this field that the shelf life of any invention is quite short and thus drives the completion of the work much more than patenting needs.[12]

One might also imagine a start-up company on a limited budget. The start-up has created a new widget that is really a combination of a number of ideas. Those ideas could merit numerous patent applications, but the company has neither enough time nor sufficient resources to devote to that effort. The company may choose to file a single application with much detail in the specification and a small number of claims, which is all that its budget allows. As the start-up has more money to spend, it can mine the specification language and use the ability to file for different types of continuations to file more claims.

Although a little trickier to accomplish, a related activity can occur after the patent is granted. With enough language planted in both the claims and the specification, one can mine that language for pieces that fit the developing markets or products. This can be useful regardless of whether the developments are made by the patent holder or by others in the field. Either as defensive or offensive weaponry, a well-loaded patent can be quite useful.

While this hypothetical scenario involves a start-up company with a tight budget, in reality no company has unlimited resources. All companies face time pressures in filing their patents, and they all must make choices along the way.

In so many areas of innovation, information continues to emerge about the invention, its application, and its limitations. The strategic inventor will want to stock the library as fully as possible to provide the necessary flexibility as developments unfold.

Consider the story of actress Hedy Lamarr and composer George Antheil. At the height of World War II, these two Hollywood icons invented a secret communications system that they hoped would help the Allies defeat Germany. They obtained a patent focused on the notion of a radio-control mechanism for torpedoes. The two were never able to convince anyone to move forward with the invention, and the idea was not implemented during the life of the patent. Their concept, however, is now at the heart of modern communication systems, including many military systems and cellular phones.[13]

Although frequently cited as a source in later patent claims, the two inventors would have a difficult time collecting royalties if their patent were still in force today. The language of the patent focused narrowly on communicating control information to torpedoes. The patent, however, did not contain broader language implicating communication systems in general.[14] Thus, as broader applications of their invention developed, the patent holders could not have reached out to cover those products. Improperly stocking the library would have left them with nothing to pull off the shelves.

Information learned along the way can be strategically omitted and strategically included. For example, the Patent Act requires that patent applicants reveal the best mode they know for carrying out their invention.[15] Under current law, however, "best mode" is measured at the time of the initial application.[16] Thus, the applicant can choose to withhold other information learned during the application process and to keep this information as a trade secret. The ability to combine patented information with information protected by trade secret enhances one's bargaining power in later licensing negotiations.

Inventors may also have more innocent reasons for withholding such information. One start-up company was developing a diagnostic for cancer and had an ongoing collaboration with a large pharmaceutical company. The collaboration involved using the start-up's diagnostic to analyze cancer samples provided by the pharmaceutical company. Under the agreement, the start-up company was obligated not to disclose information about the pharmaceutical's samples to any third party.

The start-up company was preparing a patent application for its key product, the diagnostic and methods of using it. As the papers were being prepared, the start-up's employees realized that the best mode for practicing the diagnostic method would involve the cancer samples from the pharmaceutical company. This created a difficult dilemma for them. Due to the confidentiality clause, the start-up could not disclose the method, yet it was bound by the patent law to disclose the best mode in its application.

In the end, the start-up chose to delay its filing. The researchers hoped they could nurture their relationship with the pharmaceutical company and establish a good data set before requesting waiver of the confidentiality clause.

The example again demonstrates the rapid pace of innovation and the fact that information about an invention continues to emerge over time. There is simply no way to predict when critical information will appear.

## BLOCK AND TACKLE

Language in patent drafting can be chosen for a variety of strategic purposes. Terms may be embedded not only for potential use by the patent holder but also to create obstructions for other inventors. For example, information in a patent application can serve as prior art that prevents other inventors from filing their own patents. Under current law, this may be true even if the information in the prior patent application would not be sufficient to give that applicant a patent.[17] Thus, a patent applicant could choose to strategically place information into a patent that will bring them no rights but merely block anyone else from obtaining rights. Such a strategy could be chosen either because (1) the patent holder lacks sufficient information but wants to block another inventor, (2) the patent holder is not interested in patenting the information but wants to prevent others from obtaining a right to exclude, or (3) the patent holder is simply reaching, on the off chance that the information appears substantial enough to survive court scrutiny or is at least substantial enough to provide bargaining leverage prior to a lawsuit.

The potential to prevent others from obtaining rights in the market even if one has no interest in those rights can be quite powerful. As described later, patent holders who assert their patents must be prepared to have other rights thrown back at them.[18] If I can preempt your rights by placing sufficient information in the public domain, I can block certain defensive moves you might be able to make when I try to assert my rights against you.

Patent applicants may engage in other defensive or blocking strategies as well.[19] For example, patent holders are not required to work their inventions, and, as a general matter, inventors are perfectly free to suppress what they patent.[20] Thus, inventors may choose to include language in their patent solely to block others from making products. This strategy may be particularly appealing in a crowded field where the patent holder knows that many individuals are working on the same problem.[21]

As with other aspects of patenting, the process of defensive patenting does not depend solely on work accomplished prior to submitting the initial patent application. The work continues throughout the patent application process and beyond. If the initial language is drawn broadly enough, the patent applicant may be able to amend the application by adding claims that will block variations on the invention. In addition, after a patent issues, many patent holders will file new applications on improvements or variations of the invention solely to block competing products from entering the market. One can describe this approach as defensive patenting because the patent holder is engaging in additional patent filings to protect an existing patent.

In the most innocent light, defensive patenting is a perfectly reasonable method of ensuring protection for the invention. Given uncertainties in patent law, a patent applicant must expend the necessary effort to protect the invention from a competitor who engages in no more than minor variations on it.[22] In addition, the fact that other inventors will be patenting defensively and aggressively encourages such an "arms race." From a less appealing perspective, defensive patenting exploits the uncertainties in the patent system to construct not just a stronger fortress but more expansive territory around the invention as well. From either perspective, the process of inventing and defining that invention extends well beyond the initial patent application.

The prior discussion involved defensive patenting, in which patent holders file additional patents solely for the purpose of protecting an existing patented product. Companies can also engage in filing solely for offensive purposes. For example, suppose I have a product idea, and I discover that manufacturing the product would infringe someone's patent. One possible strategy would be to try to invent an alternative or a variation on the approach and patent it. Even if my new approach is deemed to be no more than an improvement on the original patent, I am still in a better position.[23] True, my improvement patent will be considered "subservient" to the original patent, and the two will be blocking each other. Nevertheless, I have gained leveraging power in negotiating with the original patent holder. In addition, if negotiations fail, and I am judged to be an infringer in the long run, my damages may be reduced. I may be able to argue that my sales were based at least in part on my improvement.

Whether engaging in defensive or offensive filings, such patents are a far cry from the traditional image of patenting, in which an inventor comes up with an idea and receives a patent. They are, however, an indication of the strategic complexity involved in patenting and of the bargaining that takes place.

## LIMITATIONS ON THE QUALITY OF THE PATENT DOCUMENT

Finally, limitations on government resources make it unlikely that the patent document emerging from the PTO will be drawn with the level of exactitude that one might hope for. The volume of claims and the small number of PTO examiners makes meticulous review of claims and prior art literature impossible. With nearly half a million patent applications submitted every year,[24] one scholar estimates that the average amount of time an examiner spends on an application is eighteen hours, spread over two to three years.

A recent Federal Circuit case revealed the extent to which the PTO does not expect perfection from its examiners even as to the limited level of examination they perform. In the *Asokkumar Pal* case, the Federal Circuit upheld the PTO's decision to fire a quality-assurance specialist whose job was to review patent examiners' decisions.[25] The specialist was fired when an audit of his work showed a 37.5% error rate.[26] Most interestingly, the opinion noted that a 25% error rate would have been acceptable.[27]

This is not to suggest that throwing vast amounts of resources at the PTO examination process would allow for a precise limitation of the claims. As chapter 1 explains, it would be impossible to nail down the boundaries of the claims, given the limited information available at the time of the grant. Nevertheless, the limited government resources can enhance the bargaining opportunities within the system.

## Bargaining with the Patent in Hand

Regardless of what may happen during the patenting process, the traditional view of patenting holds that the bargaining stops with the grant of the patent. At that moment, an inventor's fate is sealed, and the boundaries of the rights are largely identified by the language of the claims. In the real world of patents, however, the bargaining has just begun.

The preceding examples may hint at the bargaining opportunities that lie ahead for the patent holder. The actual unfolding of the patent bargain, however, is extraordinarily complex. A patent sitting by itself is of little value. The patent holder must find a way to obtain value from the power to exclude others. Consider first the inventor who wishes to find someone to license the patented invention.

It is important to remember that the patent power is not a power to create but rather a power to exclude. Actual creation may require considerable investment to find marketable applications of the invention—not to mention the approval of various regulatory agencies. Exclusion, however, is a far simpler process to initiate.

### SCANNING THE MARKET

As a starting point, the power to exclude can be exercised against those who are already engaged in the market and have much to lose if they are cut off. One who has incurred sunk costs in an enterprise may have an incentive to pay for a license rather than risk being excluded by a finding of patent infringement.

This might seem very strange to one unfamiliar with the patent system. If a patent is supposed to be granted only for those things that are new, how can a patent holder possibly find market actors to go after? If others are already using an invention, the invention must not be new. The answer can be traced to three factors: the time lag between applying for an invention and receiving a patent; the speed of change in innovation markets; and the presence of information gaps. On average, the PTO takes almost three years to grant a patent.[28] Although most patents applications are available to the public eighteen months after the application is submitted, considerable changes that will affect the final language may occur during this time.[29] In the rapidly changing world of innovation markets, potentially infringing products can easily emerge in eighteen months.

The delay between the patent application and the grant of the patent provides strategic opportunities for inventors. Patent applicants may monitor the relevant markets during the patent application process and adjust the claims language along the way.[30] In theory, inventors cannot expand the scope of the language once the patent has been filed.[31] As described earlier, however, a carefully crafted patent application will contain a library of terms that the inventor can draw upon. As products emerge in the market, the inventor can choose from this library to emphasize different terms as the negotiating process unfolds at the PTO.

Strategic opportunities were far greater when the clock did not begin running until the patent was granted rather than starting when the application was filed and when patent applications were not published until the time of the grant. Reforms in both of these areas have reduced the opportunity for what became known as *submarine patents*.[32] With submarine patents, applicants delayed the process for many years, waiting silently under the radar. When a successful product appeared on the market, the patent applicant would conclude the process and emerge, patent in hand.

Although submarine patents no longer haunt the seas, monitoring the market and adjusting one's patent in response to new developments during the application process is considered perfectly normal behavior and is even acknowledged by the courts. In 1988, for example, a Federal Circuit panel noted that amending a claim to cover a competitor's product that the applicant's attorney learned about during the prosecution of the patent is not at all improper as long as the amendment meets all of the statutory and regulatory requirements.[33] Again, this approach reflects a vision of the patent system in which an invention is somehow fixed at the moment of invention and in which words and concepts lack malleability.

Even after the patent issues, market actors can easily introduce products without having a clue that they may be infringing someone's patent. Patents are published, and that publication is intended to give notice to society of the rights that have been granted.[34] The reality, nevertheless, is far from that utopian vision of universal notice.[35] The number and complexity of patents is so great that it would be impossible for even the most diligent company to fully monitor all emerging patents. From a different perspective, the extent of the prior art searching that a patent holder engages in at any particular time in the life of the patent is a matter of tactics and asset management. As one commentator has suggested, the amount a small company should spend on prior art searching during patent prosecution may be different from how much they should spend before entering negotiations or litigation.[36] In addition to questions of resource management, there are advantages to ignorance in the patent system. Infringers who know about a valid patent can be subject to treble damages, whereas those who do not know or those who have a good-faith belief that the patent is not valid pay simple damages.[37] Willfulness, however, is based on "objective recklessness" and not state of mind.[38]

In addition, as described earlier, regardless of what one believes the source of the problem to be, patent language is malleable and unclear. Even with great effort, it may be challenging to understand which patents may be applied to one's product.

It would be so easy to assume that one of the parties did something wrong. Either the infringing party brazenly used someone else's ideas or the patent holder is an evil night creature, waiting in the shadows to suck the life out of a hard-working company. The truth often falls far from either extreme. With the complexity of modern technological products and the vast number of patents issued, it is impossible to identify every patent that might in any way suggest rights to any part of a particular device. When a product becomes visible or successful in a field, that success offers a great incentive. Patent holders in the field may scrutinize their patents for any claim that might plausibly cover any part of the device or its manufacture.

In addition, a market actor who faces a vast number of patents and uncertainty of terms may have little incentive to try to determine whether a particular patent might be applicable to the product. The patent holder may do nothing with the patent or may target someone else's product. Outside of a broad-brush search or a search that focuses on direct competitors or major market actors, why invest the massive amount of resources it would take to resolve a question that might not need to be answered? The holder of the patent is the party with the incentive to investigate the potential applications of the right. Other parties are more likely to wait for the process to unfold.

Finally, variability in interpreting and applying a patent may come strongly into play when a patent comes to be owned by someone other than the original inventor. With new ownership, the claims may now be pushed to cover something that was not at all conscious in the mind of the original inventor or even the original owner. This may be true particularly if the new owner is operating in a slightly different commercial space from that of the original owner. Looking across a different commercial field may provide new inspiration for products against which one can assert the patent. As with the truncated language of poetry, a new reader may see different things in the same words of the claim.

In short, for an inventor holding a newly minted patent, those already in the market may offer the easiest way to create value from the right to exclude. As one practitioner commented to me, you cannot simply walk up to people and say, "license my patent and start something with it." There must be some basis of interest, some market, some interested participants.

## THE COMPANION TRADE SECRET LICENSE

The extent to which information continues to unfold after the grant of the patent is evident in the companion agreements that often accompany a patent license. Those wishing to license a patent license frequently receive other licenses in addition, such as trade secret, or know-how and show-how licenses. Such information could include what experimentation had been done in the past, how to solve technical complications that arise when a patent is applied to a product, and what types of approaches are advantageous. Such licenses may reflect the fact that there is considerable information outside of what is revealed in the patent. Given that the information is designated a "trade secret" rather than part of the patent, the information need not necessarily have been developed at the time of the patent but could, and often does, emerge later.

There are many reasons why having a trade secret license as a companion to a patent license may be advantageous, and not all of them relate to the fact that information may develop after patenting. Valuable trade secret information may have emerged prior to the patent, and the patent holder has a perfectly legitimate reason to treat that information separately. In addition, a license that encompasses both patent and trade secret information may provide a defense against patent misuse. Patent misuse is the impermissible attempt to extend the time or scope of one's patent. Provisions that could risk an accusation of patent misuse can be attributable to the transfer of trade secrets rather than the transfer of patented information, for example, if the agreement were to last longer than the term of the patent. Nevertheless, the companion agreements, in addition, do provide a method of sharing the additional information that may develop after the patent grant and ensuring the continued cooperation of inventors as those who apply the product try to learn more about the nature of the invention. The agreements provide some evidence that parties expect additional knowledge to emerge over time and certainly do not look to the patent to provide all of the necessary information.

This combination of factors provides attractive opportunities for patent holders to exercise their right to exclude by asserting it against those already in the market as a veiled threat with the offer of a license. Even if no one is currently infringing the patent, actors in the relevant market are also likely targets of approach. Those who are already invested in a particular market may have the greatest interest in making the investment to license an advancement of a product they already have—either as a method of improving their product or as a method of forestalling others from challenging them.

### CROSSING THE VALLEY OF DEATH

Of course, an inventor could always try to directly create and sell a product from the invention rather than licensing it to anyone. Even if no likely licensing prospects exist in the market, surely venture funding should be available for a truly innovative invention. A tremendous gap exists, however, between a patented invention and a saleable product. Making the transition presents challenges that make licensing or partnering with an established entity an appealing prospect—at least for individual inventors and smaller entities. The same is true for academic institutions, which are rarely interested in starting their own manufacturing plants.

To understand the problem, one must appreciate the complex relationship between a patent and a product.[39] A patented innovation does not necessarily translate into a single product or, in fact, into any product at all. As technology transfer officers and technology lawyers will attest, a tremendous chasm separates a patent from any marketable product. Few patent holders successfully cross that what is known as the "valley of death." Those who do are likely to need continued research to understand the invention's properties and applications and to either continue the inventive work or partner with others who will do so.

Part of the problem involves determining what to do with an invention. A novel discovery in the lab, for example, must be translated into something for which customers exist and that they will be able to afford. Most of the patented inventions at academic institutions never make the transition to some type of actual product.

Not only must a product be identified, but it must also be developed in such a way that it can be mass-produced in sufficient quality and quantity. Making a few specimens in a lab or a working model for the patent drafters does not ensure that something can be mass-produced in a stable, efficient manner. Nor does it guarantee that such production will be cost effective or that there will be sufficient demand to support its production.

In addition, the eventual product is likely to flow from numerous patented technologies in most cases. Such technologies may be present in the invention itself, in the process of making the invention, or in the processes that occur when the invention is used. Consider the popular communication device called the BlackBerry. The company holds patents on the physical components such as the keyboard and the LCD screen.[40] It also holds patents on elements of its functionality, such as its BlackBerry Single Mailbox Integration, which allows BlackBerry users to seamlessly integrate their mobile phones with their e-mail accounts.[41] A company producing the final product must either hold all of those patents itself or negotiate with others who hold those rights.

Multiplicity in patent interactions is not limited to the electronics field. Creation of genetically improved plants for crops, for example, requires the use of dozens of discrete and individually protected technologies.[42] Navigating that minefield can be quite difficult for an individual inventor or a start-up company, and it will surely involve interacting with other patent holders or working around existing patents.

It is certainly possible that a patented invention may involve no additional rights. Even in that case, however, an inventor may not be able to ascertain how to turn the patent into something that is stable enough for mass production and distribution or that fits within market needs sufficiently to make it cost effective.

In short, no matter how brilliant the invention, the newly minted patent holder is a long way from turning that it into a saleable product. It will take many additional steps to understand what a patented idea can be turned into, carry that notion through to a mass-produced and widely desired product, and accomplish all of this while coordinating the additional rights necessary to bring a final product to market.

## The Dance of the Sugar Plum Letter

Finding a potential licensing target sets off the complicated bargaining process that is familiar to anyone in the patenting world. Recall the inventor of the biodegradable grocery bags described in chapter 1. Suppose the inventor believes that grocery bags from Whole Foods Market are infringing the patent and wants the grocery chain to pay a license fee. If the patent holder behaves in any manner that creates a substantial controversy of sufficient immediacy with Whole Foods Market, the grocery chain can file a declaratory judgment attacking the patent's validity.[43] The inventor must find a way to enter licensing negotiations without putting the patent at risk. This is a particular concern for start-up companies or smaller inventors, who may not have the resources to defend even a strong patent. The problem is of some concern for any patent holder, however, given the high costs of patent suits and uncertainty about the limitations of any patent and any individual claim.[44]

As a result, correspondence is carefully phrased with language such as "you might be interested in reviewing the attached patents" or "you might be interested in learning about our patents." Other language might suggest that the parties "may have some areas of mutual interest that would be worth exploring." The goal is to project one's voice without speaking—or at least without speaking loudly enough to trigger an invalidity challenge.

The risk of having a declaratory judgment action filed is not just that one's patent may be challenged; it is also that the patent holder may cede control of that challenge. Forum rules for patents are quite flexible with regard to where the suit may be filed, but the choice belongs to the person who initiates the action.[45] If a patent holder files an infringement suit, that individual can choose the forum. If another party files a declaratory judgment against the patent, however, that party chooses the forum.[46]

Choice of forum matters, among other reasons, for timing. Time is often on the side of those accused of infringement rather than the patent holder. The longer one looks, the greater the chance of finding something in the patent, in the prior art, or in the prosecution history to invalidate the patent or undermine a particular claim. Given that forums vary considerably in terms of their speed,[47] giving up the choice of forum can result in significant costs. Thus, patent holders must gauge the entire dance to either avoid triggering a declaratory judgment suit or file an infringement action first, if the declaratory suit seems imminent.

Some of the "negotiating" dance may be one-sided. For example, a company receiving a sugar plum letter could choose not to respond. Patent holders do not always sue, and the company may make a calculated assessment that either the patent claim is weak or the risk of follow-through is minimal. This does not necessarily mean that the company is ignoring the letter. If the letter implies, for example, that the company's products are being made in a way that infringes a patent, the company could try to alter the manufacturing process in order to design around the patent or fall more closely within patents held by the company itself. Thus, if the patent holder sues, damages will at least be limited to products produced before the product change.

It is possible that a one-sided exchange may affect the boundaries of the patent. Suppose the accused company has its own patents that might arguably cover its products. If it chooses to redesign anyway, the company may be effectively relinquishing any interpretation of its own patents that might cover its own products as originally designed. In that circumstance, it is relinquishing a potential interpretation in the face of rights held by others who have expressed a willingness to assert those rights. By ceding the territory, albeit silently, the company has set a boundary on its rights that is more limited than what the language in the patent might imply.

Exploratory letters are part of the intricate strategies that unfold as patent holders navigate among their own patents and those held by others. Actualizing one's patent is not a matter of simply asserting a set of rights memorialized in the grant. It is also a matter of assessing one's strengths and vulnerabilities in relation to other players in the field. Declaratory judgments are not the only threat to patent holders who try to license their technology— they must also worry that the target may come up with grounds to request a reexamination of the patent from the Patent and Trademark Office. For example, when licensing talks failed between Microsoft and patent holder Avistar, Microsoft asked the PTO to reexamine twenty-nine of Avistar's patents.[48] In the resulting fallout, Avistar was forced to fire 25% of its work force a month later.[49]

Patent holders must worry not only about actions to declare their patents invalid but also about whether the other party holds any patents that could be asserted against them in counterclaim. Thinking back to the grocery-bag example given earlier, Whole Foods may hold its own patents on bag technology. In response to an inquiry by the biodegradable bag inventor, Whole Foods could reply with a long list of its own patents. The grocery chain is essentially saying to the inventor, "If you come after us, not only do you put your patent at risk of being invalidated, but you also risk an infringement suit against any bags you make or license others to make."

The greater the number of patents a party holds, the wider the array of potential threats. For example, suppose a computer-chip manufacturer wishes to assert a patent against a personal computer maker, and the PC maker responds by waving a rather weak or tangential patent back at the chip company. The chip company could laugh it off, knowing that the counterpatent may not be much of a threat. Nevertheless, if the PC maker holds thousands of patents, the threat is more ominous. In theory, the PC maker could assert numerous patents against the chip manufacturer, all together or one after another. Eventually, a claim from one of them might gain traction in the courts. Even if it does not, the cost of defending against the onslaught could be daunting to the chip company.

Beyond the general value of intimidation, numbers of patents can matter in very tangible ways.[50] For example, a scholar who has chronicled the history of cross-licensing agreements among the major companies in the computer hard-drive industry describes the following interaction.[51] After initially struggling with each other over patent infringement issues, the companies granted blanket cross licenses covering everyone's entire patent portfolios. When the agreements were renewed, the companies frequently counted their patents and asked for royalties from those who held fewer patents. Thus, the sheer number of patents, regardless of their coverage, affected the level of return.

Patent strategies are as numerous and creative as the inventors themselves. One technology executive described his company's patent strategy to me as the following: The company surveys the competitors in their field, identifying areas of technology that are critical to the competitor's success. These areas are designated as "pain points." The company then buys up patents that in some way relate to these pain points. If the competitor threatens a lawsuit, the company can simply pull out its pain point patents and threaten to countersue.

As described earlier, preparations for these battles begin at the filing stage and even at the research stage, in which one decides what areas to investigate. Having a series of patents within an area can provide both a defensive and an offensive arsenal.

One might imagine that the strongest position from which to launch a patent negotiation would be held by those who are entrenched in a particular field. After all, the established players may hold many patents that can be rattled as a threatened counterstrike against those who would challenge their products or would ignore the assertion of their rights. Accumulating patents to assert in an area and amassing power, however, is not the only strategy for patent negotiation. Those whose products are in unrelated fields and those who have few assets at all may actually have strong bargaining positions. For a simple example, imagine a company, ChocolateCo, that makes chocolate but holds a patent on telephone technology. ChocolateCo may have an interesting bargaining position. It can assert the patents against a telecommunications company without any fear that the telecom company can pull out its own patents and aim them at ChocolateCo's products. Although chocolate and telephones are an unlikely business mix for a firm's strategy, in the fast-paced world of start-ups, companies can find themselves holding patents in diverse fields as a result of mergers and acquisitions.

Peripheral technologies have been known to develop outside of the start-up world as well. Research on ceramics for the European space shuttle *Hermes,* for example, led to applications in the automobile industry.[52]

Analogous to the case of a firm licensing peripheral rather than core technologies, a firm with limited products and assets may also be in a better position in patent negotiations. The firm has less to lose and is a less appealing target for an infringement counterclaim because there will be little to collect if the claim succeeds.

Thus, in the complex world of patent negotiation, companies may marshal resources for the battle that are beyond the patent itself. They may look to other patents they own, their strengths and weaknesses as an entity, and their market position. Again, preparations for these encounters may dictate what language is placed in a patent application, what language is relinquished during the patent prosecution process, and what positions are taken in negotiations after receipt of the patent.

For example, various entities will be able to pursue different interpretations of a particular patent. A small company may not be in a position to fight for a strong interpretation of the boundaries of its patent, while a non-producing entity may have strengths and vulnerabilities better suited to the dispute. Consider a patent owned by a company too small to pay much in the way of litigation costs. Given its size, major manufacturers with products that may infringe the patent will ignore its licensing approaches and snicker at its enforcement threats. If a larger company buys the patent, however, the same manufacturers will take a different approach. Knowing that the larger company can afford to litigate, the manufacturers will actually evaluate the patent on its merits, and the scope of that patent in the context of the manufacturer's products will be explored and tested. The questions raised about the patent, as well as the definition of rights that results, will depend on who owns it.

The source of capital for an enterprise can also affect patenting choices. Those who need venture funding or alternate risk capital may have a tendency to write broad claims during initial filing as a response to the pressures of capital markets. Venture capitalists (VCs) consider patents important when deciding whether to fund an enterprise and are aware of the potential to claim widely.[53] This can act as a feedback echo by encouraging start-up companies to adopt an expansive position. As one start-up lawyer explained, if you do not begin by claiming widely, the VCs will ask why you did not try to reach farther with the patent. This encourages inventors to reach for the stars, knowing that although they may hit the roof, some of those far-reaching claims will actually survive.

Small companies, even those that do not require venture funding, may also feel the need to puff out their chest. They will need to create the illusion of being aggressive and having as much power as possible in order to do battle with larger, more powerful creatures. Thus, a small company may have an incentive to claim more and to claim more broadly. The same may be true for a university. Although certainly not a small entity, the portion of resources represented in the licensing aspect of a university is quite small in relation to the resources dedicated to its core mission. Thus, one may see universities reaching farther and claiming more broadly, while established entities may claim more tightly.

A stark example of this can be seen by comparing the patents held by the parties in the case of *University of Rochester v. Searle*.[54] The case pitted a research university against a large pharmaceutical. The innovation concerned reducing the side effects of over-the-counter painkillers, such as ibuprofen, aspirin, and naproxen. Painkillers in this category may carry the risk of side effects, including stomach upset, irritation, ulcers, and bleeding, particularly for chronically ill patients with arthritis, who use the medications repeatedly and long term. Researchers discovered that the problem occurred because the medicines that blocked the pain also blocked two bodily processes that occur in the stomach lining. They hypothesized that one could avoid these side effects by inhibiting only one of these processes but not the other. In other words, one would try to prohibit the response to inflammatory stimuli but not the beneficial response that protected the stomach lining.

The university developed and patented screening assays to identify compounds that would selectively inhibit only what was necessary for pain treatment and not what was necessary to protect the stomach. The patent also described what may be done with any compounds potentially identified through these assays, such as formulation into pharmaceuticals, estimation of effective dosages, and dosage forms. However, the patent neglected to disclose *which* compounds had the desired characteristics of inhibiting the inflammatory process. In other words, the university claimed the class of all compounds discovered using the assaying methods and the resulting treatments without identifying any members of the class. The Federal Circuit eventually rejected the claims, although not without considerable wrangling among the various judges.[55]

In contrast to the university's tremendously broad claims, consider the claims in the relevant patents held by the pharmaceutical company. Although the patents were not at issue in the opinion,[56] the pharmaceutical company held patents on the drug in question, Celebrex. The company's claims in those patents consisted of the relatively less aggressive and less risky method and composition of matter claims.

The contrast is not surprising given the position of the two players in the field.[57] A university technology transfer department generally has no manufacturing capacity. It is faced with a plethora of broad, unapplied patents. In the decades to come, only a few of these will play a role in a major invention and yield significant returns. With few possibilities for earning revenue from the patents and patents scattered among many fields, the university may choose to write claims more broadly and aggressively.

In contrast to start-ups and universities, those with established market positions who have other types of weapons may choose different strategies in claiming and relinquishing claim language. For example, tension always exists in patent drafting between claiming broadly, to reach as far as possible, and claiming narrowly, to reduce the possibility that the claim will be invalidated for lack of support. Companies can navigate around that choice by contemplating other assets and options. Consider the case of AstraZeneca, which manufactures the blockbuster drug Prilosec. The company obtained patents on the next-generation formulation of Prilosec, which it named Nexium. The claims in the Nexium patent are similar to, but narrower than, the type of claims in the Prilosec patents. As chapter 5 explains, AstraZeneca used the power already created by its blockbuster drug to shift the market to its next-generation version. The strategy would only work, however, if there were narrower claims in the follow-on patent.

Battles may take place between others in addition to the patent holder and the potential infringer. Increasing the number of parties naturally increases the range of bargaining strategies and pressure points. Modern technology battles, for example, may involve skirmishes over interactions with standards bodies and claims of improper behavior related to the adoption of standards.[58] Having one's patented technology chosen as a standard in the industry can be enormously important for patent holders. The resulting power is so substantial that it can easily tempt patent holders to manipulate the process or convince others to raise a cry of manipulation even if the charges are unfounded.

Patent holders may also choose to send letters not only to the infringer but also to the infringer's customers. Such letters may be sweetly phrased to do no more than indicate what is claimed in the patent, informing the customers that they may be purchasing from someone whose rights are in doubt. Even a letter with a light touch can have a devastating effect on sales. Customers may be perfectly happy to switch to another supplier if they see any possibility of getting caught in the middle of a fight. As one commentator noted, sending letters about intellectual property rights to the infringer's customers may yield far more than suing the infringer. By chasing away the other party's customers, the rights holder can effectively gain a temporary restraining order, thereby preventing the other party from engaging in its business.[59] Such an order would be very difficult to obtain in an infringement lawsuit.

Like the sugar plum letters, customer approaches must be delicately calibrated. A careless approach could result in the loss of forum advantage. In the *Miale* case, for example, the patent holder visited a trade show, attempted to have products removed, and told customers that the products were infringing.[60] The Federal Circuit—against the wishes of the patent holder—allowed the lawsuit to go forward where the trade show had taken place. In upholding the long-arm statute allowing jurisdiction in the state where the trade show occurred, the Federal Circuit noted that although sending letters to another state is not sufficient to create personal jurisdiction, the facts of the case constituted attempts at "extra-judicial patent enforcement," which were sufficient to create jurisdiction for the purposes of the case.[61]

Although patent holders may have to worry about forum choice or validity challenges in sending letters to a potential infringer's customers, they have far less to worry about in terms of whether the infringement allegations actually have any merit. In theory, a patent holder might be charged with anticompetitive conduct under either state or federal laws.[62] The standards in such cases, however, are quite difficult to meet. In *GP Industries v. Eran*, for example, the Federal Circuit considered cease-and-desist letters sent to a competitor's distributors and contractors alleging patent infringement and misappropriation of trade secrets.[63] The letters contained quite harsh language, including allegations that the competitor's actions constituted mail fraud, interstate transportation of stolen property, and an unlawful pattern of racketeering activity in violation of the Racketeer Influenced and Corrupt Organizations Act (RICO). The letters ended with the following admonition:

> [T]his letter is intended to place you on notice that Eran Industries will consider naming your company as an additional defendant unless you either demonstrate that your company is not selling or offering for sale [the patent holder's] products or agrees to promptly forever cease selling or offering for sale those products.[64]

The Federal Circuit overturned a lower court injunction against sending additional such letters. Although crediting the lower court's finding that the patent holder's activities approached the threshold of bad faith and had a taint of retaliatory action, the Federal Circuit noted that the patent holder's actions had to be both objectively and subjectively baseless.[65] The lower court had failed to apply the objectively baseless prong of the test, which required that "no reasonable litigant could realistically expect success on the merits."[66]

All areas of law are burdened by the possibility of aggressive litigation threats aimed at adversaries or third parties. It is difficult to stop such behavior because the threshold for proving anticompetitive conduct due to litigious behavior is quite high regardless of the doctrinal basis of the threat. In the patent arena, nevertheless, such activity may be particularly free of consequences. Given the open-ended nature of patent determinations, one would have great difficulty establishing that the patent holder had no reasonable possibility at all of anticipating success.

## Never Having to Say Good-Bye

One might imagine that, having received a patent, the patent holder would wave a fond farewell to the patent office and walk out, claims in hand, never to return. Such is not the case. Patent holders are subject to being summoned back to the PTO to have the patents reviewed and potentially revised or reversed after reexamination.[67] For some time third parties have been able to file a request for reexamination at any time during the patent's period of enforceability by alleging that a particular piece of prior art, not considered by the patent office, would render the patent invalid.[68] If the patent office determines that the prior art does, in fact, raise a "substantial new question of patentability," it will order a reexamination.[69] The third party initiating the process can submit the request either *ex parte,* which ends its participation after the request and prior art are submitted, or *inter partes,* which allows it to file additional arguments in response to the patentee's filings.[70] The director of the PTO can also initiate the reexamination process at any time if patents or publications raise significant new questions of patentability.[71] The America Invents Act, which was signed into law in the fall of 2011, creates additional pathways for reexamination.

For example, the University of Wisconsin, in the form of the Wisconsin Alumni Research Foundation (WARF), holds pioneering patents in the field of embryonic stem-cell research. Those patents were subjected to reexamination following public outcry that the patents were overbroad and would block downstream research in the area.[72] Two of the Wisconsin patents were ultimately reaffirmed, although after some adjustment of the claims language, and a third was finally invalidated by the Board of Patent Appeals and Interferences.[73]

From a bargaining perspective, the Wisconsin case highlights the continued negotiation over the reach of a patent. Given that the language of a patent is subject to adjustment after the patent has been issued, those who enter the bargaining fray can—as a bargaining chip—threaten to initiate a reexamination procedure or to create public pressure for one.

In addition to being summoned back to the patent office, patent holders can voluntarily return. A patent holder can file for reissuance of a patent within two years of the patent grant to broaden the scope of the patent to include subject matter erroneously excluded from the patent.[74] Reissuance is subject to limitations, including that the original disclosure must support the reissued claims and the patent holder must not have surrendered during the prosecution of the original patent what it is now trying to recapture through reissuance.[75] Despite these limitations, reissuance in some circumstances can be an effective vehicle for adjusting the reach of one's patent to achieve optimal coverage over time. For an example of the use of reissuance during litigation, see the discussion of the *Aspex Eyewear* case at the end of this chapter.

The potential value of the reissuance procedure is not lost on modern-day patent holders, and the company Intellectual Ventures is a wonderful example.[76] Intellectual Ventures is a heavily funded organization that acquires inventions and related intellectual property rights. Founded by a group that includes the former chief technical officer of Microsoft and the former assistant general counsel of Intel, the company is one of the top fifty patent filers in the United States.[77] Funders include Microsoft, Intel, Sony, Nokia, Apple, Google, and eBay.[78]

Studying the complex transactions and shell companies that compose Intellectual Ventures suggests that the company held between 25,000 and 50,000 patents worldwide as of the end of 2009, although the number is based on certain projections and estimates.[79] A common practice for Intellectual Ventures is to file broadening reissue applications for the patents as it acquires a particular portfolio.[80]

Even the length of the patent term is subject to negotiation, at least between the inventor and the sovereign. In 1984 Congress passed the Drug Price Competition and Patent Restoration Act, also known as the Hatch-Waxman Act. The act added Section 156 to the Patent Act, providing an extension to patent terms for patents on products that are subject to regulatory review prior to commercial marketing or use. In essence, the act reimburses a patentee for a portion of the patent term, during which time the patentee is prohibited from selling or marketing a product while awaiting government approval, such as the Food and Drug Administration's review of a prescription drug.

Modern patent law also provides for an adjustment in the length of the patent term to take into account delays in the prosecution of the patent.[81] In 2009 a survey suggested that numerous patents receive this benefit.[82] Of the roughly three thousand patents granted on a particular day in 2009, 75%

received a patent term adjustment. The average length was fifteen months, and the longest was more than five years.

Patent term adjustment can be one of the complex strategies that enable patent holders to use multiple patents with different types of claims to pursue their goals. For example, three commentators have prepared a wonderful piece describing the value of dual patenting strategies that can be used when a patent holder would like to have both an early grant date and a late termination date.[83]

These complexities add to the bargaining possibilities for patent holders, who may then have multiple types of claims with varying language and differing implications for emerging products. Even the sheer number of available patents and potential patent claims can provide bargaining leverage.

## Facts on the Ground

The critical vehicle for defining the extent of a patent may be a contract rather than a court opinion. In drafting a license contract, there is always a tension between crafting a license that grants rights to do something specific or crafting one that grants a general right to infringe the patent. If the patent holder describes the patent in terms of the right to do a specific set of activities, the parties may, in effect, have contractually construed the claims. In other words, the parties are agreeing that the patent covers what is described in the license.

Of course, the strategy may not work. In licensing negotiations, adopting an aggressive interpretation of one's patents is no guarantee of obtaining that reach. The other side may decline to join one's interpretation. In addition, under current Supreme Court doctrines, the person licensing your technology may be able to challenge the validity of a patent despite having signed an agreement to license.

Nevertheless, if the parties do agree on an interpretation, they may have contractually sorted out ambiguities in the patent language as it relates to other products and inventions that emerge over time. In addition, if the parties choose to reveal their agreements—and they may not—the agreements can influence the way those rights are viewed in the field.

Of course, attempts to create facts on the ground are not always welcome or successful. Microsoft, the operating-system giant, tried for years to convince those who made products related to the open-source operating system Linux to sign covenants and licenses related to patents.[84] Microsoft insisted on the provisions as part of any agreement to make Linux-based products operate more effectively with Microsoft products. The covenants and licensing provisions could have given credence to Microsoft's claim that Linux actually infringes Microsoft's patents and that the patents are valid. More important, the covenants could have undermined the open nature of the Linux system. Although one major player agreed to sign, another refused, and Microsoft eventually relented.

Similarly, clever drafting and negotiating can create de facto interpretations of the language even if that interpretation is unlikely to withhold scrutiny in court. With uncertainty of language interpretation, fast-paced bargaining, and much of the bargaining taking place outside of the courthouse, parties may be able to secure an expansive interpretation of their rights. One practitioner offered the following example. He was asked to review a patent portfolio that a client wanted to purchase. The core patents in the portfolio included an original patent, whose specification language was considered too thin for the purposes at hand, and a continuation application of that patent. The language in the continuation was very detailed and well targeted for what the client wanted to accomplish but had a much later filing date.

In theory, patent holders should not be able to do this. Continuation applications should not expand beyond what was included in the original application. In the bargaining world of patents, however, the patent holder had been able to use the two documents together quite effectively. Bargaining with the two in hand, he had been able to obtain an expansive definition dating back to an earlier time. It was a double-sided benefit that neither filing could have generated alone and one that could have faced significant obstacles in an infringement lawsuit. In other words, a narrow, weak patent had nevertheless resulted in a broad interpretation on the ground.

Of course, clever negotiating and creative use of any asset may result in more value for the asset than it might obtain in other circumstances. Nevertheless, the bargaining atmosphere of the patent world, combined with its fast pace and the uncertainty of language interpretation, make the patent world particularly ripe for this type of result.

## Bargaining at the Courthouse and Beyond

A license, of course, is no more than an agreement not to sue. Thus, bargaining over licensing and bargaining during a lawsuit are part of the same continuum. The courthouse is merely an extension of the action in which patent holders actualize their rights.

As many of the earlier examples have shown, if the parties proceed to court, the bargaining will continue within the litigation as the parties sue and countersue, arguing over the coverage of their respective patents in light of the products that have emerged. Some of the bargaining will play out in agreements between the parties during the litigation. Stipulations of the meaning of certain terms or claims and settlement agreements are themselves a form of contract, in which the parties agree to a definition of the reach of their rights. When such agreements are not reached, the court will offer its own interpretation of the scope of the rights, a process that can easily involve questions that were unexplored or unexplorable at the time of the invention or at the time of the grant.

Consider the case of *Chiron v. Genentech*.[85] The case concerned antibodies that could be used to fight off breast cancer.[86] Antibodies are Y-shaped proteins that defend the body against harmful agents by binding with those agents and rendering them inactive.[87] At the time of the invention in the Chiron case, scientists had succeeded only in creating antibodies from mouse cells, and the invention in the case was created in that manner.[88] Antibody science, however, had advanced considerably during the life of the patent at issue. In particular, the case concerned an infringement suit against another company with an antibody created predominantly from human genetic coding materials, a so-called humanized antibody.[89] The court had to grapple with questions related to the reach of the original antibody patent in light of the emerging information.

Throughout the bargaining life of any individual patent, the action may weave in and out of the courtroom.[90] Consider the case of *New Medium v. Barco*, which involved infringement claims related to eleven patents against a number of defendants.[91] The patents had been subject to a reexamination proceeding at the PTO. The case included a trail of cease-and-desist letters, as well as complex motions related to jurisdiction, ownership of the patents, and claim construction. In a 2008 decision Judge Posner, sitting by designation, held that the patent holder had engaged in inequitable conduct during the reexamination when he stated that he had never met or talked to any of the experts prior to the litigation.[92] On the contrary, the patent holder had solicited and paid for a bid from one of the experts seven years earlier.[93]

Judge Posner's finding of inequitable conduct rendered the patents entirely unenforceable against any party. Following the decision, the parties settled the case with an agreement that included vacating the order of inequitable conduct. Thus, the settlement had the effect of reinstating the patents so that the patent holder could proceed against other alleged infringers. In other words, a decision invalidating patents was nullified by agreement among the parties, reviving the action and transferring it back to further negotiations and perhaps further litigation among other parties.

As with any legal issue, bargaining may take place in other forums outside of the courtroom in which the case is being heard, as the parties try to affect the legal rules that could better support their desired interpretations. Patent holders may feel moved to file amicus briefs in other cases or may resort to the court of public opinion for encouraging or resisting legal change. Of particular note in recent years, the *Bilski* case in the Supreme Court drew more than sixty amicus briefs, including ones from individual companies in various industries and from industry organizations.[94] Battles over testing for genetic mutations related to breast cancer have led to outraged op-ed pieces in the popular press, proposed legislation to forbid patenting of any genes, and a lawsuit challenging the patentability of isolated and purified genes.[95] Thinking back to the analogy of patents as a license for hunting bears, such approaches allow one, in the middle of the hunt, to bargain for increasing the allotted hunting territory.

From the perspective of the sovereign weaving in and out of the process, patent law could benefit from the insights of Mnookin and Kornhauser in their classic article, "Bargaining in the Shadow of the Law: The Case of Divorce."[96] Mnookin and Kornhauser examined the extent to which divorcing couples do not require courtroom adjudication of their disputes but would be better served by private ordering or by alternative dispute forums.[97] In examining the question, the authors considered the effects that various standards might have in granting bargaining endowments to a particular party, thereby influencing the outcomes.[98]

Mnookin and Kornhauser approached the issue as a question of the extent to which law should authorize private ordering of disputes in place of legal adjudication. The bargain aspect suggests, however, that, at least for patent law, bargaining either with or without direct sovereign presence is the same process of negotiating the contours of the rights the parties can secure.

## Business Negotiations or Rights Bargaining?

This chapter has described examples of the bargaining that takes place within the patent system. In the rampant bargaining that is the hallmark of the modern patent system, much activity will occur that is not directly related to defining the contours of the rights. Bargaining certainly occurs over the value of the rights rather than the definition of the rights themselves, and some of it may appear more closely related to the maneuvering that any business might engage in to maximize the value of any asset.

Nevertheless, in many aspects of the patent bargaining, the contours of the rights emerge because their interpretation is on the table. Ordinary business-asset negotiations take on a different hue when the definition of the asset rather than simply its value is at issue.

The descriptive chapter of the book likely seems quite familiar to those in the trenches of patent law. For example, after hearing a discussion of the bargain aspect concept, one patent practitioner enthusiastically offered the following analogy of the patent system.[99]

One should view the patent system as a bakery. The "invention farmer" delivers raw ingredients to a patent bakery. Those who work on the ingredients at the bakery include the owner of the shop, the investor, the business consultant, and the patent attorney. The patent attorney will typically want to refine the raw invention to remove those parts that are not patentable and add to the raw invention some filler that will give the final product a longer, useful shelf life and broader consumer appeal. Both the owner of the bakery and the investor will normally want to stretch the invention dough to cover some perceived profitable business area while also providing cost constraints on the whole process. This semirefined product is then submitted to the patent office, which owns the only oven in the town. The government lops off bits of invention dough that it perceives to be old. This is why most actors submit loaves that lop way over the pan, and if the government bakers do not notice, then so much the better. What pops out of the government oven is supposed to be a finished loaf. Nevertheless, the use one can make of the product may depend as much on extrinsic factors as on the quality of the loaf. In the patent world, one sees sandwiches made out of cake slices and wedding cakes made from crackers.

## Summing Up the Bargaining Landscape

This chapter has described a number of examples in which modern patent holders bargain over the definition of rights in a patent in diverse ways. Patent holders are likely to engage in a number of these activities over the life of any individual patent. The following example nicely demonstrates the dynamic action in the modern patent world.

The example describes various lawsuits among three eyeglass manufacturers. Throughout the lawsuits, all three manufacturers are circling each other, testing the limits of each of the patents, the claims within those patents, and the potential interpretations of those claims in light of the product lines being developed. The definitions and the boundary lines of each patent claim develop as the parties pursue or abandon a variety of interpretations during the negotiations.

The example is not from a complex bioscience invention, in which much scientific information is unknown. Nor is it from the fast-paced world of computer software and electronics, in which inventions can become obsolete almost as quickly as inventors can dream them up. It is an example from a set of simple mechanical patents relating to how eyeglass frames are held together. Even in that context, bargaining over the extent of the rights is a fact of life.

The example centers on the Aspex Eyewear company, which manufactures eyeglass frames that are held together with studs and magnets.[100] Aspex is the exclusive licensee of a series of patents related to these magnetically attached frames.

In 2003 a competitor introduced a line of magnetically attached eyeglass frames. Aspex sent a series of cease-and-desist letters to the competitor, identifying five Aspex patents that the competitor might be infringing, including the '747 patent.

The competitor asked for clarification on which of the claims within these patents Aspex believed might cover the products, and Aspex identified claims in only two of the patents. Although the '747 patent was listed in a cease-and-desist letter sent prior to the request for clarification, no claims from that patent were mentioned in response to the clarification request.

Four years later Aspex sued the competitor for infringement based on claims within the '747 patent. The district court granted summary judgment against Aspex, finding that Aspex's silence and inaction estopped it from enforcing its claims.[101]

During the same period of time, Aspex itself was engaged in extensive litigation with another eyeglass manufacturer who also held patents related to magnetically attached frames. The two companies filed suits and counterclaims, each accusing the other of patent infringement and defending on the grounds that the other party's patents were invalid or that their own products did not infringe. The set of cases is complex and fascinating, but a key exchange in the battle includes the following: In 1999 Aspex sued Revolution Eyewear for infringement of a patent.[102] Aspex lost the case when the court agreed with the competitor's summary judgment motion that the company's eyewear did not infringe the claims of Aspex's patent.[103]

While the case was pending, Aspex filed for reissuance of its patent with the Patent and Trademark Office.[104] The reissue request was still pending when the litigation ended.[105] Although Aspex's original patent had contained only two claims, the reissued patent contained thirty-four claims.[106]

In 2002 Revolution sued Aspex for infringement of its own patents related to magnetic eyewear.[107] When Aspex received its reissued patent, Aspex filed counterclaims against Revolution for infringement of the newly minted claims.[108] Revolution's original infringement claim was dismissed for lack of standing, but the counterclaim went forward.[109] In other words, in choosing to file an infringement suit, Revolution ended up in a tough position. Revolution's claims were dismissed, and the company then found itself facing counterclaims from a newly reissued patent, whose words could have been crafted with Revolution's product in mind.

During the counterclaim lawsuit and related cases, the court had to consider whether the term "magnetic" should be understood as different from the notion of "magnetic material" and whether the phrase "forming appendages extending from either side of said auxiliary eyeglasses" meant "an appendage to each side of the auxiliary eyeglasses" or "two or more appendages . . . on at least one side of the auxiliary eyeglasses."[110]

In the countersuit Aspex initially argued that Revolution infringed three of the thirty-four claims it had received in the reissued patent. Aspex later declined to pursue two of these, but the company eventually succeeded on the third.[111]

At the end of the day, the handful of claims and patents Aspex held when its various pieces of litigation began in 2002 and 2003 were only the beginning of defining the company's rights. The company abandoned some of those claims in cease-and-desist bargaining, expanded the number of claims, altered claims language through reissuance, dropped some of those new claims, focused on particular portions of other claims after the court had defined certain phrases, and ultimately succeeded in an infringement suit—at least against one company. Most important, all of the altered language and shifting of position occurred as Aspex monitored the market for the emergence of competing products.

The *Aspex* case and other examples demonstrate that any descriptive analysis of the modern patent system would be replete with bargaining over the contours of the rights of individual patents. That description is consistent with what one would expect from the theoretical perspectives of bargain theory. Given the problems of newness, the patent cannot possibly delineate the contours of the rights at the moment of the grant. The lack of a shared conception, the difficulties of language, and problems related to lack of information at the grant fixation all ensure that the patent grant will leave much to be defined in the case of most patents. The process of definition occurs as the relevant parties vie with each other, negotiating according to their strengths, weaknesses and potentially overlapping rights. The modern description of the patent system displays the type of bargaining and navigating that one might expect in a rapidly changing environment in which the rights are unclear.

# 3

## Implications of the Bargain Aspect
## for Current Debates

With the bargain aspect in mind, one would have a radically different image of patents from what is reflected in the common academic wisdom. Common wisdom suggests that patents delineate the rights granted and that the courts interpret those rights. In the conventional view of patent law, the critical moment is the grant of the patent. After that, we are left with the postgame show to rehash and interpret the events of the day. In contrast, the bargain aspect suggests that the game is only beginning. The patent grant is a single moment in a complex process during which the inventor and others will bargain over the contours of the rights they will receive.

To be fair, the conventional view of patents does not suggest that the sovereign's role ends with the grant of the patent. Patent law and scholarship direct tremendous energy toward the development of rules that will be applied after a patent is granted for determining whether the patent has been granted properly and precisely what has been granted. Nevertheless, the inquiry remains distinctly out of focus in its failure to recognize both the uncertainty inherent in any grant and the dynamic nature of the process.

How then should we think about the role of the legal system in this process? What can envisioning the bargain aspect add to modern struggles within patent law? The bargain aspect suggests that legal doctrines should be designed to promote the best development of rights for the life of the patent. Each individual question we ask, whether it is about the boundaries of a particular bargain, the rules for setting the boundaries of bargains, or the rules for acceptable bargaining by the parties, should be framed in terms of whether it will promote the development of the best rights boundaries during the life of the patent. What, then, should constitute "best?"

Even framing the question in this manner reflects to some extent the orientation of the U.S. patent system. Modern U.S. patent law is explicitly and unabashedly utilitarian. Although some scholars have argued that early aspects of U.S. history reflect varying strains of thought, and some of our treaty obligations related to copyright echo European notions of moral rights,[1] U.S. patent law has rested firmly on utilitarian grounds for centuries.[2] As the Supreme Court noted in *Graham v. John Deere*, "[t]he patent monopoly was not designed to secure to the inventor his natural right in his discoveries. Rather, it was a reward, an inducement, to bring forth new knowledge."[3]

One might begin by asking, in more precise fashion, just what utilitarianism means. Utilitarianism and the particular brand of utilitarianism that appears in patent law are offshoots of the more general moral theory of consequentialism, which holds that actions should be evaluated on the basis of the state of affairs that will result from those actions.[4] Consequentialism stands in contrast to nonconsequentialism, which holds that actions may be right or wrong independent of their resulting consequences.[5]

Different approaches to consequentialism offer varying views on how to evaluate the state of affairs that will result from a particular action. It would be possible, for example, to argue that any bad effects, no matter how small, would disqualify a course of action,[6] although this particular approach might prove quite paralyzing for anyone trying to make a consequentially ethical decision. One could also follow a general balancing notion, in which an action is proper if engaging in it would produce a total amount of good effects that at least outweigh the total amount of bad effects.[7]

A further refined notion of balancing, and the one that is undoubtedly most familiar to modern readers, is maximization. With maximization, an action is proper if it would lead to at least as great a balance of good over evil as all other possible courses of action, including inaction.

The general notion of maximization, however, does not specify whose "good" should be counted. For example, one could follow the maximization principles of ethical egoism, which holds that individuals should maximize what is good for themselves.[8] Ethical universalism, more commonly known as utilitarianism, holds that one should try to maximize the amount of good for the community as a whole.[9] Thus, utilitarianism holds that one should evaluate an action by the state of affairs that would result and that an action is proper if the balance of good and bad consequences for the community as a whole is at least as beneficial as that of any other course of action.

Even the form of consequentialism that we know as utilitarianism, however, does not define what is "good." It is left to each individual utilitarian system to supply such a definition. Law and economics, for example, defines the "good" as a person's well-being. It measures that well-being in terms of the ability of individuals to satisfy their preferences in the marketplace through wealth.[10] Scholars have argued extensively over the limitations of the law and economics definition of the good and its form of measurement.[11] Without some way of weighting preferences, for example, one would have to attach the same value to a person's enjoyment of food and shelter as to a person's enjoyment of torturing someone else.[12]

American patent law, however, begins with its own explicit definition of the "good" that is to be maximized. The authorizing language of the Constitution describes the purpose of the patent system as promoting the progress of the useful arts.[13] In more modern parlance, one could think of this as promoting applied inventions. Thus, the utilitarian vision in the American system would evaluate a patent law issue on the basis of whether it would maximize the creation of applied inventions—although some might prefer the less precise but more familiar phrase "promoting innovation" to the more cumbersome "promoting applied inventions"—with the understanding that the American system aims to protect applied innovation rather than basic science.

A patent system need not necessarily conform to a utilitarian vision but could flow from nonconsequentialist perspectives. One could imagine granting patent rights out of respect for the inventor's moral rights. Such a notion might presuppose that inventors possess inherent rights in their inventions as the creations of their mind and labor. Thus, the individual rights of the inventor would be core rights that should not be violated regardless of any possible pleasant consequences that might accrue for promoting innovation. The moral rights concepts of some European intellectual property laws, for example, contain nonconsequentialist notions.

Similarly, one could grant patents from the perspective of fairness and equity. In this vision, fairness and equity are moral norms in society that should not be violated regardless of any positive consequences. In contrast to the maximizing perspectives of utilitarianism, such pure nonconsequentialist approaches would not sacrifice core rights even for what is, on balance, a good result.[14] Thus, from a nonconsequentialist perspective, one might be reluctant to impose upon the rights of one inventor even if the result was to preserve the rights of many other inventors, let alone if it promoted innovation.

The American system, nevertheless, is explicitly utilitarian. We grant patent rights not because we recognize the moral rights of the inventors or because we feel it is only fair to grant rights to inventors but because we want to promote the progress of innovation. Within that context, questions about the appropriateness of actions are framed in terms of whether those actions will best promote innovation.

This is not to suggest that promotion of innovation or even patent rights will reign unchecked. Our legal system encompasses competing rights and values. These will play a role both inside and outside the patent system as patent holders interact with holders of other types of rights. We would not, for example, allow you to enslave a group of people no matter how beneficial the results might be for innovation. Our distaste for anyone's control over the life and liberty of others—decidedly nonconsequential notions—would prevent patents on human beings from ever falling within patentable subject matter. This is likely to remain true despite the fact that patents have been granted on other forms of life, such as genetically altered cows.[15] Nor would we allow you to use your patent rights in payment for the murder of your mother-in-law. In many contexts, competing rights and values will interact with and limit the extent of the rights granted and the bargaining permitted. Nevertheless, patent law is unusual both for its explicit utilitarianism and for its built-in definition of what qualifies as the good to which the system should aspire.

In light of this framework, if it were possible for a patent grant to set the definitive boundaries, one might ask what the optimal scope of the grant might be for promoting innovation. Fascinating literature has been devoted to this question, which in itself is difficult and intriguing even assuming patent grants were definitive.[16] As described earlier, however, definitive boundaries cannot be determined at the outset, and we are granting no more than an opportunity to negotiate those boundaries. Thus, society's goal in the patent arena must be to craft a system that will lead to the development of the best boundaries during the life of the patent, with "best" defined in terms of the impact on innovation. We make these choices with the understanding that much will take place outside the purview of the sovereign. The sovereign may weave in and out of this process, but for much of it, the sovereign's participation will be indirect at best.

One might also ask about the normative implications of bargaining itself. Is bargaining good for the patent system, bad for it, or simply neutral? In theory, a system in which all of the parties know the precise boundaries of patent rights would be far more efficient than one in which rampant bargaining reigns. At the very least, the transaction costs incurred at each step, as the parties navigate around each other to determine their rights, represent a waste of resources.

One could possibly construct a model to suggest that, given the large number of patents and the fact that the sovereign cannot be present for all critical determinations, bargaining might create efficiencies.[17] At a fundamental level, however, a system of perfect information about rights would be more efficient than one in which the boundaries of rights are determined through extensive, multiparty negotiations. In this context, bargaining is not an unmitigated positive aspect of our system, although it is certainly possible that some aspects of bargaining are efficiency enhancing, given other aspects of the system. Thus, at a very general level, doctrines that limit the bargaining, as well as those that produce a more efficient bargaining process, may be preferable to the sovereign, assuming those doctrines are consistent with the overarching goal of promoting innovation.

In this discussion I am assuming, of course, that the sovereign and its actions represent the interests of the society it governs as a whole. One could easily argue to the contrary. Given the possibility of industry capture, agency capture, errors in human judgment, lack of information, and other difficulties, the sovereign may indeed be a poor approximation of the interests of society as a whole even in a democracy.[18] Moreover, some theorists would deny the validity of any construct involving a collective activity or a general will attributable to society as a whole. Nevertheless, it is helpful to have some starting point. The discrepancy between society's interests and the sovereign's ability to recognize and internalize those interests, not to mention the possibility that the society may have no collective interests at all, is a can of worms I will leave to others.

One should also be aware that the participation of the sovereign at a given point does not necessarily create a definitive boundary. To some extent, sovereign participation may be seen as recasting or redirecting the bargain. Although decisions undoubtedly are made, the effect may be simply to close off one avenue or open another. Definitive answers will be known at the end of the patent term but not necessarily along the way. Limited life span again distinguishes patents from many other types of rights. Having an end point provides the possibility that at some point all of the questions that can be answered in that period will be answered. Thus, patent law allows a somewhat defined time for observing the bargaining and its effects and for determining where everyone will end up when the music stops.

I say "a somewhat defined time" because there are some, although limited, possibilities for temporal extension of the power granted with a patent. Some of these extensions are explicit. For example, the U.S. Patent and Trade Office (USPTO) currently extends patent terms for delays at the office, such as a failure to act upon an application within fourteen months of filing.[19] Additionally, the USPTO will grant patent term extensions for products that cannot be marketed prior to approval from a regulatory agency or for undue delays at the patent office itself.[20]

Other extensions are more subtle. Consider the interaction of trademarks and patents. Trademarks are fundamentally intended to communicate source. Accurate information about the source of a product helps consumers make an informed choice about the quality of the product and encourages producers to invest in a reputation for quality goods. When a pioneering product is patented, however, the trademark may become associated with the product itself in the mind of the consumer, given that the patent holder is the only one making the product.[21] For example, consider a patented medication that is heavily advertised and associated with a particular color. If the patent holder is allowed to obtain protection under trademark-related doctrines for the color of the pill, generic companies will be unable to make their pill in the same distinctive color. Thus, even after the patent expires and generics have entered the market, consumers might continue to reach for the familiar color because they associate it with something they know will work.[22] This would indirectly extend the power of the patent beyond the grant.[23]

The patent holder may argue that it has earned a reputation for quality during the term of the patent and that consumers are merely responding to that reputation. In theory, if the original medication had been of low quality, consumers might have welcomed an alternative. The patent holder has had the entire period of time to develop a reputation, however, and has been able to do so without any competition at all. How would we know, for example, what a good-quality pill might be if we have only seen one? In addition, the consumer may not be responding to a reputation for quality but simply acting out of habit, inertia, or, in the case of health-care products, fear of the unknown. Even with my shoe brand, I may be unwilling to risk the discomfort of trying something new, although the issue is certainly less than life threatening.

The point is simply that the patent holder has had an exclusive period of time to develop consumer familiarity. Fair or not, that familiarity can extend the power of the patent beyond what appears to be a firm temporal line.[24] Thus, the notion that a patent ends is not always quite as definitive as it appears.

With the time dimension, however, at least we have a target for what is intended. Right or wrong, optimal or suboptimal, we have made a societal decision of the bounds. Having discovered that the dimension of time, one that we might have assumed to be fixed, may be subject to subtle extension, we may want to be sensitive to aspects of the system that can reinforce the boundary if patent holders appear to be stretching or extending it. This does not mean we should never extend the patent term. If the sovereign, in the form of legislature, decides to extend the boundary in certain cases, theorists can argue over the appropriateness, but it is a societal choice. When patent holders exploit opportunities within the rules to extend the time of the patent, however, their actions may signify one result of bargaining power that the sovereign did not intend to convey or allow. It could indicate the need for a revision of rules, that is, if such a revision could be accomplished without unappealing collateral results. As always, there are bargains to be made.

The same could be said of the dimension of scope. On a broad level, understanding that we are giving something less firmly bounded than we have previously considered could suggest that we may want to be more careful about how broadly we allow the possible reach. In particular, the bargain aspect suggests that we cannot set precise boundaries with a patent grant. We know that much. Given this aspect of patents, the relevant question to ask is how the legal system can best operate in an environment in which patent boundaries cannot be known until the end of the patent term.

Even without being able to set the boundaries at the time of patenting, one can analyze issues in terms of whether varying approaches are more or less likely to lead to effective outcomes in the bargaining process that will unfold. In looking at doctrinal questions, for example, one could ask whether a particular approach might grant a troubling amount of bargaining power to certain parties, either to patent holders in general, to particular types of patent holders, or to those who challenge them.

This approach could certainly affect issues related to process, such as patent examination and reexamination or the question of whether third-party opposition should be allowed at a particular time. Similarly, shifting the rules that determine when parties can file declaratory judgment actions to challenge the validity of a patent can have a significant effect on patent bargaining.[25] Recognizing the unknowns at the time of the patent grant and the negotiation inherent in the patent system could provide useful perspectives for answering such process-oriented questions.

Nevertheless, the insights that can be gained from considering the bargain aspect relate to far more than simply process questions. Consider those associated with allowing particular types of grant language. Would it be better, for example, to require broad language, narrow language, or a particular type of language? With the bargain aspect in mind, one might consider which approach has the potential to lead to a better result when boundaries cannot be known at the outset and the sovereign is likely to weave in and out of the process of developing those boundaries.

In thinking about the aspects of the patent system that have unwanted effects on the bargaining, one should also be mindful of potential abuses of the sovereign presence. The threat of sovereign intervention may be a positive factor if it moves the bargaining in a way that promotes innovation. Where evidence suggests that the threat is being used to deter innovation, a reexamination of the rules may be in order.

In addition to considering aspects of the patent system that might give too much bargaining power to one type of entity at the expense of another, one should also consider aspects that might give too much bargaining power to the sovereign or the sovereign's representatives as they weave in and out of the process. Too much flexibility for judges or examiners might create too great an ability to alter the bargaining midstream in a way that could deter those who would enter the game. Problems include disturbing settled expectations, as well as never allowing expectations to settle at all, as things shift at the whim of the designated decision makers. With rules that are arbitrary, unfathomable, or laughable, the sovereign loses the respect of the governed. The next generation of great minds, not to mention the risk capital those minds must attract, may choose to focus on something other than scientific innovation.

One could argue that if the patent system is essentially a bargaining process, we should not expend so much effort fine-tuning the legal doctrines related to properly interpreting a patent and defining the scope of the rights. Perhaps we are wasting our time trying to pin down and define the indefinable. It cannot be done, and the doctrines we choose are no more than part of the bargaining in any event.

In a similar vein, one might be tempted to take a pure Coasian approach and argue that no matter what doctrines we impose, the parties will bargain to the proper solution. As chapter 1 explains, it was Coase who first suggested that, absent significant transaction costs, two parties in a private dispute will bargain to an efficient outcome regardless of the initial assignment of legal liability. Perhaps our efforts are irrelevant, particularly in a context of intense bargaining.

Even Coase, however, recognized immediately that a world without transaction costs is an illusion. Similarly, economists have noted that transaction costs are particularly important in industries related to technology and knowledge.[26] Coase used his insight to suggest ways that the legal system could reduce transaction costs and encourage an efficient outcome, arguing that law should assign liability to the party best able to cost-effectively engage in precautions.[27] The point for my purposes is not so much that perfection exists in an abstract way but that our efforts in the real world should encourage movement toward the best result possible under the circumstances.

Finally, it is important to emphasize that even in the face of uncertainty, boundaries remain relevant. Despite our inability to know where the edges will be, we can at least understand what is outside any boundaries that might be set. Patents may be uncertain, but they are not infinite. One who tries to assert that Boeing's jet engines infringe a patent on Gummi Bear flavorings is unlikely to succeed. There will be logical limits, and those limits will be grounded in the invention itself, although any individual invention will be subject to a vast amount of play.

One could argue that I am taking the easy route and identifying only outer boundaries, thereby leaving out the difficult cases. Perhaps that is the point. On both a micro- and a macrolevel, clear boundaries do not exist. Uncertainties do. Change will occur, and trying to resolve all of the issues in advance is likely to be unproductive.

As I have discussed on a more general level in the past, doctrinal structures in law are not eternal. Those wishing to escape the confines of any doctrinal structure in law will seek the open spaces within whatever has been decided, rendering that structure insufficient for resolving the question.[28] New structures will emerge, bounded by our fidelity to precedent and the need to persuade others that the new structure observes that fidelity. Despite the natural tendency of change within law, it is possible to develop the broader perspectives and flexibility of mind that will allow us to adequately approach questions as they arise.

In particular, the fact that bargaining and uncertainty exist is not a reason to abandon efforts to influence the definition of rights that will eventually emerge. Our inability to delineate patent rights up front may be an inevitable result of how the system must function, but that does not relieve us of the responsibility to appropriately direct the enterprise. We can certainly have an effect, although perhaps not with the level of precision frequently contemplated and fervently desired. This enterprise is the subject of the remaining sections of the book.

Let me begin by offering a simple example of how the bargain aspect of patents might affect one's thinking about modern patent dilemmas. The example involves the tremendously contentious issue of measuring damages and the enormous damage awards dotting the landscape of modern patent law.

Prior to 1990 U.S. courts had granted only one damage award greater than one hundred million dollars. Since 1990, however, approximately fifteen have been granted, at least five of which topped five hundred million dollars.[29] Recent awards have reached into the billions of dollars.[30] The size and the increasing frequency of such superawards have raised concerns about the nature of the doctrinal structure for calculating damages in patent law.

Damage calculation begins with the words of the Patent Act, which directs courts to award damages "adequate to compensate for the infringement, but in no event less than a reasonable royalty for the use made of the invention."[31] Courts interpreting this law have settled on two modes of damage calculation: lost profits from sales the patent holder would have made "but for" the infringement and reasonable royalties on the infringing sales.[32]

As the name suggests, lost profits are simply the profits from sales that the patent holder would have made if the infringer had not interfered. To prove lost profits, Federal Circuit law requires that the patent holder prove the following: (1) the extent of the demand for the patented product; (2) the absence of noninfringing substitutes; (3) the patent holder's ability to meet the additional demand by expanding manufacturing capacity; and (4) the extent of profits the patentee would have made.[33] Patent holders can prove all of these elements only if they are already using and selling the invention in the market.

If patent holders cannot prove all of the elements of lost profits, they can request a reasonable royalty on the sales made by the infringer.[34] It is the calculation of reasonable royalties that has caused so much consternation in recent years.

Calculating a reasonable royalty begins with a very simple notion. The court multiplies the infringer's total sales of the infringing product (royalty base) by the reasonable royalty rate (royalty rate). Consider a patent on a bread-making process. A court might determine that a reasonable royalty rate for the process would be 1%. Damages would then be 1% of the bread company's total sales.

Although quite simple in the abstract, the process of actually determining the royalty rate and the proper sales base is quite difficult. A number of courts have approached this through the notion of a hypothetical negotiation. Under this approach, a reasonable royalty is the court-determined licensing deal that would have taken place between the parties if the deal had occurred before the patent infringement.[35]

As described in the opening chapters of this book, however, patent negotiating is an extraordinarily complex and unpredictable endeavor. Trying to replicate the results of such an endeavor is an activity fraught with uncertainty. Moreover, the court is asked to replicate the outcome of this complex human interchange as if what has transpired—in the market and between these parties—had never transpired. This is a remarkably treacherous exercise, and it is no wonder that the process has yielded uncomfortable results.

In particular, the details of determining the proper royalty rate and base of sales provide little assurance of an accurate outcome. Numerous courts follow the so-called *Georgia-Pacific* factors, an elaborate fifteen-part test enumerated by a district court in 1970. The fifteen factors, listed in the footnote to this sentence, range far and wide. Not all of the factors are relevant in all circumstances, and courts do not always follow all of the factors.[36]

One practitioner describes the *Georgia-Pacific* test as more often involving the talents of a conjurer than those of a judge.[37] This hypothetical, or some would say mythical, bargaining is intended to lead to a reasonable approximation of the damages from infringement. Nevertheless, scholars and commentators have complained that it all too often leads to ridiculous results.[38]

In particular, with complicated multicomponent inventions, patent infringement of minor components can result in awards that are disproportionate to the contribution of that component to the overall invention. A prominent example is a case involving the ubiquitous BlackBerry, a popular mobile phone that also provides e-mail and data services. A patent holder sued the BlackBerry supplier, alleging that the device infringed several of the company's patents. The patent holder alleged that its patents broadly covered systems and methods for remote e-mail delivery. E-mail delivery is an important component of Research In Motion's (RIM) BlackBerry devices, although it is only one part of the multicomponent device and numerous technologies are included in its construction and operation.

The patent holder prevailed in court, and a jury awarded past damages based on a royalty rate of 5.7%. In addition, an injunction order against future infringement threatened to shut down the BlackBerry's system.[39] Following the decision, the parties settled, and the BlackBerry supplier paid $612.5 million in exchange for a license to all of the other company's patents.[40] At the end of the day, one component of a complex, multicomponent invention commanded an enormous damage reward.

Much of the controversy in the BlackBerry case revolves around the rate of royalty and the hypothetical negotiation process. As described earlier, however, the current reasonable royalty test has a second component as well: the sales base to which that royalty base will be applied. A skewed royalty base can also lead to disproportionate damage awards.

One example of problems with the royalty base is the case of *Alcatel-Lucent SA v. Microsoft*. In *Microsoft,* the jury found that Microsoft's Windows Media Player infringed on Alcatel-Lucent's *software* by violating two patents related to the popular MP3 digital-music format. The result was a record damage award: a federal jury ordered Microsoft to pay $1.52 billion. The award was based on an amount equal to one-half of 1% of the average price for Windows-based *computers* sold since the second half of 2003. Thus, the royalty base was calculated from the sale of *computers* instead of the much lower value of the Windows *software*. A new trial over damages has since been ordered, but the case nevertheless demonstrates the enormous potential for damage awards.

Both the BlackBerry case and *Microsoft* demonstrate the problem of disproportionate damage awards. How can a patent holder whose invention constitutes only a small part of a successful product be awarded such a large proportion of the product's profits?

The root of the problem has been described in different ways. Some argue that the problem stems from the base number from which royalties are determined, as in *Microsoft*. If a patent holder has invented a new intermittent windshield wiper, the argument goes, damages should be portioned on the basis of the value of the intermittent windshield wiper alone, not on the basis of the value of the car with the windshield wiper.[41] Following this logic, the damage award in *Microsoft* should have been based on the *software,* not the entire *computer*. From this perspective, the question should be framed in terms of the value of the specific patented component and not attributed to the value of the entire multicomponent product.[42]

Another approach frames the issue from the perspective of royalty stacking.[43] Making a product may implicate dozens of patents, including both product and process patents. The value of all of those technologies is embodied in the sales, along with the value of unpatented technologies and the value added by the infringer in putting everything together and getting the product to market. If every patented component of an invention received a monstrous award, like the one granted in the BlackBerry case, the total would far exceed the value of the product itself. This does not even consider the value of unpatented technologies included in the product, not to mention the value added by the infringer in putting everything together and getting it to market. The high awards for an individual component cannot possibly be accurate.

In response to these concerns, industry groups and legislators have pushed for patent reform in damages as part of recent comprehensive patent reform bills.[44] The provisions were watered down along the way and then eventually dropped.[45]

In addition, incoming chief judge of the Federal Circuit, Randall Rader, sitting by designation as a trial judge, has engaged in what some are calling judicial patent reform, questioning the rule used by a plaintiff's expert in one case[46] and reducing an award by nearly two-thirds in another case.[47] His colleagues on the Federal Circuit, however, have not necessarily followed his lead.[48]

The true impact of disproportionate damage awards, however, lies outside any case or court decree. The process of developing a definition of a patent's boundaries involves a long and complex series of negotiations, and much of the interaction takes place outside the purview of the sovereign. When patent holders can threaten to inflict more harm than their patent could ever be worth, they wield a weapon of inappropriate size. It is the type of system distortion that one would condemn if looking from the perspective of the bargain aspect of patents. It suggests that reform efforts are essential and should ensure that patent holders cannot bargain with tools more powerful than their contribution to the enterprise would suggest. Thus, while an understanding of the bargain aspect of patents may not illuminate the perfect doctrinal language, it can provide a different perspective on the extent of the distortions occurring under the current system and on the necessity of doctrinal reform.

Following the same approach, the remaining chapters of the book apply insights from viewing the bargain aspect to some of the most challenging questions facing patent law today. These questions include whether a patent should reach beyond the state of the art at the time of the invention, how one should differentiate between processes of nature and processes created by human inventors, and what the proper relationship of patent, antitrust, and contract law should be.

As the discussion of damage awards suggests, despite the uncertainty inherent in the definition of a patent and the bargaining that naturally results, some legal rules will be better than others. When considering issues from the perspective of the bargaining aspect of patents, one should generally look for solutions that, in the interest of promoting innovation, will lead to a more efficient and effective bargaining system. Thus, chapter 4 explains how software, business method, and biotechnology inventions have become such a tightly tangled mess in the area of patentable subject matter that some have suggested abandoning subject matter entirely. In contrast, the chapter argues that patentable subject matter plays an important role and that a logically consistent and intellectually satisfying test is possible. In particular, with certain categories of invention, so few examples are likely to be legitimate and the potential damage through bargaining opportunities could be so great that we choose to eliminate the category entirely. Although bargaining over the boundary points will still occur, subject matter categories indicate when it is less likely that an invention is within the possible realm. With this in mind, the chapter suggests a test that would create coherence in the area and then applies it to the field of personalized medicine, where computers and biotechnology are combined to create new approaches to health care.

Chapter 5 examines the intricate intersection of patent, antitrust, and contract law. It suggests that in an intense bargaining environment, especially one that takes place largely outside the sovereign's purview, the law should be sensitive to circumstances that allow parties to use one area of law to distort the limitations imposed by another. The chapter provides an overview of patent misuse, the first sale doctrine, licensee estoppel, and a key regulatory regime, all of which are essential for understanding how patent, antitrust, and contract law intersect. With this background, the chapter then applies insights from the bargain aspect of patents to the current battles over generic pharmaceuticals.

Chapter 6 offers an example from the biologic arts in which the failure to properly acknowledge information limitations is wreaking havoc in the substantive doctrines. In the example, patent holders are allowed to reach beyond the state of the art at the time of the invention. However, when boundaries are uncertain, such reaching can create trouble. The temptation to restrain that reach leads to strange doctrinal twists and an unworkable body of law.

The substantive rules can be reformed, however, so as to limit the footprint of patents in this area and bring logic and coherence to five doctrines.

This example, therefore, demonstrates that despite the inherent uncertainty in the definition of an invention, one can use substantive rules to cabin the reach of an individual invention and reduce the range of the bargaining.

Finally, the chapters utilize an approach that is frequently absent in the patent arena. Patent scholarship and commentary tend to approach problems by tinkering with the minutiae of patent doctrines. Perhaps it flows from our proximity to and sympathy for the inventors we are trying to help, who themselves often adopt this approach—adjust one nut, fix one bolt, and the machine will operate more effectively. In contrast, the remaining sections of the book take a step back and focus on the broader picture of patent law by looking at how the pieces fit together in the hope that this approach will provide a more theoretically sound and workable patent system.

Finally, it is important to note that the book is not intended to solve all questions related to patent law, nor is it intended to provide a blueprint for answering those questions. Rather, I hope to start a conversation about what we know, what we do not know, and how we might be able to operate within those parameters.

# 4

## Where Do Processes of Nature End and Processes of Human Inventions Begin?

This chapter looks at the tremendously challenging question of what types of inventions should fall within patentable subject matter in the case of process patents. The question brings together issues related to the patenting of software, business methods, and biotechnology inventions. The area is so challenging and controversial that the Supreme Court, which took almost ten months in 2010 and 2011 to write the *Bilski* opinion in this arena, was unable to agree on much at all. The Court's opinion was able to draw five votes only as to certain portions, and the opinion pointedly noted that the Court disagreed with everything the Federal Circuit has said about the topic over the last decade. Major players in the field have suggested that we simply abandon patentable subject matter, and a recent opinion from the chief judge of the Federal Circuit recommends that the Patent and Trademark Office direct its efforts to issues other than patentable subject matter.

Nevertheless, this chapter suggests that patentable subject matter plays an important role in light of the bargaining aspect of patents. Tracing the history, the chapter identifies key points at which patentable subject matter lost its way and provides a test to bring coherence to the area.

## "[A]nything under the Sun That Is Made by Man"

In describing the wide breadth of things that may be patented, courts and commentators often enthusiastically quote language from the legislative history of the 1952 Patent Act, which states that patents "may include anything under the sun that is made by man."[1] The quote, however, is generally taken out of context. It actually suggests the opposite. The actual quote is the following: "A person may have 'invented' a machine or a manufacture, which may include anything under the sun that is made by man, but it is not necessarily patentable under section 101 [detailing patentable subject matter] unless the conditions of the title are fulfilled."[2] Thus, the full quote indicates not an expansive notion of patentable subject matter but a limitation on its reach.

Not all innovations fall within patentable subject matter. Scientists and inventors have come up with many wonderful things over the years that have failed to satisfy the notion of the types of subject matter that are eligible for protection under the U.S. patent system. The fact that something gives great benefit to society does not necessarily mean that it is eligible for a patent.[3]

As a general matter, U.S. patent law has traditionally excluded inventions that constitute laws of nature, abstract ideas, mental steps, and mathematical formulas from the list of things that are patent eligible, no matter how useful, insightful, ingenious, and revolutionary they might be. This list of exclusions has developed as a matter of common law rather than statutory law.[4] The logic for these exclusions to patentable subject matter, however, can be understood from constitutional, historic, theoretic, and practical perspectives.

The constitutional language giving Congress the power to establish copyrights and patents authorizes Congress "to promote the Progress of Science and useful Arts, by securing for limited Times to Authors and Inventors the exclusive Right to their respective Writings and Discoveries."[5] Given the language of the time and parallel construction within the sentence, science, authors, and writings are interpreted as applying to copyright, while useful arts, inventors, and discoveries are interpreted as applying to patents.

As the Supreme Court has noted, the constitutional clause serves both as a grant of power and a limitation on it.[6] Congress's power is limited to those acts that will promote progress, reflecting the distinctly utilitarian approach in this country. Patents are limited to the useful arts, and the grant must be for limited times. Finally, although it is not generally discussed in the literature,[7] the notion of granting rights to inventors for "their respective . . . Discoveries," could be read as a limitation because it suggests that inventors should have rights only to those things that can truly be deemed theirs.[8]

These constitutional limitations provide a backdrop for the historic, theoretic, and practical considerations that have led to the common law exceptions to patentable subject matter. The interplay between the constitutional language and the various exceptions is discussed in this chapter.

The notion that proper subject matter for patents excludes laws of nature and abstract principles has deep roots in the U.S. common law system. As early as the 1850s the Supreme Court noted that abstract ideas and laws of nature could not be patented.[9] These early cases reflect a separation between the notion of applied science and basic science. General ideas, or basic science and research, would not be the subject of patent protection. Only applied ideas would be eligible to receive the patent bounty.

The Supreme Court waxed poetic about this distinction in dicta in an 1852 case related to lead pipe: "A principle, in the abstract, is a fundamental truth; an original cause; a motive; these cannot be patented, as no one can claim in either of them an exclusive right. . . . The same may be said of electricity, and of any other power in nature, which is alike open to all, and may be applied to useful purposes by the use of machinery. . . . The elements of the power exist; the invention is not in discovering them, but in applying them to useful objects."[10]

The distinction between the discovery of basic laws of nature, which are outside the subject matter of patent law, and the application of laws of nature, which are within patentable subject matter, has echoed strongly in Supreme Court and lower court language over the years. As the Court noted in the *Funk Bros. Seed* case in 1948, "He who discovers a hitherto unknown phenomenon of nature has no claim to a monopoly of it which the law recognizes. If there is to be invention from such a discovery, it must come from the application of the law of nature to a new and useful end."[11]

This perspective finds constitutional support in two ways. First, the constitutional language gives Congress the power to promote the progress of the useful arts. Although not a model of clarity, such language suggests that the universe of patents should include those inventions that are of practical use to society rather than fundamental laws and abstractions. As one jurist has noted, "There is little evidence in the historical record about what is meant by the 'useful arts,' but it appears intended to refer to 'arts' used in industry and the production of goods."[12]

As a side point, it is important to note the difference between "abstract" in the sense that one has an idea not yet reduced to practice and "abstract" in the sense that one's invention falls outside patentable subject matter. Parts of a patent application, for example, may be based on a constructive reduction to practice rather than an actual reduction to practice.[13] An inventor who has an idea related to the construction of vacuum cleaners may constructively reduce the invention to practice by simply describing the innovation in a patent application in sufficient detail that a skilled mechanical engineer could build it. Building a sample vacuum cleaner would be called an actual, rather than a constructive, reduction to practice.

With abstractions that are not considered patentable subject matter, however, the patent system is using the term to differentiate an abstract concept from an applied one. In that sense, an abstract idea or invention is akin to a law of nature or a formula and thereby omitted from patentable subject matter. Following the earlier example, a new theory on the physics of suction force would be akin to a law of nature and as such would not be patentable unless it was applied in a vacuum cleaner or a vacuuming process.

Although a little more tenuous, one could also rest a constitutional argument on the notion that language refers to granting rights to "their" (i.e., the inventors') innovations. One could argue that uncovering a fundamental principle or a law of nature is not something that an inventor has derived but something that comes from nature. Inventors can claim as "theirs" only something that they have developed by applying what nature has provided. Discussions by courts and commentators are infused with this notion that a law of nature, an abstraction, or a mathematical formula is an invention of nature, not of humans, although the connection to the constitutional word "their" is not explicitly spelled out.[14]

The problem in resting this argument on the constitutional language is that the full language refers to granting inventors rights to "their Discoveries." One could argue that the language refers to an inventor's discovery of a basic law of nature or a principle just as easily as it refers to an inventor's discovery of an application of that principle. Nevertheless, perhaps due to the notion of "useful arts" or to contemporary understandings carried down through the centuries, patentable subject matter is understood to reach only to practical applications and not to basic laws of nature or abstract principles. The courts follow this distinction despite acknowledging that it leaves out many valuable insights of science. As the Federal Circuit noted recently in an *en banc* opinion:

> [P]atent law has always been directed to the "useful Arts," U.S. Const. art. I, § 8, cl. 8, meaning inventions with a practical use, see Brenner v. Manson, 383 U.S. 519, 532–36 (1966). Much university research relates to basic research, including research into scientific principles and mechanisms of action, see, e.g., Rochester, 358 F.3d 916, and universities may not have the resources or inclination to work out the practical implications of all such research, i.e., finding and identifying compounds able to affect the mechanism discovered. That is no failure of the law's interpretation, but its intention.[15]

The distinction between introducing information and creation echoes to some extent another historic distinction in U.S. patent law. At one time, British patent law rewarded not just the act of creation but also the act of rendering information accessible to British society.[16] Importers and inventors, for example, were once treated the same under English patent law on the theory that information first brought to British society was as valuable as new inventions.[17] The United States, however, has always focused directly on the notion of original creation rather than the notion of rendering information accessible. The distinction between introducing information and original creation also plays out in the development of categories excluded from patentable invention.

The preceding section describes the constitutional roots of excluding certain categories from patent law. Leaving laws of nature and abstract ideas out of patentable subject matter can be expressed in theoretic terms as well. Formulas, laws of nature, and natural phenomena are the building blocks of all science and innovation. All inventions to some extent rely on and use laws of nature, laws of physics, and other natural phenomena. These are the raw materials out of which all inventions are formed. Allowing individual inventors to tie up the basic building blocks of innovation poses a threat to the progress of innovation on which the patent system is based.[18]

One can look at abstract mental steps in a similar light. The process of thinking and imagining abstractions is at the heart of much innovation. Granting an inventor control over certain mental steps would impede the innovation we wish to stimulate, although the prohibition against mental steps may best be understood by practical considerations discussed later.

Reflecting this theoretical perspective, the Supreme Court has explained that "patents cannot issue for the discovery of the phenomena of nature" because such phenomena "are part of the storehouse of knowledge of all men. They are manifestations of laws of nature, free to all men and reserved exclusively to none."[19] Allowing one inventor to capture these elements would hamper innovation and block further development in a number of fields.

In 1853, for example, the Supreme Court rejected a claim from the inventor of the telegraph that would have covered all uses of "electromagnetism, however, developed for marking or printing intelligible characters, signs, or letters, at any distances." In denying patentability, the Court noted the following:

> For aught that we now know some future inventor, in the onward march of science, may discover a mode of writing or printing at a distance by means of the electric or galvanic current, without using any part of the process or combination set forth in the plaintiff's specification. . . . [T]he inventor could not use it, nor the public have the benefit of it without the permission of this patentee.
>
> Nor is this all, while he shuts the door against inventions of other persons, the patentee would be able to avail himself of new discoveries in the properties and powers of electro-magnetism which scientific men might bring to light.[20]

Thus, the patent system sequesters the raw materials of invention, thereby ensuring access for all current and future inventors.

Some of the areas excluded from patentable subject matter can be understood in practical terms as well. If an area is too difficult or uncomfortable to detect and control, it may be impractical to include that area in patentable subject matter. This notion is not well articulated or deeply entrenched in our collective understanding of the patent system, but it is beginning to appear at the edges of modern discussions.[21]

For example, abstract ideas have traditionally been excluded from patentable subject matter. Inventions involving mental steps have also been generally excluded, although as I discuss later, our understanding of the term has shifted uncomfortably at times. Both mental steps and abstract ideas could fall within the realm of things that would be difficult to control or that we would not want to control. It may simply be too difficult for courts to manage infringement claims that relate to an accused infringer's mental processes. This is not to say that we grant patent rights to only those things that are relatively easy to police. Much in patent law is difficult to police effectively, particularly when one is talking about trying to determine what laboratory process a particular company may have used in the development of its product.

Even with products already on the market, it may be difficult to determine whether particular process patents are being infringed. For example, much of the web-based technology we encounter every day, such as webpage search algorithms, security algorithms, or machine-translation algorithms, are run as "back end" programs on the servers of the companies that offer these services. Given that different algorithms may produce the same or similar results, it is very difficult to detect infringement. Nevertheless, trying to police the realm of thought and the abstract would be particularly challenging and could place courts in the unenviable position of policing the mind.

The notion of refusing to grant patents to inventions composed of mental steps may also touch on our reluctance to tell citizens what they can and cannot think. Granting patents in this realm may tread too closely on our First Amendment notions. Although the First Amendment specifically protects freedom of speech and communication, the notion of freedom of thought is implicit.[22] Granting patents in a way that impinges on people's mental processes goes against our instincts in this area.

In sum, for constitutional, theoretic, and practical reasons, patentable subject matter traditionally has not included laws of nature, natural phenomena, abstract ideas, mental steps, or formulas. One can apply a law of nature, for example, to a particular invention within a particular context. What a patent holder may *not* do is occupy that law of nature in a way that excludes current and future inventors. This occupation or preemption forms an important boundary line for patentability and is the driving force of the subject matter requirement.

## Applying Insights from the Bargain Aspect of Patents

The definition of the proper subject matter for patents is a subject of great controversy at the moment, and some scholars have suggested eliminating the subject matter inquiry from patent law or at least severely limiting it. They argue that reining in objectionable patents can be accomplished by the use of the other elements of patentability—novelty, utility, obviousness, and proper disclosure.[23]

Excluding certain areas from patentable subject matter, however, may make sense in light of the bargain aspect of patents. As chapter 1 explains, the bargain aspect of patents suggests that the boundaries of the patent grant cannot be known at the time of the grant. Given the lack of a shared understanding of new concepts, the limitations of language, and problems related to fixation in time, the boundaries of a particular invention cannot be fixed with any degree of precision at the moment of the grant. Rather than delineating precise boundaries, a patent provides an opportunity, during the life of the patent, to bargain over the outer boundaries of the rights. Those boundaries will be affected by, among other things, what products develop during the lifetime of the patent, what aspects of the definition are explored, and how our understanding of the invention—and the language used to describe it—unfolds.

Given the extent of bargaining that is likely to occur, we should be wary of allowing patent holders to wield a weapon in a way that could block an entire natural phenomenon from exploration or preempt human thought. This is particularly true in light of the fact that much of the patent bargaining takes place privately, beyond the reach of the sovereign. The potential for overreaching with certain types of patents could suggest that those areas should remain outside the patent system.

One could also think of the subject matter inquiry in instrumental terms. Yes, we might be able to choke off inappropriate patents through the novelty and obviousness inquiries, for example. Nevertheless, with certain categories of patents, so few things within that space are likely to survive close scrutiny that we cordon off the area for all. If we had a system in which we could quickly and easily identify which ones can survive scrutiny, we might give inventors license to wander into that territory. Given that many of the boundaries established and the power exercised will occur outside the sovereign's purview, however, allowing those categories poses too great a risk. One can think of this as roughly analogous to per se rules in antitrust law. Given that so few examples are likely to be legitimate and the potential damage is likely to be so great, we choose to eliminate the category entirely.

Of course, subject matter inquiries themselves may lead to bargaining over the boundaries. Even after declaring that certain areas are outside patentability given their subject matter, bargaining may still take place over whether the edges of the invention touch the edges of the forbidden categories. Nevertheless, identifying general categories can eliminate some, if not all, of these cases. In addition, the subject matter patentability categories may serve as warning bells and set off alarms as the parties approach them. This may cabin the bargaining even if it cannot entirely eliminate it.

The need for limitations may be particularly acute in the realm of process patents, which are at the heart of the current controversies over subject matter patentability. Patents are generally divided into two types: product and process patents. In very general terms, product patents are granted on a particular device or machine, while process patents are granted on a method of doing something.

When patent language identifies the boundaries of an invention that constitutes a device or a substance, that language is an abstraction of something concrete. When patent language identifies the boundaries of an invention that constitutes a way of doing something, that language may be an abstraction of an abstraction. The need for warning signals is particularly great when the discussion is quite far removed from anything that we can contemplate in concrete terms.

Finally, framing the issues in terms of subject matter patentability in certain cases may help focus our attention on what is truly of concern and prevent us from getting caught in difficult side inquiries. The *Ariad* case, which is discussed more fully later on, is a useful example.[24] *Ariad* concerns patent claims related to the discovery of a pathway through which a cell controls gene expression. In rejecting the claims, the Federal Circuit focused on questions of proper disclosure. The court found the patent invalid because the patent holder failed to include experimental data that showed any means by which the activity of the relevant pathway could be altered so as to lead to reduced activity of the pathway in controlling gene expression.[25] In other words, the court objected to the fact that the inventors were trying to gain control of a group of things for which they had not provided sufficient examples.

A larger and more troubling issue was at stake, however. The patent holder had certainly identified something important in nature and was making a great contribution to science. However, the patent holder then attempted to occupy everything that might relate to that natural occurrence by tying up an entire natural pathway—in all of the ways that such a pathway might operate. This is a classic subject matter problem, in which an inventor tries to tie up a natural phenomenon and preempt all inventions related to that phenomenon. It would have been much more effective to put the disclosure issue to the side.

In choosing to move forward on disclosure grounds, however, the Federal Circuit waded into much trickier territory by focusing on issues that are more difficult in the long run. Framing the case in disclosure terms implicates extremely difficult questions related to claiming groups such as whether describing some members of a group would entitle the patent holder to the entire group, how many members are enough, and what relationship must exist among them. These are questions that the Federal Circuit has struggled mightily over without resolving.[26] It is far easier and more directly focused on the problem in the case to conclude that a patent holder simply cannot preempt a natural pathway.

One can speculate that the Federal Circuit approached the *Ariad* case as a disclosure case because it was looking for a vehicle to quell a bubbling controversy over whether a separate written description requirement exists within disclosure. The case was indeed taken *en banc* and produced an opinion that reaffirmed the existence of a separate written description requirement. *Ariad* may have appeared too tempting a vehicle for making a point about disclosure. Taking this approach, however, misses the underlying problem in allowing this type of claim in the first place.

## Understanding the Current Controversy in Subject Matter Patentability

The bargain aspect of patents suggests that limits on subject matter patentability can play an important role in patent law. To cabin the bargaining, it may be useful to choose default rules to push back the possible roaming space and prevent patent holders from preempting areas that for historic, theoretic, and practical reasons should be available to all. This framework can help in puzzling through one of the most controversial and challenging areas of modern patent law—patentable subject matter for process patents.

As explained earlier, process patents, also known as method patents, are the topic of a series of controversies over what types of processes constitute the proper subject matter for a patent. As a general matter, patentable subject matter for process patents is an area in search of sustainable logic. The lack of clear doctrines and firm, logical underpinnings is creating problems throughout a wide variety of cases and in a large number of industries and technologies. Although brewing for some time, the controversies erupted in 2006 with the Supreme Court's aborted attempt to wade into the topic of patentable subject matter for method patents in the case of *LabCorp v. Metabolite*.[27]

The case concerned the amino acid homocysteine, a natural substance produced by the body. Scientists have known since the 1960s that high levels of homocysteine are associated with many health problems, including heart disease, kidney disease, lupus, and vitamin B6 deficiency. In this case, the inventors claimed to be the first to figure out that high levels of homocysteine correlate with vitamin B12 (cobalamin) and folic acid (folate) deficiencies.

Knowledge of this correlation is tremendously important for a variety of health-care issues. Insufficient folic acid in pregnant women, for example, is linked to the severe birth defect spina bifida. It is difficult to test directly for vitamin B12 and folic acid insufficiencies, and a correlation with overall homocysteine levels would thus be very useful.

The inventors in this case had developed a test kit for measuring levels of total homocysteine. The test kit is a product, and the patent claims related to it were not problematic. In addition to claims related to the test kit, however, the company filed method claims, including one fateful claim that became the subject of the Supreme Court case. In essence, the language claimed no more than testing a body fluid for elevated homocysteine and correlating that level with a deficiency of B12 or folic acid. The claim, in its entirety, said the following: "A method for detecting a deficiency of cobalamin or folate in warm-blooded animals comprising the steps of: 'assaying a body fluid for an elevated level of total homocysteine'; and 'correlating an elevated level of total homocysteine in said body fluid with a deficiency of cobalamin or folate.'"[28]

The Federal Circuit upheld the patent, the Supreme Court granted certiorari, and everyone had something to say about the case. Academics weighed in, arguing that the connection between these two things, higher levels of homocysteine and vitamin deficiencies, was no more than a natural phenomenon. Thus, the claim was an attempt to patent a natural phenomenon and constituted a back-door approach to preempting a part of nature. As one commentator complained, the ruling would allow inventors to patent methods comprising the "[1] collecting [of] data related to a law of nature and [2] thinking about the law of nature."[29]

Complaining that the claims preempted thought and interfered with medical treatment, medical professionals argued the following. Suppose a physician has a patient, orders a panel of blood tests, and notices a high level of homocysteine.[30] The moment the physician gets the panel back and realizes that a vitamin deficiency may exist, the physician has violated the patent in forming that thought. The claim literally says "assaying" and "correlating," but how can one violate a patent simply by thinking?

The biotech industry supported the patent and expressed concern that overturning the lower court opinion would invalidate a wealth of diagnostic and correlation patents in the medical field.[31] Numerous patents have been granted that essentially comprise either a correlation of a natural phenomenon, such as a connection between a disease and a drug, or a correlation between a genetic market and a disease for diagnostic companies.[32] These patents are of great value to the biotechnology and pharmaceutical industries.

The case also attracted attention from far beyond the biotech and health fields. Business organizations and financial services companies chimed in as well because of their concern about the implications for business method patents. Financial services companies, for example, hold business method patents on ways of calculating derivative assets and hedging investments. If patents on testing something and making a correlation or a calculation are just patents on natural phenomena, perhaps such business method patents are as well. Perhaps methods of calculating risk, for example, merely embody a recognition of natural phenomena related to risk.

Computer and software companies were worried as well. The line of cases allowing patents on most types of software had never been tested in the Supreme Court. Perhaps the type of calculations involved in software could be considered analogous to the correlations in the *LabCorp* case. Concerns in the area of software were particularly strong given that the logic in the lower court line of cases finding software to be patentable subject matter was tenuous at best and that the courts had struggled to define what software should be patentable and why.

As I explain later, a number of questions are lurking in the area of software patentability, but one was particularly troubling. In the 1968 case of *In re Prater*, the predecessor court to the Federal Circuit held that a spectrum existed between purely mental steps and purely physical ones and that each process claim should be evaluated on a case-by-case basis to determine whether it falls in the patentable end of the spectrum.[33] The opinion left much uncertainty about the nature of that supposed spectrum and where particular types of inventions might fall. This uncertainty, along with other difficulties of software patenting, resulted in questions about the logic underlying the patenting of software and the viability of software patents.

*LabCorp* threatened to stir up the software mess. If the correlations involved in *LabCorp* rendered the invention unpatentable, then perhaps inventions that involve any steps that could be performed mentally but are being performed by a computer are unpatentable. Worse yet, do inventions whose foundations rest on activities that appear to be analogous to mental calculations fall outside of patentable subject matter? If so, all software patents could be invalid, even those involving calculations that the human mind would be incapable of performing.

In short, anything the Supreme Court said about patentable subject matter could potentially implicate thousands of patents in a wide range of both industries and patentable subject matter issues. Perhaps in response to this mess, when the infringer first requested certiorari, the Solicitor General's office suggested ducking the case altogether on the grounds that the issues had not been properly raised and fully briefed. In its brief to the Supreme

Court, the Solicitor General argued that "if this Court were to consider re-evaluating almost a quarter-century of administrative practice and lower court jurisprudence, it should do so based on a full record."[34]

The Supreme Court initially ignored the Solicitor General's suggestion, granted certiorari, and heard oral argument in the case. Following oral argument, however, the Court followed the advice and dismissed the case, saying only that it had been improvidently granted. Three justices, however, filed an extensive dissenting opinion, arguing that the patent should have been invalidated as an unpatentable natural phenomenon.[35] The dissenting opinion foreshadowed the fact that the question of what constitutes patentable subject matter—as opposed to a law of nature, a formula, or a natural phenomenon—would persist. In fact, the issue continued to bubble up in numerous cases in various industries including software, the Internet, financial services, health services, pharmaceuticals, legal services, and satellite imagery. The intricate intersection of all of these areas threatened to create a Gordian knot that would be impossible to untie.

Despite the challenges, I believe it is possible to make sense out of the area by returning to a critical moment in technological history. In making this journey in the remainder of the chapter I am reminded of Shakespeare's classic line, "Though this be Madness, yet there is method in't."[36]

## Blame the Computer

Although much good in our lives can be credited to the invention of the computer, the current crisis in patentable subject matter can be traced to that moment as well. Even though it is certainly true that difficulties concerning subject matter patentability for method patents reach back at least to the early 1800s, the modern controversies have their roots in uncertainty over how to handle the emergence of computer technology in the American industrial landscape.

Computers and digital technology are so deeply entrenched in our modern lives that it is difficult to remember the relative newness of the invention. The first programmable electronic computer was completed in the 1940s, but the possibility of having a personal desktop computer did not emerge until the 1980s. The federal courts would not squarely address questions related to the patentability of computer programs until the late 1960s and early 1970s.[37]

Computer programs brushed up against a number of prohibitions in subject matter patentability. First, a computer program looks a great deal like a formula or pure math. If mathematical formulas are unpatentable, how can a computer program be patentable? Second, computers often seem to be doing what the human mind can do, simply doing it faster and more efficiently. If human mental steps are unpatentable, how does this affect computer programs? Finally, as a general matter, computer programs seem to be operating in an abstract manner. They employ algorithms, which in the computer-science arts are understood as a series of steps performed on input data.[38] Where are the concrete elements that we are accustomed to seeing in the world of patents? Where are the chemicals, the machines for cutting leather, the vehicles that we physically touch? Input data seem awfully close to abstractions.

One could see the Supreme Court struggling with these issues as it denied patent protection in the early cases concerning the patentability of inventions related to computers. Consider, for example, the 1972 case of *Gottschalk v. Benson*.[39]

Determining the nature of the invention in *Benson* requires an understanding of the basics of digital computer processing. In computer processing, simple language commands, such as "print the letter K" or "move to the next line," are first converted into the numerical information of our ordinary decimal system. The numerical information may then be represented in the form of timed electrical impulses, magnetized spots on the surface of tapes or discs, or the presence or absence of punched holes on paper cards, among other methods.[40] Each of these methods is based on something that can exist in two distinct states, such as the presence or absence of holes or two distinct voltage levels. Finally, the two distinct states of such impulses, spots, or holes are converted into the digital language of zeros and ones (for example, one for presence, zero for absence) to trigger machine functions.

There are different approaches to encoding full numerical information in the digital language of ones and zeros. The *Benson* case concerned the BCD system and the pure binary system.[41] In everyday life we represent numbers in base ten, moving to the next place after we have reached the number 9. Both the BCD system and the pure binary system take numbers as they would be familiar to us and translate them into base two, so that they can be represented using only zeros and ones.

For our purposes the key difference to understand is the following: In the BCD system the numerals 0–9 must *each* be represented by a different sequence. For example, the number "15" would be broken down into a "1" and a "5," each of which would be represented in base two. Thus, the "1" would be represented by the sequence "0001," and the "5" would be represented by the sequence "0101." Therefore, in BCD, "15" becomes "0001 0101."

In contrast, using the pure binary system, the full number "15" would be represented in base two rather than first translating the "1" into base two and then translating the "5" into base two. Thus, in the pure binary system, "15" becomes "1111."

Binary numerals and BCD numerals each have advantages. The latter are more easily converted into characters for printing and screen display. Binary numerals, however, are smaller and therefore take up less storage space, or memory. As a result, computer operations frequently convert numbers from one type of encoding to another for different purposes.

The invention in *Benson* concerned a process for programming a computer to convert numbers from BCD into pure binary form. The Supreme Court held that the invention did not constitute patentable subject matter. In denying patentability, the Court emphasized the similarity between the invention and categories traditionally excluded from patentability, noting that "[a] procedure for solving a given type of mathematical problem is known as an 'algorithm'" and that "[t]he procedures set forth in the present claims are of that kind; that is to say, they are a generalized formulation for programs to solve mathematical problems."[42]

The Supreme Court also struggled in the case with the issue of how to prevent patents from preempting laws of nature or entire areas of natural phenomena, particularly for dimensions that inhabit less concrete domains. The Court noted in particular that chemical processes or physical acts that transform raw materials are sufficient to confine the patent monopoly within "rather definite bounds," whereas inventions that do not involve such transformation may not have those basic limitations.[43] The Court hinted vaguely that some forms of limitation on the reach of the claims might be helpful and noted at the outset of the opinion that the claims were neither directed to any particular art or technology nor limited to any particular type of machine or end.[44]

The *Benson* opinion also included language that would eventually come to dominate Federal Circuit jurisprudence. In discussing prior cases, the opinion stated that "transformation and reduction of an article 'to a different state or thing' is *the* clue to the patentability of a process claim that does not include particular machines."[45] The Court backed away from that language later in the opinion, however: "It is argued that a process patent must either be tied to a particular machine or apparatus or must operate to change articles or materials to a 'different state or thing.' We do not hold that no process patent could ever qualify if it did not meet the requirements of our prior precedents."[46]

Nevertheless, the Federal Circuit would later ignore the Supreme Court's admonition and rule that inventions satisfy subject matter patentability only if they are tied to a machine or involve transformation of a physical article. The so-called machine-or-transformation test is discussed later.

The Supreme Court's decision in the 1978 case of *Parker v. Flook*[47] evidenced the same struggle over the similarity between computer-processing inventions and areas traditionally excluded from patent law. The *Flook* case concerned a method of calculating an alarm limit during the process of catalytic conversion. Catalytic conversion changes harmful pollutants into less harmful emissions before they exit a mechanical system, and it is probably most familiar to readers in the context of an automobile's exhaust system.[48]

During the process, temperature, pressure, and flow rates are constantly monitored for signs of inefficiency or danger. This calculation is more complex during critical stages such as start-up, when the factors may fluctuate. The patent in the *Flook* case claimed a method of updating alarm limits in the catalytic conversion of hydrocarbons following a particular formula and set of steps by which the alarm limit would be recalculated.

In rejecting patentability in *Flook*, the Court reasoned that a phenomenon of nature or a mathematical formula is unpatentable; only an inventive application of such can be the subject of a patent.[49] In exploring this concept as applied to algorithms for computer-related inventions, the Court held further that one must consider the algorithm itself to be part of prior art and then ask whether the implementation in the patent is somehow innovative.[50]

Leaving aside the algorithm, the Court saw no such innovation in the patent. Everything else was well known, including the chemical process for catalytic conversion, the practice of monitoring the three variables, the use of alarm limits to trigger alarms, the notion of calculation and readjustment of alarm limits, and even the use of computers for performing automatic monitoring and alarm functions.[51] Thus, having found that the algorithm was the only new part of the application and that an algorithm itself should always be considered prior art, the Court had no difficulty denying patentability.

The patent holder tried to argue that the activity of altering the alarm limit once the new limit had been calculated added a layer of activity and that such post-solution activity should be considered sufficient to move the invention out of the realm of patenting formulas. The Court, however, disagreed, arguing that one could always find ways to attach some insignificant post-solution activity. This notion of "insignificant post-solution activities" would ring throughout subsequent Federal Circuit opinions, as explained later.

In short, initial Supreme Court forays into the topic of the patentability of computer programs resulted in denials of patentability. Computer programs, however, were rapidly becoming integral to the type of industrial products and processes that had always been the subject of patent protection, and judges' discomfort with denying patent protection increased. In this context such programs looked much more like part of the applied arts than the academic inquiries of basic research. Denying protection to one area of innovation within our applied arts seemed increasingly odd, but it was difficult to move past the traditional prohibitions enshrined in our patent system.

## Initial Responses

As the march of computer technology continued, inventors tried different ways to help the courts understand the importance of the inventions, their role in society, and the need for protection. In looking for a way out of the traditional prohibitions, perhaps the clearest message from the courts was the need to avoid the forbidden territory of algorithms. A number of lower court opinions, as well as key Supreme Court cases, had made it clear that being branded an algorithm was the kiss of death.

The problem, of course, was that it was not exactly clear what an algorithm was. An algorithm, in its broadest sense, is any sequence of steps taken to produce a result. That definition, however, would cover just about everything that receives a process patent.

In the field of computer science, the term "algorithm," in its broadest sense, refers to a series of steps that a computer performs on input data.[52] In a narrower sense, the study of algorithms in computer science often describes a theoretical area of the field in which sets of operations are formalized in mathematical notation.[53] The number of operations necessary to produce the correct output generally determines the efficiency of the algorithm, given that significantly larger numbers of operations may take longer and require more processing power.[54]

If the courts truly intended to exclude from patentable subject matter anything that can be understood as a set of steps formalized in mathematical notation, huge swaths of modern innovation would be eliminated from the patent system. The courts themselves, however, were not clear about what they meant. By the 1980s the Supreme Court had used the terms "mathematical algorithm," "mathematical formula," and "mathematical equation" to describe types of nonstatutory mathematical subject matter without explaining whether the terms are interchangeable or different.[55] As the Federal Circuit lamented in the *Alappat* case, "The Supreme Court has not set forth . . . any consistent or clear explanation of what it intended by such terms or how these terms are related, if at all."[56]

The message was clear, however, that if an innovation was ever going to survive a court challenge, it had to avoid being labeled an algorithm or looking too much like math. The result was an attempt to describe the process of what was happening in simple English terms by moving the description of the process to an even more abstract plane. If successful, the approach would have the advantage of allowing the inventor to tie up an even larger swath of territory, given that broad, abstract language had the potential to cover many different ways of accomplishing the same result. For example, an algorithm designed to operate on digital images may be claimed by the simple language of what it is intended to do, thus covering a far wider territory than mathematically describing the algorithm itself.

Another part of the attempt to avoid rejection involved trying to connect the invention to an industrial endeavor or a particular kind of machine. This could focus a court's attention on the industrial art involved in the invention as a whole and not on the appearance of math or abstractions. In other words, it provided a way to say to the court, "We are not just doing silly math abstractions here. We are in a particular technological art."

These approaches were encouraged by the landmark Supreme Court opinion in *Diamond v. Diehr* in 1981.[57] The invention in *Diehr* related to a process for molding raw, synthetic rubber into cured precision products. The proper process for obtaining a perfectly cured product depends on the thickness of the item to be molded, the temperature, and the time the item remains in the press. In theory, one can calculate the necessary length of time for the curing process through a well-known formula known as the Arrhenius equation. Calculating the appropriate time of completion had proven difficult in the industry, however, because it was impossible to continually measure the internal temperature without opening the mold and disturbing the temperature. Thus, the industry relied on estimations of the shortest time in which it was likely that all of the parts would be sufficiently cured, a less than perfect solution.

The claimed invention involved the process of constantly measuring the actual temperature inside the mold with an internal thermometer that would automatically feed those measurements into a computer. The computer would repeatedly recalculate the cure time using the Arrhenius equation and then signal the press to open at the proper moment.

The Supreme Court upheld the patent in *Diehr,* describing the invention as "a process for curing rubber which includes in several of its steps the use of a mathematical formula and a programmed digital computer."[58] In finding that the claims satisfied the requirements for patentable subject matter, the Court noted the following:

> Respondents here do not seek to patent a mathematical formula. Instead, they seek patent protection for a process of curing synthetic rubber. Their process admittedly employs a well-known mathematical equation, but they do not seek to pre-empt the use of that equation. Rather, they seek only to foreclose from others the use of that equation in conjunction with all of the other steps in their claimed process.[59]

Finally, the Court noted that in determining whether a claimed process satisfies patentable subject matter, the claims must be considered as a whole:

> [W]hen a claim containing a mathematical formula implements or applies that formula in a structure or process which, when considered as a whole, is performing a function which the pat-

ent laws were designed to protect (*e.g.,* transforming or reducing an article to a different state or thing), then the claim satisfies the requirements.[60]

The Court concluded by noting that the claims were not an attempt to patent a mathematical formula but rather were drawn to an industrial process for the molding of rubber products.[61]

The difference between the *Diehr* case and the *Flook* case seemed illusory at best. In fact, one could argue that the difference rested on better lawyering rather than any distinction in the character of the inventions. As the dissent in *Diehr* noted dryly, "Their method of updating the curing time calculation is strikingly reminiscent of the method of updating alarm limits [in *Flook*]."[62]

Buoyed by success in the *Diehr* case, inventors and the courts moved forward in trying to find ways to patent the type of computer-processing inventions that had been problematic. In an effort to mold an invention to the hints in the case law, patent holders looked for ways to characterize their inventions as something other than an algorithm; abstract the process using English language terms rather than mathematical terms; and connect the invention to a specific endeavor and a particular kind of machine. These approaches, admirable though they may have been in their attempts to lead us out of the morass, have simply taken us deeper and deeper into the quagmire.

For example, once one begins looking at an invention as a whole, almost everything can be described as being part of some type of applied, concrete industrial art. The goal in *Diehr* was curing rubber; the goal in *Flook* was operating hydrocarbon machinery; the goal in *LabCorp* was treating patients with vitamin B12 and folic-acid deficiencies. Framing in that manner does not provide much in the way of a dividing line for separating what is patentable from what is unpatentable. Referencing a particular machine provides little as a dividing line. As machines increasingly dominate our lives, not to mention the industrial arts, one can almost always find a machine involved at some point, particularly if one is free to look at the invention as a whole.

Most troubling, the incentive to describe what is happening in linguistic rather than mathematical terms could also provide a tremendously wide footprint for each patent. For example, consider the applicant who would now simply use the claims language "applying a statistical model" rather than providing the notation of the actual statistical model or formula that is used. The general term "statistical model" will have very broad coverage if it is not strictly defined.

The problem of such expansive claiming was exacerbated by a shift in an entirely different area of patentable subject matter. For some time appellate courts had held that methods of doing business could not constitute patentable subject matter. The rule had been cited in denying protection for inventions such as a method for deciding how salespeople can best handle customers,[63] a system for helping a neurologist diagnose patients,[64] and a system for cash registering and account checking to prevent fraud and theft by waiters and cashiers in hotels and restaurants.[65]

In 1998, however, the Federal Circuit overturned the so-called business-method exception in the *State Street* case.[66] The case concerned a computerized hub-and-spoke accounting system for structuring mutual-fund investments. In the patented system, mutual funds would pool their assets in an investment hub, which would be organized as a partnership. The arrangement offered economies of scale combined with the tax advantages of a partnership.

The Federal Circuit upheld the patent, overturning the prohibition on patenting business methods. The court held that prior cases applying the business-method exception had actually rested on objections related to obviousness or concern that the invention was no more than an abstract idea or a mathematical algorithm. The court replaced the business-method exception with a more general rule for method patents, which is discussed in the following section.

In the wake of the *State Street* opinion, courts and commentators have engaged in a heated debate over whether the prohibition on patenting business methods was a traditional part of our patent law or a more modern addition.[67] It is possible that the history in this area is unclear or that one or both sides is engaging in some degree of hyperbole. It is also possible that the early history is of minimal help in sorting through our more modern dilemmas. What is quite clear, however, is that throughout much of the twentieth century, patents on methods of doing business were not permitted, and the *State Street* opinion opened the floodgates to applications on business-method patents.

The fallout from the opinion created increasing discomfort for courts and commentators. As one federal-circuit judge noted in a dissenting opinion, "Patents granted in the wake of *State Street* have ranged from the somewhat ridiculous to the truly absurd . . . producing a thunderous chorus of criticism."[68] For example, patents have been granted on inventions including methods of training janitors to dust and vacuum using video displays,[69] a method for selling expert advice,[70] a method of enticing customers to order additional food at a fast-food restaurant,[71] a method of using color-coded bracelets to designate dating status in order to limit the embarrassment of rejection,[72] and a system for toilet reservations.[73] Allowing patents for such broad, abstract concepts increasingly appeared to be absolute folly. Moreover, given that *State Street* emerged during the same era as the movement to express computer-software patents in broad, overview language, *State Street* and its progeny threatened to drag software patents into the maelstrom of discontent over business-methods patents.

## Series of Failed Tests

In the decades since the introduction of the computer, the judiciary has struggled to develop a test that will allow patenting of computer-related innovations in a logical manner, one that can also be applied rationally in emerging areas of biology and business methods. The trail is littered with failed attempts, as one after another, the tests have been unable to provide a satisfactory sorting mechanism. The following section describes some of the approaches undertaken and explains the logical problems lurking within each.

The judiciary's first tentative steps toward patenting computer-related innovations centered on being able to describe an invention in terms of a physical transformation of something. In particular, when denying patentability in *Benson*, the Supreme Court focused on the difference between the activity of transforming binary numbers and the activity of chemical processes or physical acts that transform raw materials.[74] In contrast, when finding patentability in *Diehr*, the Court framed the invention as part of a process for curing rubber.[75] The language in both cases, however, left the door open to other types of criteria, and the lower courts quickly determined that requiring a physical transformation created too narrow a test.[76]

The judiciary's next foray into the area involved what became known as the "useful, concrete, and tangible" test. Although the test is frequently associated with *State Street* and business-method patents, it was first articulated by the Federal Circuit in *Alappat*. The invention in *Alappat* was called a "rasterizer," which is essentially an algorithm for converting vector list data into smooth waveforms.[77] It can be understood in more simplified terms in the following manner: Images on a screen are created by a series of dots. The rasterizer algorithm calculates how to space those dots so that the eye believes it is seeing a continuous line. Rasterizers are widely used in computer graphics and can be implemented as software or as hardware.[78]

In finding that the rasterizer was patentable subject matter, the Federal Circuit in *Alappat* commented that the claimed process was directed to "a specific machine that produced a useful, concrete, and tangible result."[79] The Federal Circuit's *State Street* business-methods decision formalized the statement into a test.[80]

The new test required that the result of an invention be "useful, concrete, and tangible." It is not a rigorous three-prong test but has more of a subjective standard, and the terms themselves are less than a model of clarity. As a starting point, the term "useful" merely restates the utility requirement that has historically been considered a patentability issue separate from patentable subject matter.[81] As the late Honorable Giles S. Rich, an author of the 1952 Patent Act, explained, "Section 101 states three requirements: novelty, utility, and statutory subject matter. The understanding that these three requirements are separate and distinct is long-standing and has been universally accepted."[82]

The other terms, "concrete" and "tangible," are synonyms. More important, they have not been particularly helpful in separating the patentable from the unpatentable. For example, "concrete and tangible" can be read narrowly to apply only to data that represent physical objects. However, courts have also read the terms as including types of data that are far more abstract. In particular, when describing results that would be considered "useful, concrete, and tangible," the Federal Circuit in *State Street* mentioned final share prices.[83] One might be hard pressed to understand what the terms "concrete and tangible" mean if share prices are examples of things tangible.

It is possible that the courts were trying to find a way to avoid preemption by asking whether an invention could be understood as a specific, practical application of a broad concept, formula, or algorithm. Perhaps this would be helpful in avoiding the problem of granting patents on broad, basic concepts or formulas that raised the threat of preemption.

In fact, the Federal Circuit may have had these ideas in mind in the *Alappat* case. For example, in articulating the test, the *Alappat* court explained that the algorithm was acceptable as patentable subject matter because it did not preempt an area of technology given that the claims were limited to specific structural elements.[84]

If the Federal Circuit was trying to find a way to articulate the notion of a specific practical application, it was not very successful. The question of whether an invention is a specific, practical application of a broad concept is not well represented by the words "concrete" and "tangible." An invention can constitute a specific, practical application of a concept and still embody an intangible result. For example, toilet reservations certainly constitute a specific, practical application as opposed to a broad, scientific concept. Nevertheless, a reservation of any kind is not something one would think of as concrete and tangible.

As a method of determining the existence of a specific, practical application, the terms were woefully inadequate and simply added more layers of confusion. For example, when the concrete, useful, and tangible test is applied to computer software, should courts ask whether it is the input data or the output that represents something tangible? Should courts ignore both questions under the test and just ask whether the result is a practical application?

Finally, the notion of whether an invention involves a specific, practical application is itself a poor proxy for preemption because it provides an inadequate sorting mechanism. Just about anything can be described as having some form of practical application, and by the time the courts grew tired of the "useful, concrete, and tangible" test, clever patent lawyers had indeed tried to fit just about everything into the test.

In the 2008 *Bilski* opinion the Federal Circuit sitting *en banc* finally overturned the "useful, concrete, and tangible" test.[85] The *Bilski* case involved a method of managing risk in commodities trading. The claimed invention essentially consisted of "(1) initiating a series of sales between a broker and a purchaser where the purchaser buys the commodity at a fixed rate based on historical prices, (2) identifying the sellers or producers of the commodity, and (3) initiating a series of sales between the broker and the sellers/produc-ers of the commodity at another fixed rate, so that the seller's and purchas-er's respective risk balance one another."[86]

The Federal Circuit also reminded readers of the Supreme Court lan-guage in the case of *Diehr* that drew a distinction between claims seeking to preempt the use of a fundamental principle and claims seeking only a par-ticular application of that principle.[87] The Federal Circuit concluded that the best way to determine whether an invention constituted an unpatentable principle would be to apply what quickly became known as "the machine-or-transformation test." Under the machine-or-transformation test, an in-vention constitutes patentable subject matter only if it is tied to a particular machine or apparatus or it transforms a particular article into a different state.[88] The Federal Circuit noted further that mere recital of a machine or transformation would be insufficient. If the machine or transformation is not central to the claimed process, it should be dismissed as "post-solution activity."[89]

The machine-or-transformation test quickly proved as confusing and ineffective as the prior test. For example, one might think that the transfor-mation prong would require an invention related to some type of physical transformation of a substance, such as the process of curing rubber. The Federal Circuit indicated as much by reiterating old Supreme Court lan-guage that an invention would constitute patentable subject matter if the invention involved a transformation such as a chemical process or a physical act that transforms raw material.[90] What the Federal Circuit proclaimed clearly in one breath, however, it withdrew in another. In further describing the transformation prong, the Federal Circuit explained that CAT-scan data would satisfy the transformation test because data representing bones, or-gans, and other body tissues were transformed. The act of displaying CAT-scan data on a screen bears little resemblance to a chemical process or a process that physically transforms raw materials. Thus, while the test pro-fesses to be about a physical transformation of something, it is not.

Alternatively, one might think, from the CAT-scan example, that the test is really asking whether input data represent something physical. In other words, it is not about whether something physical is changed in a physical sense. Rather, it is simply about whether input data that started out representing something physical are "transformed" into a different state. From that perspective, the Federal Circuit might have intended to limit computer-related technology to only those programs that create data representations of physical items. This approach seems to be the best way to make sense of the idea that CAT-scan data satisfy the transformation test.

Such a distinction, however, would not be very helpful as a demarcation line. One can argue that almost any data represent something physical in some way. For example, one would think that interest rates and carbon credits are abstractions rather than physical items. Interest rates, however, represent cash payments of dollar bills, and carbon credits represent volumes of carbon that are not emitted into the atmosphere. Just about anything could arguably satisfy a test this broad.[91]

Taking an entirely different approach, one might imagine that to satisfy the transformation portion of the test, the core of the invention itself must relate to a physical transformation. Some of the Federal Circuit language in *Bilski* suggested this by noting that if the machine or transformation is not central to the claimed process, it should be dismissed as "post-solution activity."[92] Within a year, however, the Federal Circuit found patentable subject matter under the transformation prong in a case that stretched both the boundaries of centrality and the entire concept of transformation. The case, *Prometheus v. Mayo*, which I have previously discussed in detail,[93] concerned a diagnostic method of determining the efficacy of drug treatment.[94] The invention in *Prometheus* is a classic example of the burgeoning field of personalized medicine, in which types of treatments and treatment levels are calibrated to a patient's genetic and metabolic variations.

The *Prometheus* invention involved treating a patient with one of a category of drugs designed for a particular gastrointestinal disorder, allowing the patient to metabolize the drug, and then measuring the metabolite level. (A metabolite is essentially the chemical form that a substance changes into as the substance is broken down by the body.) Finally, the physician adjusts the amounts of the drug given until the patient reaches the proper metabolite level.

Looking at the invention as a whole, one could argue that the key discovery involved identifying the proper range of metabolite that physicians should aim for in treating patients. The company developed these ranges by monitoring levels of drug metabolites in large groups of patients over an extended period of treatment (at least four months) and identifying the ranges of metabolites that correlated with favorable clinical outcomes.[95]

In *Prometheus*, the patent holder argued that the test involved a physical transformation because the drugs were metabolized by patients and the patients themselves were transformed by the administration of the drug.[96] The Federal Circuit agreed, finding that this transformation was the type of physical transformation deemed patent eligible in *Bilski*.[97]

This is arguably a stretch of both the notion of centrality and that of transformation. From the standpoint of centrality, treating the patient with the drug is not truly the invention. The drug already existed. What is new is the idea of correlating the range of metabolite measured to the amount of drug administered. Knowing a drug dosage range alone or comparing results to the drug range does not involve a transformation.

From the standpoint of transformation the opinion could suggest a sweeping result. Using the logic of the opinion, one could argue that all inventions related in any way to the field of medicine satisfy the transformation test because the patient will ultimately be transformed in the healing process. If so, the test cannot exclude anything in the medical field as unpatentable, no matter how abstract the claimed invention may be and regardless of whether the invention in essence claims a law of nature.

To fully understand *Prometheus*, one must understand the context in which the opinion was delivered. At the time, the Federal Circuit's *Bilski* opinion, which established the machine-or-transformation test, was pending at the Supreme Court. Numerous amicus briefs had been submitted to the Supreme Court in *Bilski*, including a number arguing that the test would be terribly damaging to the biotech industry. *Prometheus* can be understood as the Federal Circuit's message to the Supreme Court. It was a way of saying, "Don't worry. Everything is fine here. Biotech has nothing to worry about, so you can just go ahead and uphold our test."

The way in which the Federal Circuit protected biotechnology under the test, however, merely highlighted the problems with the test. The machine-or-transformation test has no underlying logic and no ability to delineate categories of inventions other than by subjective application of what a particular court believes to be the right result.

The same subjectivity and lack of clarity are evident in the machine prong of the machine-or-transformation test. This prong specifies that an invention can constitute patentable subject matter if it is "tied to a particular machine." Although the Supreme Court may have had some idea of a distinction in mind in earlier opinions involving machines for a specific purpose, such as curing rubber, the Federal Circuit in *Alappat* eliminated any such distinction. *Alappat* concerned a program for making lines on a computer appear smooth to the human eye.[98] The Federal Circuit found that the invention constituted one related to a specific machine because the invention had the specific purpose of being a machine that produced smooth lines on the display.[99] By this logic, any invention related to a computer automatically makes that computer a specific machine. One cannot distinguish between inventions related to a specific or particular machine, which should be patentable, and those related to machines in general, which should not be patentable.

With the approach in *Alappat* drafters can easily come up with similar linguistic solutions in just about any case. For example, a general-purpose computer programmed to calculate derivatives is called a "derivate calculator." In these cases the only thing that distinguishes between a specific machine and a general machine is the construction of a noun that describes what the invention does, thereby suggesting that the real creativity occurs when the patent lawyer figures out how to draft the claim.

The truth, one might suspect, is that the Federal Circuit tried to devise some type of test specifically tailored to produce the result that it wanted in a handful of cases. The test, however, rested on clever wordplay without clear logic. As such, it was little more than a license for the Federal Circuit judges to declare that "We know it when we see it." Such subjectivity is bound to wreak havoc, and the havoc began almost immediately after the Federal Circuit's decision in *Bilski*.

As explained earlier, the machine-or-transformation test as applied in *Prometheus* could be interpreted as finding that all inventions related to medicine constitute patentable subject matter. Swinging in the opposite direction, the Patent and Trademark Office took advantage of the lack of clarity in the test to interpret it in a tremendously narrow way. The PTO's approach would reject many inventions in the personal diagnostics field and lead to remarkably strange results. Specifically, the PTO has interpreted *Prometheus* to mean that the patentability of diagnostic tests turns on the timing of the treatment determination.[100] If the diagnostic criteria are based on a series of baseline characteristics before treatment rather than reading similar characteristics during treatment, the invention would not be patentable. Presumably, the theory is that if a physician decides *not* to administer a drug to a particular patient, one cannot say that the patient's body has been transformed by the treatment. Thus, for example, if I use a personalized-medicine method to look at your genetic, metabolic, and clinical characteristics, and I conclude that you should not take a drug, that invention is unpatentable. If, however, I use a personalized-medicine invention that looks at the same set of genetic characteristics before you take the drug, starts you on the drug, interprets the characteristics, and—after determining that the drug is not effective—takes you off the drug, that invention is patentable. The only difference between the two inventions is whether measurement takes place before the drug is administered or before and after the drug is administered. From the standpoint of whether the invention should be considered as doing no more than identifying a natural phenomenon or whether the computer program that is being patented as part of the invention constitutes a mathematical formula, the PTO's distinction is arbitrary. The distinction does serve the instrumental function of narrowing the more sweeping implications of the Federal Circuit's decision in *Prometheus,* but the foundational logic is lacking.

In a later iteration of *Prometheus,* the Federal Circuit broadened its transformation holding by concluding that the invention involves transformation not only of the human body but also of a sample of human blood or tissue. This, presumably, would ease the problem of disallowing patents for personalized-medicine methods in which a physician decides *not* to use a particular treatment because the entire process would involve analysis of some human-tissue sample at some point, and analysis of the tissue would constitute transformation. This approach, however, just leads back to blanket approval of any biotech invention regardless of how broad or preemptive.

Given the expansive reach of its holding, the Federal Circuit had to strain mightily to distinguish *Prometheus* from the Court's earlier case, *In re Grams.*[101] The inventor in *Grams* had claimed a sweepingly broad invention reminiscent of some of the troubling business-method patents. Specifically, the inventor claimed a process that involved (1) performing a clinical test on individuals, (2) based on the data from that test, determining whether an abnormality existed, and (3) determining possible causes of any abnormality by using an algorithm.[102] Despite its breathtaking sweep, the invention in *Grams* did include a clinical test that would involve transformation of a human tissue. In struggling to clarify the reason the invention in *Prometheus* was unpatentable whereas the invention in *Grams* was not, the Federal Circuit explained that the clinical tests in *Grams* were just for the purpose of obtaining data whereas the clinical tests in *Prometheus* were for the purpose of treating the patient.[103] Given that the examined claims in both inventions were aimed at treating an individual patient, the Federal Circuit's distinction is remarkably difficult to discern.

The cases are far less difficult to distinguish when focusing on the question of preemption. The inventor in *Grams* expressed a claim that covered the broad concept of testing for clinical parameters and determining appropriate treatment. As I have noted in previous work discussing gene patents, when testing for patentable subject matter, one should ask whether, when considering the limitations of the patent system as a whole, we are likely to have preemption problems with the subject matter of a particular patent.[104] The *Grams* claim clearly raises preemption problems by threatening to block an entire approach to medical treatment in general. As such, the claim falls outside patentable subject matter. To reach this conclusion, one does not need to get tangled up in searching for transformations or arguing about whether those transformations are sufficiently central.

One should remember that the Federal Circuit's test focuses the inquiry specifically on the presence of machines or transformations rather than the presence of laws of nature, natural phenomena, mental steps, or abstract concepts. If the Federal Circuit's approach to the transformation prong of the machine-or-transformation test spills over onto the machine prong of the test, the results could be quite troubling. In particular, the Federal Circuit's approach suggests that a court should be satisfied if it finds a transformation occurring anywhere in the invention. Imagine the possibilities in the machine prong of the test if a court must simply ask whether a specific-purpose machine is involved in any way. Consider the following invention for improving the reliability of a printer: (1) Stand in front of the printer; (2) close eyes and pray that the printer does not jam; (3) press print button; (4) retrieve printed sheet. The invention certainly involves a machine, and one for a specific purpose, namely printing. For that matter, the invention involves a physical transformation, given that ink appears on the paper in the form of characters. Thus, it could pass the test with flying colors. Although somewhat exaggerated, the example suggests the dangers of forgetting the concepts underlying the short-cut proxies that the court believes it has found.

In short, in overturning the "useful, concrete, and tangible" test and adopting the "machine-or-transformation" test, the Federal Circuit simply replaced one fuzzy and ineffective test with another. Most important, the machine-or-transformation test provides no guarantee of accomplishing its described goal of drawing a distinction between claims that seek to preempt the use of a fundamental principle and claims that seek only to prevent others from using a particular application of that principle.[105] Consider the process in the *Ariad* case that is described at the beginning of this chapter. The *Ariad* case involved claims related to the discovery of a pathway through which a cell controls gene expression. The patent claimed the process of reducing NF-κB activity in a cell. The claim would satisfy the transformation prong of the machine-or-transformation test, given that the reducing activity in a cell involves a physical transformation of the cell. Nevertheless, by trying to control anything related to a pathway in the human body, the invention preempts a broad area of human genetics and essentially tries to occupy that entire phenomenon. In the end, the machine-or-transformation test does not solve the problems of patentable subject matter any better than its predecessor tests.

Although the patent world held its collective breath while waiting for the Supreme Court decision in *Bilski,* the Court's decision solved very little.[106] All nine members of the Court agreed with the Federal Circuit that the inventor's method of managing commodities trading fell outside the category of patentable subject matter. There was little agreement, however, on anything else. Three opinions were filed. Justice Kennedy authored the opinion of the Court, in which three other justices joined in full and a fourth joined for all but sections II-B-2 and II-C-2. The other four justices signed an opinion written by Justice Stevens, concurring in the judgment but using slightly different reasoning. Another of the concurring justices, Justice Breyer, filed a separate opinion, which was joined in only one part by Justice Scalia, the justice who had joined some, but not all, of the majority opinion. I suspect that most readers would have appreciated an algorithm to figure out what issues everyone, or even a majority, agreed on, what words have precedential value, and what approaches are likely to appeal to the Court in the future.

A few key issues can be discerned in the portion of the opinion of the Court signed by five justices. First, the Federal Circuit erred in finding that the machine-or-transformation test is the sole measure of whether a method satisfies the requirements of subject matter patentability. The machine-or-transformation test may be "an important and useful clue" and "an investigative tool," but it is certainly not the sole test.[107] Second, although this business-method patent was ineligible, the words of the Patent Act do not forbid all business-method patents. Third, the Court left future development of other tests up to the Federal Circuit, although the Court specifically rejected *State Street* and suggested that it disagreed with just about everything else the Federal Circuit had said in this arena. Specifically, the Court said, "And nothing in today's opinion should be read as endorsing interpretations of §101 that the Court of Appeals for the Federal Circuit has used in the past."[108]

In terms of the specific invention at issue in the case, the majority opinion found that it fell outside patentable subject matter because it was an attempt to patent abstract concepts. Some of the claims simply explain the basic concept of hedging risk by reducing the concept to an abstract formula. Allowing the inventor to succeed in these claims would "pre-empt the use of [risk hedging] in all fields and would effectively grant a monopoly of an abstract idea."[109]

The remaining claims simply try to patent the use of the abstract idea of hedging risk in the energy market by turning that concept into a simple mathematical equation and the use of well-known random-analysis techniques to help establish some of the inputs of the equation. The Court felt that none of this added much to the underlying principles in the area, which itself should be unpatentable.

The Supreme Court granted certiorari, vacated, and remanded the Federal Circuit's original decision in *Prometheus* on June 29, 2010, to be reconsidered in light of the Court's opinion in *Bilski*.[110] On remand, the Federal Circuit again held that Prometheus's patent claims were valid according to its earlier analysis because the Court in *Bilski* had not invalidated the machine-or-transformation test to determine patentability.[111] Thus, the

Federal Circuit reaffirmed that *Prometheus*'s claims involve transformative steps that, rather than preempting a law of nature, rely on a specific application of naturally occurring correlations.[112] The Supreme Court again granted certiorari in the case, and the case is still pending as of the printing of this book.

Reading the tea leaves of the *Bilski* opinion will occupy lawyers and legal scholars for some time to come. Perhaps the clearest message of the *Bilski* opinion is that much remains undecided on the question of what constitutes patentable subject matter for a method patent.

## How Do We Solve This Mess?

Finding the proper approach to deciding what processes should constitute patentable subject matter continues to frustrate the courts despite decades of effort. With the introduction of digital technology, which then became coupled with our forays into allowing business-method patents and the rapid emergence of more abstract and intangible financial and business structures, and the modern development of biomedical and computer inventions, the courts have remained entangled in the web that connects all of these issues. The difficulties create a temptation to see a comfortable result and to craft a test that reaches that result without coming to terms with the implications of the approach. The complexity of the issues and their almost impenetrable interconnections, however, make these piecemeal approaches inadequate over time, not to mention logically and theoretically unsatisfying.

The solution to untangling the mess can be found in returning to the basic underlying rationale for subject matter patentability. Insights into laws of nature may be tremendously valuable, but they do not necessarily constitute patentable subject matter. All inventions use laws of nature and natural phenomena, and many inventions can be abstracted or expressed in either mathematical terms or in prose. Shifting the terms in which inventions are expressed should not affect their patentability one way or another.

In contrast, patentable subject matter for an invention can be understood in the following manner. An invention that is the proper subject matter for a patent applies laws of nature, abstract ideas, formulas, insights into natural phenomena, and the like in a way that does not preempt current or future inventors from also utilizing those building blocks. The question is not whether a machine or math is involved. The essential questions for these difficult borderline areas of innovation are whether one has an applied invention and whether a threat of preemption exists.

The following sections present some examples of how this approach can be applied in some of the more challenging modern circumstances. Consider first the *LabCorp* case, in which the inventor claimed any method of testing a bodily fluid for elevated levels of homocysteine and correlating that level with a deficiency of B12 or folic acid.[113] In essence, the claim does no more than take note of a fact of nature, that certain levels of substance X are associated with problem Y. The inventor does not apply that fact of nature to any particular invention, such as a particular test for the levels or a particular medication for treating the deficiency. Rather, the inventor tries to gain control of that fact of nature. This is the type of claim that would be disallowed under an approach to patentable subject matter that properly focused on preemption or occupation of natural phenomena.

The addition of steps for testing and correlation does not save the claim. Examining and concluding are part of the basic elements of scientific exploration. If all one is doing is examining nature and concluding that the natural phenomenon exists, the claim has no patentable substance.

If one asks what the patent holder has brought to society, that is, what gifts the invention presents, there is no contribution here other than insight into what nature provides. That, in itself, is not patentable, although the insight may be of great value to society. Granting the patent holder control of such a natural phenomenon may prevent society from receiving the gifts that future inventors could bring by finding ways to apply that fact of nature to the creation of novel technological inventions.

Similar logic can be helpful in approaching the case of *Ariad v. Lilly*.[114] As described earlier, *Ariad* concerned claims related to the discovery of a pathway through which cells control gene expression. The claims included any method of modifying the effects of the pathway.[115] In focusing on disclosure as a vehicle for invalidating the claims, the Federal Circuit avoided the more glaring problems related to patentable subject matter. The claims simply recited a natural phenomenon, a way in which cells operate, and then claimed any method of affecting that natural phenomenon. In so doing, the patent had the effect of tying up the natural pathway for all possible inventions.

Although one could argue that it might be theoretically possible for an inventor to have discovered all of the ways of affecting a law of nature, the likelihood of such an event is extremely remote. Even then, full understanding of any such pathway would entail the characterization of natural phenomena arguably unpatentable under the rationale discussed earlier. Focusing instead on the question of whether the inventor truly has found a way of affecting the pathway or how many ways might suffice to claim enough invention to tie up the pathway misses the point that no inventor should be permitted to occupy or preempt a method in which nature operates or to tie up the natural pathway in all of the ways that such a pathway might operate or be manipulated.

The posture of the case highlights the problem of allowing this type of claim. Ariad was the patent holder of the claimed pathway invention. Prior to the grant of Ariad's patent, Lilly had patented two drugs. Scientists understood the efficacy of the drugs but not the mechanism by which the drugs worked in the body. This is not unusual in the medical field. Aspirin remains a tremendously useful medication for treating a variety of medical conditions, yet scientists are still uncertain of the mechanism by which it helps to prevent or treat certain heart problems.[116] In Lilly's case, it turned out that the company's drugs used the cell pathway highlighted in Ariad's patent. A patent on methods of affecting a pathway in general allows the inventor to occupy that natural pathway, thereby preempting not only future uses of the pathway but also any current inventions related to it.

This type of problem is particularly troubling in light of bargaining. Even if the patent claims ultimately fall, their existence provides the patent holder with significant leverage that can affect the development of other inventions. Given the intricate bargaining interactions among patent holders, even a potentially weak patent claim may be used as a weapon to effect the way the parties maneuver in their interpretation of the extent of other patent rights. In other words, I may be willing to forego pressing my rights to develop an area of patent X if you let go of claims in patent Y.

In light of the bargaining potential, it would be better to draw some end points, some warning signals that indicate when it is less likely that an invention is within the possible realm of patentability or that other patent holders will give it much credit. No boundaries will be perfect, but an effort to carve out areas that do not belong in the patent system may help cabin the bargaining range. When the potential for navigating is such that whole swaths of nature may be blocked, those areas should be placed out of reach of patents.

The earlier discussion explained why a claim that preempts a natural phenomenon should be excluded from patentable subject matter. In a similar manner, the basic activities of scientific exploration, particularly those that involve human thought, should also be unpatentable subject matter. As a scientist, one should be able to think and explore. Patents on exploration, as well as those that impinge on or preempt thought, should be problematic.

I do not mean to suggest that a patent falls outside patentable subject matter if it is too important to exploration in an area. At any given time, patents may exist that claim key elements of the current methods of exploration. Such is the nature of the patent system. An inventor may legitimately hold the patent on a microscope even if the microscope is the only current method available for investigation of things that cannot be observed by the naked eye. This does not mean, however, that one can patent the general activities of thought or exploration. Thus, although a microscope patent would fall within patentable subject matter, an inventor may not patent "any method of observing particles too small to be seen by the naked eye" or, even more broadly, "any method of study and observation" of something. Thought, study, and observation are basic elements of human endeavor and scientific exploration.

Following this approach could be helpful in analyzing other recent troubling cases. For example, in the 2007 case of In re Comiskey,[117] the patent claimed a method for a mandatory arbitration system regarding documents. The system was described in tremendously broad and general terms and consisted of nothing more than steps such as: (1) enabling people to register themselves and documents; (2) providing any arbitration language for the documents; (3) conducting arbitration; and (4) determining a final award or decision.[118]

A Federal Circuit panel, in finding that the claims fell outside patentable subject matter, used language that touched on the fundamental problem. Rather than getting hung up on whether machines were involved or focusing on other red herrings, the panel found that "the patent statute does not allow patents on particular systems that depend for their operation on human intelligence alone."[119] Something that is no more than an approach for thinking through and solving problems should be beyond patentable subject matter. While the patent and its claims may have suffered from other problems as well, the possibility of tying up an approach to problem solving should be clearly beyond the pale.

Similar to methods of thought is the process of exploration. Inventions that impinge on exploration not by claiming a specific method but by claiming exploration in general are problematic. For example, the case of *Classen v. Biogen*[120] concerned claims to a method of determining whether an immunization schedule affects the incidence of chronic immune disorders. In other words, the patent holder claimed any method of testing to see whether different immunization schedules would produce greater or fewer incidences of immune disorders as side effects of any given vaccination. As the trial court noted, the patent holder did not claim any particular technology or approach for testing this but merely claimed the general inquiry of testing to determine a correlation between any immunization schedule of any substance and any resulting immune disorders.[121]

The Federal Circuit issued a one-paragraph opinion upholding the district court's denial of patentable subject matter on the grounds that the invention did not constitute a machine or transformation.[122] The problem, however, can be understood in far more direct terms. In this case the patent holder wanted to claim the general process of exploring how a drug and its side effects work in light of the timing of administering the drug. The inventor had no particular discovery of how to administer a particular drug for improved safety or a particular test that would demonstrate whether a proposed approach was safe. The inventor, in essence, claimed the process of investigating the question. Patents that attempt to tie up the general process of testing and exploration should fall outside of patentable subject matter.

Looking from the perspective of preemption can be helpful in developing an approach to many of the questions generated by the emerging field of personalized medicine. Personalized medicine is an area of applied research devoted to developing tests that operate on biological and clinical data from a patient (e.g., protein levels, genetic mutations, medical history) to provide diagnoses, prognoses, and treatment regimens specific to the patient. Cases arising in this field include *LabCorp,* which concerned correlating elevated homocysteine levels with certain deficiencies, and *Prometheus,* which concerned determining metabolite levels after administering a particular class of drugs for gastrointestinal disorders and adjusting the dosage of the drug based on the metabolite levels.

As discussed earlier, the Federal Circuit's decision in *Prometheus* seemed to suggest that most life science inventions would satisfy the requirements of patentable subject matter, while the PTO's application of *Prometheus* could lead to the rejection of numerous inventions in this arena. Neither extreme is necessary if one focuses on preemption of laws of nature and natural phenomena as the primary concern.

For example, *LabCorp* was a relatively simple application of personalized medicine. It involved one biomarker and a reasonably straightforward correlation for treatment. In contrast, most personalized-medicine diagnostics are developed using whole genome expression or sequencing arrays to identify hundreds or even thousands of biomarkers that can be used to diagnose a specific disease state. The machine learning algorithms used to identify these markers do not operate on statistical concepts as simple as linear correlation, which for some of us is complicated enough. Machine learning algorithms employ statistical models to identify different combinations or "patterns" of markers that correlate with a specific disease state. Usually these markers are selected and statistically modeled to compensate for human genetic and environmental variation.

Thus, most personalized-medicine programs are tremendously complex compared even to logistic regression and other simple forms of statistical analysis. They are not simply a reflection of a natural phenomenon; they are an interpretive model of nature. Nor are they analogous to or preemptive of human thought. It would be quite improbable for a physician to be able to sit down with a pen and paper and work out a diagnostic by applying a machine learning algorithm or logistic regression to hundreds of biomarker levels.[123]

Consider the first person who discovered that human chorionic gonadotropin (hCG) levels indicate pregnancy when they are elevated above a certain level, and assume that the inventor also created a home pregnancy test for measuring the hCG. One could think of this as a simplistic personalized diagnostic device in which a particular nongenetic marker is measured to identify a state of health. The inventor could certainly patent the kit, which would consist of the physical device with its particular components. The inventor should not, however, be allowed to patent the process of testing human urine for an elevated level of hCG and correlating that level with the state of pregnancy. The core of the invention, the fact that hCG above a particular level confirms pregnancy, is a simple reflection of nature rather than an interpretive model. To understand the difference, compare the process of measuring one marker by looking for a simple level to the average personalized invention. The modern personalized invention may utilize hundreds of biomarkers analyzed by means of statistical patterns. Even if the complex process involved in identifying the relevant biomarkers yields a limited number of biomarkers to consider for a relevant patient, that information does not relate directly to anything. For example, with a personalized medicine invention involving only a few biomarkers, each of those markers generally has confidence intervals assigned to indicate the likelihood that the presence or absence of a factor or the particular level of that marker will translate into a particular diagnosis or successful treatment. Once biomarkers are collected from a relevant patient, they must be processed by statistical modeling to determine how the various factors and confidence levels for this particular patient should be interpreted. The complexity and variability of individual humans ensures that a model like this can never be a simple reflection of nature. Rather, it is no more than an interpretation of nature, albeit one that is extremely important in the treatment of a specific disease.

In contrast, the inventor of the method of measuring hCG is looking at only one marker, and it is a marker that is elevated in the same range for pregnant women in general. Thus, it requires no complex modeling and is a direct reflection of a phenomenon of nature. As a result, it would not be patentable subject matter on the grounds that the core of the invention is no more than the discovery of a natural phenomenon.

The hCG invention should also fail on the grounds that performing the test is no more than a mental step. The method does not require complex computer analysis to interpret the data; it requires observing a particular level of a substance and reaching a conclusion from that level. Preventing human beings from looking at information and concluding something threatens to preempt simple thought.

Personalized medicine, with its marriage of biology and computer technology, provides a wonderful opportunity to understand and tease out some of the threads of patentable subject matter. These inventions demonstrate how early misconceptions about the nature of computer programs and the nature of mathematics are causing problems in modern case law.[124]

Part of the difficulty can be traced to confusion between the content of something that is being expressed and the language in which it is expressed. For example, we know that laws of nature are not patentable. Some of these laws are familiar to us in the formulaic language in which we normally see them expressed. Most people, for example, would recognize one of Einstein's laws of physics expressed as $E = MC^2$. One could express that same law in prose, however, rather than formulaic language by explaining the way in which matter and energy are interchangeable.

The choice of language is irrelevant.[125] We disallow patenting of $E = MC^2$ not because it is expressed in mathematical form but because it represents one of the building blocks of scientific exploration and endeavor. Patenting that law would preempt scientific exploration by occupying a basic concept.

In addition to laws of physics, other things can be expressed in formulaic language. Expressing something in formulaic language, however, does not mean that what is being expressed is a law of nature. Thus, the fact that computer programs are expressed in a formulaic language that looks somewhat like math to the layperson does not mean that the concepts underlying a particular program are analogous to math, let alone analogous to a law of nature. Two things expressed in the same language or the type of same language are not necessarily analogous. Comic books and the Constitution are both expressed in the English language, but they are hardly analogous. Our focus should remain on the content of what is being expressed and on the preemptive effect that might result from patenting that type of content.

Some unfortunate language in the Supreme Court's *Diehr* opinion, which flows from this misperception, makes it more difficult to properly separate software claims that should be patentable from ones that should not. In searching for logic to explain why the rubber-molding invention at issue was patentable while other apparently similar inventions had failed, the Court made the following comment: "A mathematical formula as such is not accorded the protection of our patent laws, and this principle cannot be circumvented by attempting to limit the use of the formula to a particular technological environment."[126]

Other courts have jumped on the language to declare that so-called field of use restrictions cannot save software patents.[127] Even the recent Supreme

Court opinion in *Bilski* wandered into the same territory when referencing its earlier decision in *Flook:*

> *Flook* established that limiting an abstract idea to one field of use . . . did not make the concept patentable. That is exactly what the remaining claims in petitioners' application do. These claims attempt to patent the use of the abstract idea of hedging risk in the energy market and then instruct the use of well-known random analysis techniques to help establish some of the inputs into the equation. Indeed, these claims add even less to the underlying abstract principle than the invention in *Flook* did, for the *Flook* invention was at least directed to the narrower domain of signaling dangers in operating a catalytic converter.[128]

It is true, as a general matter, that if one were to claim a law of nature, the claim would not be rendered patentable by limiting use of that law of nature to a particular field. Thus, for example, an inventor could not save a claim to all uses of $E = MC^2$ by limiting the claim to "all uses of $E = MC^2$ in the construction field."

Sliding the analogy over to software, however, involves logical errors. The logic that appears to have been used is the following. Computer programs are mathematical formulas, and mathematical formulas are laws of nature. We know that laws of nature cannot be rendered patentable by limiting their application to a particular field of use. Computer programs, therefore, cannot be rendered patentable by limiting their application to a particular field of use.

This sequence contains a number of logical errors. Computer programs may be expressed in a language that looks like math, and some do involve calculations, but they are not necessarily analogous to mathematical formulas. Most important, they are not analogous to natural laws just because both are expressed in formulaic languages. One must look to the content of the computer program and its potentially preemptive effect to determine patentability.

As described earlier, the term "algorithm" in computer science means a series of steps performed on input data by a computer. This process may or may not raise preemption concerns. Some computer "algorithms" are based on properties inherent in types of input and output data. Such broad, generic algorithms, which can be used on a variety of types of input data, may raise threats of preemption. In other words, if an inventor asks for a patent on a software program that works with whole sets of numbers or entire types of data, such a patent would not be patentable subject matter. Particularly in light of the bargaining potential that would come with such a grant, the patent would risk tying up entire types of data rather than constituting something applied.

This does not mean that all software is unpatentable. Claims to programs that are applied to a specific type of data in the pursuit of particular types of outputs do not present the same level of preemption threat. For example, a personalized medicine algorithm (i.e., series of steps) that employs a specific type of statistical model using a fixed set of markers to produce a very specific diagnosis would not threaten to preempt other methods of performing the same diagnosis that use different markers or novel types of statistical models. Such an invention should be patentable.

Computer programs may be many things, including methods of creating useful models of the world around us, methods of providing interpretations of information, and methods of sorting information. When methods of creating a particular type of model are described at a very general level, they may threaten to preempt the broad activity of exploration. However, when claimed at the level of a specific method of sorting a particular type of information for a particular pursuit, they should constitute an applied invention. Such specificity is the hallmark of what separates unpatentable abstractions from applications of those abstractions in the useful arts in a way that is worthy of patent protection.

Other strained comparisons haunt the question of whether computer-related inventions are patentable. For example, one could certainly argue that, at a very basic level, computers operate in a way that is vaguely analogous to the human brain, at least to the extent that both engage in the processing of information. Computers, however, are only loosely analogous to the human mind, and their functions range far beyond the types of tasks that even the most sophisticated human mind can accomplish. This is not simply a matter of speed or accuracy but one of task content as well. Vague similarities related to the activity of processing information do not make computer programs analogous to the human mind.

In the same vein, computer programs are undoubtedly similar to things that are intangible and abstract. Performing a series of steps on data is certainly abstract. Attempting to circumvent the ethereal nature of computer programs by looking for evidence of something concrete in any corner of the activity, however, simply invites clever drafting and creative framing of the invention.

I suspect that these types of comparisons have led some courts to fixate on the presence of a machine in the invention. A machine for a specific purpose would seem to mollify those who would object that the invention is merely an abstraction or that it constitutes no more than human thought.

The presence of a machine, however, may be totally irrelevant. If an invention is unpatentable because it is essentially human thought, one cannot save the invention by having a computer perform the task that a human ordinarily would. Thus, arguing over the presence or absence of a machine and the centrality of the machine to the invention is not helpful. What is helpful, however, is to return to the touchstone reason for removing certain categories from patentable subject matter in the first place. That reason is preemption. One should focus on the content of what is new in the invention. In that context, one should ask whether, considering the limitations of the patent system as a whole, we are likely to have preemption problems with the subject matter of this patent.

## The Interaction of Subject Matter and the Other Elements of Patentability

Part of the problem in the area of patentable subject matter is that subject matter has too often been asked to bear an excessive amount of the burden of protecting the patent system from troubling claims. Although important, subject matter need not shoulder all of the weight alone.

Some of the problems that courts and commentators complain about in the context of troubling "subject matter" cases do properly belong in other categories. For example, we may find that computer programs constitute patentable subject matter, yet an invention that uses a computer program to do something that has previously been done manually may be perfectly obvious in light of what computers have already been used for and the lack of any particular innovation in the computer application.

Patentable subject matter, however, remains an important weapon in the arsenal of patent law in its efforts to limit the reach of patent holders. Identifying general categories that are beyond the reach of patent holders may offer a direct, upfront method of keeping patent holders away from those areas that patent law has deemed fundamental to innovation and scientific endeavor. This is particularly true in light of the bargain aspect of patenting. Given the bargaining potential associated with patent claims, the patent system may benefit from establishing threshold lines: bright-line warning strips that, in their best moments, may serve to keep patent holders away from certain domains.

Of course, bargaining and navigating will remain even as applied to the application of the subject matter rules themselves. Nevertheless, the bright-line threshold rules of patentable subject matter may serve to cabin the bargaining and limit the power of those who would overreach.

# 5

## The Interaction of Patents with
## Contracts and Antitrust

In any attempt to manage the dynamics of the patent system, one must be mindful of efforts to navigate around that system. In particular, parties may be able to use systems outside of patent law to avoid bargaining limitations built into the patent system or to evade the patent system altogether. If left unchecked, such strategies could undermine whatever policies and priorities have been established in the creation of the patent system.

This is not just a matter of using inappropriate sources of power to browbeat one's negotiating opponent, although that in itself can be problematic. One must also be wary of efforts by both parties in a negotiating setting to collaborate so that, together, they can receive more than the sovereign intended to grant to either one.

One of the most difficult terrains to navigate in this area is the intersection of the patent system with antitrust law and contract law. Each of the three doctrinal areas is quite complex, and courts can easily miss the subtle interactions among them. Maintaining the integrity of the patent system, however, requires an understanding of how these systems are intertwined and an effort to manage the interactions among them.

This chapter describes ways in which modern manipulation of these critical intersections threatens to undermine the patent system. It focuses in particular on attempts to use other areas of law to avoid the restrictions of patent exhaustion and patent misuse.

## Understanding Patent Misuse

In tracing the intersections of patent, contract, and antitrust law, all roads lead to patent misuse. In fact, it is impossible to understand the complex interplay of these three areas of law without understanding patent misuse and its history.[1] The following section briefly describes the doctrine of patent misuse and its origins. The saga begins in the late nineteenth and the early twentieth century, as antitrust laws began to appear at both the state and the federal level. These laws were intended to outlaw unreasonable restraints of trade and anticompetitive behavior.

The introduction of antitrust laws posed a natural dilemma for interactions involving patents. After all, the patent holder's right to exclude others from making an invention creates an opportunity for the patent holder to develop a monopoly in the market for that invention. How can a body of law that curtails monopolization be reconciled with one that grants the opportunity to develop a monopoly?[2] Courts in the late nineteenth and the early twentieth century struggled to resolve this apparent contradiction.

A few early cases suggested avoiding the conflict by separating contract and patent law into entirely separate baskets. In cases arising under contract law, the court could look into the nature and character of the agreement, including whether it violated antitrust law. In cases arising under patent law, however, the court could not.[3] Taking this approach, if a party sued for breach of contract, the defendant would be allowed to argue that the terms of the contract violated public policies, such as the antitrust principles. If a party facing the same facts sued for patent infringement, however, the court could not review the nature of any of the agreements but would be confined to determining patentability and infringement.

As a result, patent law became a key vehicle for undermining the antitrust laws. Latching on to this marvelous principle of separation, patent holders were able to use their patents to engage in precisely the types of schemes that the antitrust laws were designed to outlaw, including price fixing and tying while avoiding application of the antitrust law. If a patent holder asserted only patent rather than contract causes of action, antitrust issues could not be raised. In fact, in striking testimony before Congress in the early 1940s, one German manufacturer commented that he had no reason to worry about U.S. antitrust laws. If he wanted to control the distribution of markets, it could be fully accomplished through patent licensing.[4]

Courts continued to struggle with this problem until the 1930s and 1940s, when the Supreme Court began to articulate what would become the basis of the reconciliation of patent and antitrust law. In this famous compromise, the Supreme Court determined that antitrust law would apply to all agreements, even those concerning patents. In the context of patents, however, antitrust law would apply only when patent holders tried to exceed the powers conferred with the patent. In short, when a patent holder acted outside of the patent grant, that behavior could be scrutinized under the antitrust laws.

What constitutes acting outside the patent grant? That notion is embodied in the doctrine of patent misuse. Patent misuse, as delineated by a series of Supreme Court cases, is an impermissible attempt to extend the time or scope of a patent.[5] Potential examples include insisting that those who want to license an invention agree to buy an unpatented item as well or extracting an agreement to pay royalties after the patent term has ended.

Identifying what it means to act outside the patent grant has proven more challenging than the Supreme Court may have anticipated. Consider an agreement to pay royalties beyond the term of the patent. It could be an impermissible attempt to extend the patent grant, which would be in violation of patent principles. However, it could also be a perfectly harmless extended payment contract, analogous to paying off a mortgage over time. Delineating the difference between the two is not easy.

Despite such difficulties, the concept of attempting to extend the time or scope of a patent formed the basis of the doctrine of patent misuse and established an important grounding for the theoretic relationship between patent and antitrust. A patent holder who acts outside the patent powers by trying to extend the patent has exceeded the authority granted under the patent. In those circumstances a court may scrutinize a patentee's conduct using antitrust doctrines that might otherwise appear to be in tension with the granting of patents.

Although I have described patent misuse here in terms of its role in identifying the interaction of patent and antitrust, patent misuse has traditionally played a role in patent law unrelated to antitrust. The basic role of patent misuse is as a defense of infringement. Specifically, accused infringers can defend on the grounds that the patent holder has misused the patent and that, as a result, the patent should not be enforced. Thus, a patent holder pursuing an infringer can face a defense of patent misuse, as well as charges of violation of the antitrust laws.

It is also important to emphasize one key point about the traditional relationship between patent misuse and antitrust violations. The two are not the same. A patent holder who engages in patent misuse by trying to extend the time or scope of the patent is subject to antitrust scrutiny, but that does not necessarily mean that an antitrust violation will be found.

Traditionally, patent misuse has been described as a broader wrong than antitrust violation, one that should be tested according to patent principles. Thus, even if no antitrust violation has occurred, a patent holder may have engaged in patent misuse. In particular, antitrust law focuses on behavior by firms that have market power, which is generally defined as the ability to raise prices and restrict supply in a relevant market. Market power, however, is something that most patent holders do not possess because, to put it simply, having a patent is no guarantee that one will have a monopoly. Substitutes may be available for the patented product, or sufficient cross-market elasticities may exist such that the patent holder does not control a large enough share of the market to constitute market power for the purposes of antitrust law. The inventor who first patented margarine, for example, still had to compete with those who made butter.

The vast majority of patent holders earn nothing from their patents.[6] Even when patents generate a high level of revenue, that revenue does not necessarily translate into market power. For example, when the patent on acetaminophen was still in force, the makers of Tylenol might have had to compete with the makers of aspirin, ibuprofen, and naproxen. The patent generated great revenue, but the company did not necessarily have market power in the market for nonprescription, anti-inflammatory drugs. A finding of market power is not required under traditional patent misuse doctrine, but it is required for establishing an antitrust violation. Thus, a finding of patent misuse does not necessarily mean that the patent holder has committed an antitrust violation.

The Federal Circuit has tried to dodge the principle of nonequivalence in recent decades by suggesting that patent misuse should be determined by the same tests as antitrust violations. It remains to be seen, however, whether the Supreme Court will swallow the Federal Circuit's revision of the rules. The story of the Federal Circuit's dance with patent misuse is a wonderful example of the Federal Circuit's less than enthusiastic embrace of Supreme Court precedent and authority.

The story begins at the Federal Circuit in the mid-1980s. Up to that time patent misuse had been defined as an impermissible attempt to extend the time or scope of a patent. This formulation followed Supreme Court language from the original cases that launched the doctrine. In 1986, however, Chief Judge Markey of the Federal Circuit added three key words to the definition. In the case of *Windsurfing v. AMF*, Judge Markey defined patent misuse as an impermissible attempt to broaden the physical or temporal scope of a patent *with anticompetitive effect*.[7] Thus, in revising the test for patent misuse, Judge Markey borrowed directly from antitrust language, making it clear that patent misuse should be tested under antitrust principles. In particular, he held that the key inquiry in patent misuse "must reveal that the overall effect of the license tends to restrain competition unlawfully in an appropriately defined relevant market."[8] Although the opinion cited the 1971 Supreme Court case of *Blonder-Tongue,* that case does not contain either *Windsurfing's* language or its test.[9]

With this change the Federal Circuit attempted to subsume patent misuse under antitrust. To be fair, Judge Markey did try to avoid a direct contradiction of Supreme Court precedent by suggesting that the new test would apply only to behaviors that the Supreme Court had not previously declared to be misuse.[10] Behaviors that the Supreme Court had previously declared to be misuse were to be treated as per se examples of misuse, while all other cases would be treated under antitrust's rule of reason.[11] Supreme Court case law, however, had spoken in terms of a general rule for all of patent misuse and had given no hint of the type of two-tiered structure Judge Markey had implemented.

Within nine months Judge Markey had retreated. In an opinion in the case of *Senza-Gel* Judge Markey returned to the prior definition of patent misuse, noting in a footnote that the Federal Circuit had to wait for Congress or the Supreme Court to enact the change he had attempted in *Wind-*

*surfing.* Judge Markey's footnote said the following: "Commentators and courts have questioned the rationale appearing in Supreme Court opinions dealing with misuse. . . . *See Windsurfing v. AMF.* We are bound, however, to adhere to existing Supreme Court guidance in the area until otherwise directed by Congress or by the Supreme Court."[12]

Congress did indeed consider the question two years later. In 1988 the Senate version of a proposed patent reform bill would have prohibited a finding of patent misuse unless the patent holder's behavior violated antitrust law.[13] The language, however, never saw the light of day. It was amended prior to passage of the act, and the final version of the 1988 Patent Act enacted a change related to only one type of patent misuse claim and only one element of that claim. Specifically, the act forbids a finding of misuse based solely on a tying claim without proof that the patent holder at least had market power.[14] The remainder of patent misuse claims and even the remaining elements of a tying claim were not affected.

Undeterred, the Federal Circuit returned to the well four years later in 1992. In the case of *Mallinckrodt v. Medipart* Judge Newman again altered the patent misuse test to require that patent misuse conform to antitrust.[15] Citing the now defunct *Windsurfing* opinion, Judge Newman held that patent misuse turns on anticompetitive effects, which are measured by the antitrust rule of reason.[16] The case did not mention the retreat from *Windsurfing,* in which Judge Markey acknowledged that the Federal Circuit lacked the power to impose this change, nor did it mention Congress's failure to pass the type of test that the Federal Circuit was now imposing.

Later cases have tried to better harmonize *Mallinckrodt* with earlier precedents. These cases repeat the mantra that patent misuse is a greater wrong than antitrust violation and may arise in circumstances in which an antitrust violation does not exist. Despite these pronouncements, the Federal Circuit currently applies an antitrust analysis to patent misuse cases and continues to describe the test for patent misuse as an impermissible attempt to extend the time or scope of a patent *with anticompetitive effect.* The Supreme Court has yet to consider the issue.

Thus, under current law, the relationship between patent and antitrust is somewhat muddy, given the Federal Circuit's decision to add an antitrust test to patent misuse. The basics of the doctrine, however, remain. When patent holders act outside the grant of the patent, they are engaging in patent misuse. Patent misuse is a wrong separate from antitrust violations and depends for its core analysis on patent doctrines. A party accused of patent infringement can raise a defense of patent misuse. In addition, when patent holders engage in misuse by acting outside the patent grant, individuals and the government may file antitrust claims against them.

In theory, the bargain aspect of patents could pose a dilemma for patent misuse. The bargain aspect suggests that one cannot know the precise definition of an invention at the time of the grant. How can a patent holder possibly exceed the scope of something that is inherently indefinable?

Although it looks like a fascinating philosophical paradox, the reality is more likely to be mundane. As described earlier, bargaining over the definition of an invention is confined, to some extent, by the nature of the invention itself. An invention related to an improved chocolate flavoring, for example, is unlikely to read on jet engines, no matter how the claims are drafted or interpreted. Inventions have some outer boundaries, although the choices within those boundaries may be quite broad.

The question that arises in most patent misuse cases is not, what are the subtleties of the definition of what you have invented? but rather, what are you doing wholly outside of any definition that might apply? For example, patent misuse may involve behaviors such as using one's patent to gain a return on someone else's invention or using a patent to suppress the development of a potentially competing product.[17] Such behaviors would exceed the rights granted with a patent, although they would not involve the definition of the claims.

In sum, patent misuse is an impermissible attempt to expand the time or scope of a patent, which under current Federal Circuit law also requires anticompetitive effects. It operates as a defense in patent infringement cases. Most important, patent misuse arose from concerns that patent holders were using their patents to skirt the antitrust laws. I now turn to the flip side of this problem: modern attempts to use other areas of law to avoid the confines of patent law. The modern version of the game requires a basic understanding of the doctrine of patent exhaustion.

## Understanding Patent Exhaustion

When the Supreme Court decided the case of *Quanta* in 2008, the Court breathed life into the doctrine of patent exhaustion, a doctrine that had just about withered away under Federal Circuit decisions.[18] The doctrine of patent exhaustion holds that a patent holder may not control a patented item once it has been released into the stream of commerce.[19] In more simplistic terms, once an item embodying an invention is sold, the patent holder must relinquish control of that item. The doctrine of exhaustion is sometimes called the "first sale" doctrine from the notion that a patent holder cannot reach beyond the first sale of a patented item to control downstream sales or uses.

The doctrine of exhaustion has roots that reach back to the law related to tangible items. Historically, the doctrine flowed from the notion that if one buys an item, one should be free to use it in any way.[20] If I buy a hammer, for example, I should be able to hit any nail that I choose or sell it to anyone I choose. The doctrine of patent exhaustion also reflects a preference for the free alienability of property and an appreciation of the benefits that accrue to commerce from such freedom.

Over time, the rationale for patent exhaustion has been described in more explicit economic terms under a theory related to total patent return. According to this theory, a patent holder should be able to receive the full value of the patent from the first sale. Allowing later restrictions and returns would generate duplicative rewards while creating bottlenecks in the flow of commerce.[21]

In recent decades the Federal Circuit had all but declared that the doctrine of exhaustion was dead. The process began with the 1992 *Mallinckrodt* decision mentioned earlier. In addition to changing the definition of patent misuse, the opinion in *Mallinckrodt* cast doubt on the vitality of the exhaustion doctrine. *Mallinckrodt* reinterpreted Supreme Court precedents related to exhaustion and concluded that those cases should not be read to forbid any postsale restrictions on the sale of a patented article. Rather, they should be understood to forbid only restrictions past the first sale if those restrictions violate other areas of law, such as antitrust.[22]

In the decades following *Mallinckrodt* many thought that the doctrine of patent exhaustion would fade into the background. That perspective changed dramatically in 2008 with the Supreme Court's unanimous opinion in *Quanta*. The Court's message echoed loudly and clearly from the opening words of the opinion. "For over 150 years," the court proclaimed, "this Court has applied the doctrine of patent exhaustion to limit the patent rights that survive the initial authorized sale of a patented item."[23] The opinion went on to reject the Federal Circuit's attempts to avoid applying patent exhaustion to the patent holder in the case: "The Court of Appeals for the Federal Circuit held that the doctrine does not apply to method patents at all and, in the alternative, that it does not apply here because the sales were not authorized by the license agreement. We disagree on both scores."[24]

The decision, authored by Justice Thomas, was consistent with the direction of other recent Supreme Court patent decisions. Since 2005 the Court has issued a series of decisions cutting back on patent holders' power.[25]

## Preventing Licensees from Challenging the Underlying Patent

After chiding the Federal Circuit in the *Quanta* opinion, however, the Supreme Court dipped its toes into treacherous waters. In a footnote to the opinion, the Court casually mentioned something that could open the door on a method of navigating not just around patent exhaustion but also around all of the constraints of patent law. In what could become a famous footnote, the Court said the following:

> [The patent holder] does not include a breach-of-contract claim, and we express no opinion on whether contract damages might be available even though exhaustion operates to eliminate patent damages. See *Keeler* v. *Standard Folding Bed Co.*, 157 U.S. 659, 666 (1895) ("Whether a patentee may protect himself and his assignees by special contracts brought home to the purchasers is not a question before us, and upon which we express no opinion. It is, however, obvious that such a question would arise as a question of contract, and not as one under the inherent meaning and effect of the patent laws").[26]

In this footnote the Court cited a case from the period of time in which some opinions flirted with the notion that contract law and patent law could be segregated into separate domains. As described earlier, that approach was abandoned over time as it became clear that separating the doctrines in this manner gave patent holders the perfect opportunity to avoid the limitations of antitrust law. In other words, patent law would be used to avoid antitrust.

Although the concern is slightly different here, the impact would be similar. Contract law would be used to avoid patent law. In particular, if patent holders can contract around the doctrine of exhaustion, they would be able to avoid the limitations inherent in that doctrine. Similarly, if patent holders can contract around patent law in the case of the exhaustion doctrine, perhaps they could contract around any other restriction in the patent law as well. If so, any of the limitations imposed by the patent system could be circumvented by drafting the issue into a contract and suing for contract damages rather than patent damages. This would allow patent holders to form contractual agreements related to their patents and frame any issues arising out of those agreements in contract terms rather than in terms of patent infringement. For example, patent holders could choose to file claims for breach of contract rather than for patent infringement. They could thereby use the contract system to avoid the restraints imposed by the patent system.

One might argue that concerns in this area are unfounded by trying to undermine the economic logic of the doctrine of patent exhaustion. Why should we worry if patent holders can reach beyond the first sale? Would patent holders really be able to use contracts to reap more than they could through the patent system? Would market forces not prevent a patent holder from getting more overall profit anyway? Consider the following example, suggested by a colleague. I have simplified it by leaving out interest. (Economic examples always assume something away.)

Suppose you are willing to pay $10 for my patented widget. I can sell it to you for $10 now, or I can sell it to you for $5 now plus an agreement from you to restrict the next sale in a way that allows me to reap $5 of value from John, the person you sell it to. Why should that make any difference? John will be willing to pay only so much when he buys the product. It will not matter to John whether I have extracted the total return on my patent at one point, as opposed to extracting part now and part later. Regardless of the timing, John will not be coaxed into paying more, and I will not be able to extract any more of an overall return on my patent.

The scenarios available to patent holders if they are allowed to contract around patents, however, are far more complex. Suppose I sell my patented widget to you for $5 now and an agreement from you to restrict the sales of the product in a way that continues after the end of the patent term, allowing me to earn additional returns then. The simple fact of allowing an inventor to search for rewards beyond the patent term may allow the patent holder to reap greater rewards overall. In the real world of patents, time limits matter. An inventor may not be able to capitalize extensively on an invention during the term of a patent for a number of reasons. The market may not be ready, the inventor may not be skilled enough, and ancillary inventions may not be sufficiently developed to allow full appreciation of the invention during the limited term. By extending the reward into the future or even indefinitely, the patent holder is expanding the time for searching out and capturing the reward. This extension potentially increases the rewards available and alters whatever trade-offs exist under the patent structure.

One may want to argue that the rewards and trade-offs under the patent structure should be set differently. That, however, is a different question from whether patent holders would be motivated to contract around patent law. As the earlier discussion demonstrates, regardless of the trade-offs and limits that exist in the patent system, if patent holders can contract around those limits, they can gain.

The doctrine of patent exhaustion could help mitigate an additional economic concern that flows directly from the bargain aspect of patents. When bargaining is cost free, the amount of bargaining or the number of bargains related to each patent is irrelevant. In the real world, however, where bargaining has substantial costs, restricting the patent holder to returns from the first sale may have efficiency-enhancing effects. In very simple form, assume that bargaining occurs in any transaction in which patent rights operate. If, in addition to the first time the product is sold, patent rights operate each time a product is resold, the total efficiency loss from the costs of bargaining will be greater. In other words, the farther a patent holder can reach in the life of an object, the more the stickiness and friction of each interaction can gum up the system. The doctrine of patent exhaustion, with its limitation on how many iterations the patent holder can reach out to, embodies a cap on the amount of friction that one patent holder can create.

As history has shown, when patent holders have an opportunity to use their patents to avoid the restraints of a particular system, they will indeed take advantage of it. One can expect nothing less if patent holders are offered an opportunity to contract around the restraints of patent law. It is not just a question of whether patent holders will be able to avoid the doctrine of exhaustion. If they can contract around patent law, any restraint imposed by patent law is up for grabs. The parties will simply be able to write a contract negating that restraint and enforce it through a breach of contract action rather than an action for patent infringement.

The problem again is particularly troubling in light of the bargain aspect of patents. In an intense bargaining environment, and one that takes place largely beyond the sovereign's purview, the law should be sensitive to circumstances that allow parties to use other systems to distort the limitations or priorities of the patent system. The issue is not simply a matter of parties' bringing in appropriate weapons to the table to pound each other into submission. Rather, both parties may be perfectly happy to subvert the patent system. In fact, it may be in the interests of both to extend the patent powers and share the rewards of that extension.

For example, suppose two parties contract in a way that would prevent a nascent technology from taking hold. Perhaps the parties agree to suppress a technology that is essential for the development of a nascent technology in exchange for some cross-licensing. By the time the patent expires, potential challengers will have been destroyed, and the parties together can share the rewards of unimpeded competition. This sharing may be true for a short while until new competitors gear up or, if network effects are strong and entry barriers are significant, for a longer period of time.[27] Either way, the two parties may share the rewards of prices above the competitive level, while society loses the benefit of a nascent technology. Thus, the bargain may be perfectly acceptable to both parties even as it undermines society's goals related to competitive pricing and fostering downstream innovation.

In theory, if patent holders try to contract around patent law, such behavior should be blocked by patent misuse. Contracting around patent law would be a classic attempt to expand the time or scope of the patent. For example, if patent law forbids applying restrictions past the first sale, and a patent holder licenses its product requiring restrictions past the first sale, that could constitute an attempt to expand the patent. Attempts to expand the patent, of course, should constitute patent misuse.

Patent misuse, however, is a defense to a charge of patent infringement. It is normally not an affirmative cause of action that one can bring in the absence of an infringement charge. Thus, the operative question would be whether a defendant can raise patent misuse as a defense to a claim of breach of contract. In other words, if a patent holder licenses a patent under terms that would constitute patent misuse but chooses to sue only for breach of contract rather than patent infringement, could the defendant raise patent misuse as a defense, or has the patent holder successfully avoided the pesky limitations of the patent system?

From a theoretical perspective, contracts involving patents should not be used as a dodge to get around patent law any more than contracts involving patents should be used as a dodge to get around antitrust law. The doctrinal question is less settled in patent law, however. Courts are not always precise in explaining whether a ruling on patent misuse is being rendered as a defense to a charge of infringement or as a defense to a charge of breach of contract,[28] and the issue has not been squarely addressed and resolved. The underlying logic, however, is similar in both of these circumstances. Courts should not allow contract law to be used to navigate around restrictions imposed on patent holders by other areas of law.

*Quanta*'s footnote contained no hint of the delicate interactions of patent, contract, and antitrust, including (1) the potential dangers of allowing patent holders to contract around the constraints of patent law, (2) the history in which patents, contracts, and antitrust were integrated to avoid that type of gamesmanship, and (3) the role of patent misuse in this context or even the existence of the doctrine. Although the footnote was a casual aside, no more than a dictum indicating an issue that the court had chosen not to think through with any great care, even raising it shows the danger of mentioning anything. The casual aside has sent firms scrambling to consider ways to contract around exhaustion, which threatens to create a tangle of legal questions that could take the courts years to unsnarl. An appreciation of the bargaining aspect of patents, combined with an appreciation of the intricate interaction of the systems, could avoid a difficult and costly mess.

## Planting the Seed for Contracting Around Patent Law

As described earlier, Justice Thomas's footnote in *Quanta* appeared to be a casual comment—a throwaway line that betrays little awareness that complex implications might flow from it. The footnote, however, was not entirely uncalculated. It echoes a discussion that appears in an earlier Thomas dissent.

The earlier discussion also implicated the question of whether parties may contract around patent law.[29]

The prior language appeared in the context of determining when parties in a patent dispute can get into court and under what circumstances. In more technical terms the question concerned whether an issue has risen to the level of "a case or controversy."[30]

The question of when and whether parties can access the courts is critically important in light of the bargain aspect of patents. Access to the sovereign and the timing of that access will deeply affect the bargaining choices parties make, as well as the ultimate outcome of the bargaining process.

With the bargain aspect in mind, one might approach questions of access to the sovereign by considering, for example, whether a particular approach might promote more efficient bargaining or whether it might discourage behaviors that are undesirable to the process. Consider the following example. If a patent holder believes that a competitor is infringing, the patent holder may bring an action for infringement. The competitor, however, does not have such unfettered access to the courts. One cannot simply file a suit to establish that one is *not* infringing a patent. Nor can one file a suit alleging that someone else's patent is invalid or asking how a particular patent should be interpreted. Reaching the courthouse requires an active controversy. If the patent holder does nothing, where is the controversy?

A competitor without access to the courts may be in a precarious position. For example, the patent holder could simply sit back, let damages accumulate, and wait to strike at a later time. The competitor would have no way to resolve the situation or gain clarity.[31] This is particularly problematic in a system in which parties cannot know the definitive boundaries of a patent at the moment of the grant. Denying or delaying another party's access to the courts may be a powerful weapon in the bargaining wars. Justice Thomas's earlier language concerning contracting around patent law appeared in a recent case involving access to the courts in the context of patent law.

## ARTICLE III JURISDICTION AND *MEDIMMUNE*

The language appeared in the case of *MedImmune v. Genentech.*[32] According to Federal Circuit doctrine at the time, one who holds a license to use a patented item and remains in good standing by paying the royalties cannot challenge the patent's validity. The Federal Circuit had reasoned that as long as the party holding the license continues to pay royalties to the patent holder, there is no threat of an infringement suit and therefore no case or controversy.[33]

This approach created an uncomfortable dilemma for license holders who believed that the patent they were being asked to pay royalties on was either weak or did not relate to the product or activity they were engaged in. In order to challenge the validity of a patent, a license holder had to stop paying royalties and invite an infringement suit, thereby risking the cost of a substantial damage award—including the possibility of punitive damages. Thus, the Federal Circuit's doctrine substantially reduced the likelihood that a license holder would challenge a patent even if that patent was quite weak or was being wielded inappropriately.

In the context of bargaining over the definition of rights, the doctrine also had the effect of shifting substantial bargaining power to the patent holder. Even if the patent holder was asking for something beyond any possible definition of the rights, the license holder could be reluctant to fight back, given the substantial economic risk involved.[34]

In the eight-to-one *MedImmune* decision, the Supreme Court overturned the Federal Circuit. The Court ruled that a licensee does not necessarily have to stop paying royalties and repudiate the license in order to challenge the patent's validity.[35] The case arose as a declaratory judgment action. In other words, the patent holder had not sued to enforce the contract or for patent infringement damages. Rather, the license holder initiated the suit, complaining that the patent covered by the license in the contract was invalid, and, thus, no patent royalties could be due. As a general rule, parties may file a declaratory judgment action to clarify their rights and obligations if the action is adequately supported by a case or controversy as described in Article III of the Constitution.

In granting standing for a license holder to challenge the underlying patent, the Supreme Court cited doctrines beyond patent law in which the law does not require parties to expose themselves to liability before challenging the basis of that liability.[36] For example, parties need not violate a law in order to challenge the constitutionality of that law.[37]

The underlying logic in the line of cases suggests that parties who are being subjected to coercion need not invite substantial risk in order to challenge the basis of that coercion. This is true not only when the coercion comes from the threat of government sanctions but also when it comes from the threat of private actions for enforcement that could have serious business consequences.[38]

In particular, the Supreme Court cited a 1913 treatise noting that an actual or threatened serious injury to business or employment by a private party can be just as coercive as other recognized forms of coercion that give rise to a declaratory judgment action.[39] As the *MedImmune* Court commented, one need not "bet the farm" by taking a forbidden action in order to challenge a restraint.[40]

In sum, prior to *MedImmune*, patent holders could rest assured that their patents could not be challenged by anyone who held a license. In *MedImmune* the Supreme Court found that under the Article III case or controversy requirement, one can actually challenge the validity of a patent while remaining a licensee in good standing.

In response to the *MedImmune* ruling, patent holders and commentators have begun to contemplate whether there are other ways to prevent licensees from challenging the validity of a patent.[41] Possible approaches could include either common law doctrines related to license contracts or contractual provisions drafted into licensing contracts themselves. Understanding the implications of Justice Thomas's language requires an understanding of this final set of background doctrines.

Readers might be forgiven at this point for thinking that if any patent holders are clever enough and patient enough to slog through so many of these doctrines to figure out how to manipulate them, then they deserve whatever bounty they can capture. The nagging goal of promoting innovation, not to mention the one about maintaining the integrity of the patent system, encourages slightly higher standards, however.

### IF NOT BY ARTICLE III, THEN BY COMMON LAW ESTOPPEL?

In addition to the now fruitless approach of an Article III challenge, another potential approach for preventing licensees from challenging the validity of a patent is a common law doctrine known as licensee estoppel. The doctrine, which had its heyday in the mid- to late 1800s, has roots in both contract law and the law of real property as it related to landlords and tenants.[42]

In broad terms, the doctrine holds as a matter of common law that a license holder cannot enjoy the benefits of a license contract while simultaneously challenging that contract.

The logic of the common law licensee estoppel doctrine, as well as its contractual roots, are evident in an old lower court case that was cited in the 1856 Supreme Court decision that first applied the doctrine of licensee estoppel:

> [The defendants] have had the license to make and sell which they agreed for; they have received proceeds from it, and they are only asked to pay over the proportion of those proceeds, which they agreed to; they have lost nothing in all this, if the patent was invalid; and why, then, should it be said that the consideration for this contract has failed?[43]

The common law estoppel doctrine was not based on any explicit agreement between the parties that the licensee would refrain from challenging the patent. In fact, early case law applied the doctrine despite the absence of contractual provisions either acknowledging the validity of the underlying patent or agreeing not to challenge its validity.[44] The logic of the early cases rested on the equitable notion that one cannot avoid the effect of an agreement after accepting its benefits.[45]

Common law licensee estoppel was never an absolute doctrine. Even in its heyday, courts allowed various events to release a licensee from the restriction on challenging the patent.[46] In addition, different versions of licensee estoppel appeared in the case law, in which some courts suggested that a license holder was not permitted to challenge the validity of a patent until the license agreement had expired, while other courts suggested that a license holder had to first stop paying royalties and lose the protection of the license before challenging the patent.[47]

By the early 1900s the Supreme Court had begun to cut back on licensee estoppel. For example, the Court allowed one license holder to concede the validity of the patent but narrow its interpretation.[48] The Court allowed another license holder to bring an antitrust challenge to a license contract that involved disputing the validity of a patent.[49]

The assault on licensee estoppel culminated in 1969 with *Lear v. Adkins*, in which the U.S. Supreme Court overturned the California Supreme Court's use of the doctrine.[50] The U.S. Supreme Court began by reviewing the history of cases in which it had applied licensee estoppel and noted that the trajectory had been one of constantly limiting and cutting back the doctrine:

> During this [forty-five year] period, each time a patentee sought to rely upon his estoppel privilege before this Court, the majority created a new exception to permit judicial scrutiny into the validity of the Patent Office's grant. Long before [a particular licensee estoppel case] was decided, the estoppel doctrine had been so eroded that it could no longer be considered the "general rule," but was only to be invoked in an ever-narrowing set of circumstances.[51]

The Court then reversed the California Supreme Court's decision and repudiated the estoppel portion of an earlier case.[52]

The language of the Supreme Court's opinion was quite broad, appearing to sweep away all of the doctrine. For example, the Court noted the following:

> Surely the equities of the licensor do not weigh very heavily when they are balanced against the important public interest in permitting full and free competition in the use of ideas which are in reality a part of the public domain. Licensees may often be the only individuals with enough economic incentive to challenge the patentability of an inventor's discovery. If they are muzzled, the public may continually be required to pay tribute to would-be monopolists without need or justification.[53]

Following these threads, the lower courts in the immediate aftermath of *Lear* operated as if the decision had eliminated all vestiges of licensee estoppel.

In recent years, however, some scholars have argued that, given the various strands of licensee estoppel floating around at the time of *Lear*, the opinion could be interpreted as eliminating only certain portions of the doctrine.[54] In particular, one scholar in an intriguing argument has suggested that although the Supreme Court perceived that it was rejecting the doctrine of licensee estoppel in 1969, it failed to comprehend the complexity of the doctrine at the time and the limitations of the case before it. Thus, *Lear* should be limited to its facts.[55]

Other scholars and commentators conclude, however, that despite the uncertainty, a modern Supreme Court would most likely read *Lear* as having repudiated the doctrine in full.[56] From that perspective, a licensee would not be estopped from challenging the validity of an underlying patent, at least not as a matter of common law doctrine. If so, patent holders must continue their search for other methods of restraining licensees from challenging the validity of an underlying patent.

## IF NOT BY COMMON LAW ESTOPPEL, THEN BY CONTRACT?

The doctrine of licensee estoppel was an attempt to impose a restriction on licensing contracts as a matter of common law. Assuming that such an approach fails, or as an alternative to such an approach, can parties simply include their own contract provisions forbidding a license holder from challenging an underlying patent or placing burdens on a license holder who chooses to mount a challenge? The question suggests that the issue of when license holders can have access to the courts leads back to the question of what types of things patent holders should be allowed to contract for and what should be considered misuse of the patent power. In other words, would contract provisions that forbid challenging the underlying patent be considered contracting around patent restrictions, and, if so, should the courts forbid them as constituting patent misuse?

The question of whether license holders can be prevented from challenging the underlying patent through explicit contract provisions is closely linked to the question of whether license holders can be prevented from challenging the underlying contract through common law estoppel. In both cases, patent holders are arguing that allowing license holders to challenge the validity of the patent alters the bargain inherent in the contract. The question, of course, is whether such a bargain should be permissible.

The link between (1) licensee estoppel implied by common law, (2) licensee estoppel explicitly stated in a contract provision, and (3) licensee estoppel imposed through the Article III case or controversy requirement is evident in one of the patent holder's arguments in *MedImmune*. Recall that

*MedImmune* was the Article III case. The contract in *MedImmune* contained no explicit contractual provisions on the issue. Nevertheless, in arguing that its license holder should be blocked from challenging the validity of the underlying patent, the patent holder offered the following analysis:

> When a licensee enters such an agreement . . . it essentially purchases an insurance policy, immunizing it from suits for infringement so long as it continues to pay royalties and does not challenge the covered patents. Permitting it to challenge the validity of the patent without terminating or breaking the agreement alters the deal, allowing the licensee to continue enjoying its immunity while bringing a suit, the elimination of which was part of the patentee's *quid pro quo*.[57]

The Supreme Court rejected that argument in the Article III *MedImmune* case, and it appears to have intended to reject the argument in *Lear* in the context of licensee estoppel implied by common law. The same argument could be made, however, by patent holders who had negotiated for and obtained a specific contractual provision prohibiting their licensees from challenging the patent. In fact, one might conclude that the logic applies more strongly to a restriction that the parties have presumably bargained for than a restriction implied by law.

From the perspective of the bargain aspect of patents, however, the distinction begs the question. Once a restriction has been applied by law, any party taking a license after that presumably knows what comes with the license. This is particularly true in the modern world of patent licensing, in which the parties tend to be represented by expert counsel. Patent licensing is not a sport for amateurs.

If it is improper coercion for a licensee to be prevented from challenging the underlying patent through a restriction implied by law, it is also coercion for the licensee to be prevented from challenging the underlying patent through a restriction in the contract. Either one represents a form of coercion that may reflect an improper use of the patent power.

As described throughout this book, bargaining and negotiating over the definition of the patent will occur over the life of the patent. The bargaining occurs, however, with certain rules in place, including the understanding that the sovereign may weigh in at some point. Allowing one party to block that entry is problematic.

One can think of the problem from two perspectives. First, preventing sovereign entry is not a right provided by the patent system, and one should not be able to use the power of the patent to obtain that right. Framed in misuse terms, broadly defined, one would be using the power of the patent to obtain a legal right outside the patent system, an act that could be considered an improper attempt to extend the scope of the patent.

Preventing sovereign entry is also problematic from the perspective of an effective bargaining system. If patent holders are using contracts to navigate around the patent system and obtain a right not provided by the patent system, this interferes with efficient bargaining and undermines an appropriate result. In short, although we may expect that parties will bargain over the definition of rights granted with a particular patent, we would not want them to be able to change the rules of the game such that the sovereign may not enter.

Allowing parties to impose by contract law what Article III and licensee estoppel cannot provide undermines the integrity of the patent system itself. The Supreme Court suggested as much in the *Lear* case in 1969:

> The parties' contract . . . is no more controlling on this issue than is the State's doctrine of estoppel, which is also rooted in contract principles. The decisive question is whether overriding federal policies would be significantly frustrated if licensees could be required to continue to pay royalties during the time they are challenging patent validity in the courts.[58]

In light of this language, lower court opinions after *Lear* have held that contract provisions forbidding license holders from challenging the underlying validity of the patent are unenforceable, although some have found that the existence of a no-challenge clause does not by itself constitute patent misuse.[59] These opinions, however, have been rendered with little or no analysis,[60] and the area is less than a model of clarity. In addition, the question has become more complicated. Modern no-challenge provisions have arisen not just in the form of a contract but also in the form of negotiated settlements to active cases or in the form of court decrees. In addition, some modern no-challenge provisions impose various penalties for challenging the validity of the patent rather than creating a simple prohibition on challenges.[61]

This brings us back to Justice Thomas. As described previously, the Supreme Court held in the 2007 case of *MedImmune* that a license holder who wishes to challenge the underlying validity of a patent has an appropriate case or controversy for Article III jurisdiction. The majority ruled that the threat of an infringement suit constitutes coercion and that a license holder need not invite substantial business risk to challenge the basis of that coercion.

In his dissent in the *MedImmune* case, Justice Thomas disagreed that sufficient coercion existed and argued that the Court was improperly extending its coercion precedents "to apply to voluntarily accepted contractual obligations between private parties."[62] In so doing, Justice Thomas once again hinted at his willingness to allow parties to contract around the obligations of the patent system.

Although Justice Thomas was the lone dissenter in *MedImmune,* even the *MedImmune* majority left room to revisit the question of contracting around patent law. The majority left for another day the question of whether common law estoppel can prevent a patent holder from challenging an underlying patent, not even mentioning the more difficult question of whether parties can contract to prevent or burden a challenge. Most important, Justice Thomas's minority view in *MedImmune* echoes in his majority opinion later in *Quanta*. There, lurking in a seemingly casual footnote, the opinion leaves room for future consideration of whether contractual provisions to prevent patent exhaustion might be effective.[63]

In short, these Supreme Court snippets hint that the Court may be moving toward facing the broader issue of whether parties should be allowed to contract around the restrictions of the patent system and whether those contractual provisions involve the first sale doctrine, the possibility of challenging a patent's validity, or other limitations. As the issue of contracting around patent law arises, it will be critical to recognize how the disparate pieces of the puzzle fit together. Although the law must have appropriate respect for agreements freely negotiated between sophisticated parties, the agreements at issue here must be understood in the broader context of the intersection of various areas of law. Given the inherent bargaining aspect of patents, the legal system should be wary of doctrines that allow parties to use other systems to distort the limitations of the patent system. The lessons of the early twentieth century, as parties used patents to move around the limitations of the antitrust system, should sound a warning bell for modern courts as they consider these complex problems.

## Drug Wars: The Battle over Generic Pharmaceuticals

Lessons of the early twentieth century may be particularly helpful to us in understanding the implications of various maneuverings in the field of pharmaceutical patents. The issue involves the interaction of patent law, FDA regulatory approval, antitrust, and even contract law at points.[64]

The issue appears in many forms, but the key in every context is to understand how these areas of law fit together. Similar to the situation when patent holders reach beyond the state of the art of invention, only the broader picture can illuminate the ways in which parties may be manipulating different areas of law to undermine the restraints in each of them. Courts that do not recognize the role of bargaining in the patent system, both its expected role and the necessary limitations on it, are at risk of allowing parties to use multiple legal systems to navigate around all of them.

In the maneuvering described later on, patent holders try to extend the life of a patent as its expiration approaches or to delay challenges to a weak patent. As with many end-of-life circumstances, the final years of a patent generate a flurry of frantic activity intended to extend the benefits as long as possible. This may be true regardless of whether the patent's life is ending after a full term or whether it is ending prematurely. As with all patent maneuvering, of course, preparation for the end-of-life bargaining may begin long before the patent is in its death throes or even before it is granted.

The following sections consider techniques that pharmaceutical patent holders engage in, either alone or in conjunction with others, to extend the life of a patent. Examples abound, but I examine three techniques: reverse payments; filing staggered or multiple suits; and evergreening, that is, refreshing by filing a variation of the original patent.

Different approaches may be appropriate if courts wish to rein in each of the behaviors discussed. Some may involve more fully applying the sections of antitrust law that address collusive behavior between competitors. Others may involve a different approach to antitrust law doctrines related to sham litigation. Still others may rely on the court's ability to properly interpret prior art such that the first patent will be considered to foreclose the second.

In each of these circumstances, however, it will be critical for courts to recognize that the parties are using the interaction of multiple legal systems to undermine the restrictions of each. Just as courts of the early twentieth century learned to forbid the use of patents to avoid antitrust, courts of the early twenty-first century must determine how to thwart ever more sophisticated attempts to use patent, antitrust, and regulatory doctrines to accomplish more than any of these doctrines are intended to permit.

## Setting the Stage: The Hatch-Waxman Regime

Hatch-Waxman is a regulatory plan initiated by congressional legislation in 1984. It amended the Federal Food, Drug, and Cosmetic Act. The Hatch-Waxman Act was initiated in response to concerns over the high cost of prescription medications and hopes that the benefits of generic competition could be brought to the public as soon as possible for each medication. In particular, studies have shown that the price of a drug drops 20–30% when the first generic enters the market and may drop 50% or more when additional generics join in.[65]

Within that context the Hatch-Waxman Act makes it easier for generic companies to prepare to enter the market as soon as the patent on the branded drug expires. Prior to passage of the act, generic companies could not even begin to experiment with, develop, or get approval for the generic version of a drug until the patent on the drug had expired because each of these activities constitutes an infringement on the patent right. This had the effect of extending the time of the patent holder's dominance, given that it takes a significant length of time for new entrants to gear up and secure FDA approval. If the starting point is the moment that a patent ends, the actual entry point for generics will be delayed. Hatch-Waxman allowed generics to begin their preparation before the end of the patent. It also significantly streamlined the approval process for a generic entrant. Finally, in its quest to bring generics to the market more quickly, the Hatch-Waxman Act also provided incentives for generic companies to challenge either the validity of a patent or the application of that patent to the drug at issue.

The Hatch-Waxman Act and the resulting regulatory scheme are extraordinarily complex. As so often is the case, complexity breeds opportunity, and clever lawyers have been exploiting the details of the act since its inception. As one former government official noted wryly, one could argue that some of the most creative thinking in pharmaceutical companies is occurring not in the R&D department but in the legal department.

In 2003 Congress attempted to stem the flow of schemes with a set of revisions to the act.[66] At the time, Congressman Henry Waxman, one of the original authors of the act, addressed the following comments to the pharmaceutical industry: "I call upon the brand-name industry to cease and desist from inventing new games, that they work with us to re-balance the brand-name and generic systems, and that they return to the scientific research that they are good at and that has been their real contribution."[67] Neither passage of the revisions nor Congressman Waxman's pleas have stemmed the tide.[68] The games have simply become more complex and ever more sophisticated.

For example, the Hatch-Waxman Act lets manufacturers of a new version of a medication engage in a streamlined regulatory approval process, essentially piggybacking on the safety and efficacy data produced when the original drug was approved. New drug manufacturers need show only that the generic version has the same active ingredient, has the same effect in the body, and is bioequivalent to the original drug.[69] New drug manufacturers may also begin experimenting with the drug and entering the approval process prior to the expiration of the drug's patent.[70] These provisions allow generic drug manufacturers to hit the ground running and enter the market as soon as the patent on the branded drug expires.

Other provisions, however, encourage generics to get to the market even before the patent expires. Specifically, Hatch-Waxman gives generics the opportunity and the incentive to assert that the patent on the underlying drug is invalid or that, even if the patent is valid, it does not cover the particular drug at issue.[71]

Questions related to whether the patent covers the drug often revolve around what is commonly known as the Orange Book. When original drug manufacturers apply for regulatory approval of a new drug, the FDA requires a list of all of the patents that the manufacturer could assert against someone who might try to make or use the drug in an unauthorized manner. Among other things, the list serves as a warning for those who might enter the market. This information is published monthly by the FDA in the Orange Book.[72]

Much modern skirmishing has surrounded the question of whether particular patents are appropriately listed in the Orange Book. The FDA does not review the patents listed to determine whether they actually do support the drug as claimed, yet the mere listing of those patents can have a powerful effect.[73]

Other games and manipulations revolve around two key aspects of Hatch-Waxman. First, Hatch-Waxman offers a six-month period of market exclusivity to the first generic to successfully challenge the validity of the underlying patent or its application to the drug in question.[74] In other words, after a successful challenge, no other generic may enter the market until the first generic has operated for six months. The provision is intended to give generic companies an incentive to do battle against the big guns.

Second, when a would-be generic company files a suit alleging that a patent is invalid or does not validly cover the drug, the act gives the original drug manufacturer an opportunity to sue the generic company to resolve the matter.[75] These two provisions have been the subject of a remarkable number of attempts to manipulate the patent, litigation, and regulatory systems.

## REVERSE PAYMENTS

An endless amount of ink has been spilled on the topic of reverse payments in recent years, and I describe it only briefly here.[76] The practice exploits the fact that the first generic to challenge the patent gets a six-month period of exclusivity as a generic on the market. That exclusivity does not begin, however, until the generic comes to market. As a result, patent holders have been engaging in various forms of settlements with generics, in which the generic agrees to stay out of the market for a period of years in exchange for a payment.

From an economic perspective, such settlements may be troubling. If the patent is weak or should not be read as covering the drug, the patent holder may be preserving an undeserved monopoly in the drug for a period of years. Successful drugs can be extremely lucrative, and the patent holder pays for this undeserved stream of revenue by sharing some of the monopoly rents with the generic challenger. The agreement is perfectly acceptable to the generic filer, who gets to share in the monopoly rent today and still enjoys six months of market exclusivity when the term of the settlement ends. Thus, it is a win-win situation for everyone, except, of course, the consumer, who continues to pay high prices for the drug.

Reverse payment settlements are becoming increasingly complex. One scholar, Scott Hemphill, has noted that with some of the more sophisticated settlements now passing muster in the courts, patent holders are effectively permitted to buy private-term extensions to their patents.[77] Hemphill offers the Pfizer case as an example.[78]

The Pfizer litigation concerned the company's blockbuster cholesterol drug, Lipitor. Following the Hatch-Waxman structure, Pfizer sued the first generic filer, alleging that the generic would infringe its two key patents. One patent was set to expire in March 2010, and the other was set to expire in June 2011.[79] The court upheld Pfizer's infringement claim related to the patent expiring in 2010 but not to the one expiring in 2011.[80] The parties then settled, agreeing that no generic entry would enter the market until November 2011.[81] In other words, Pfizer was able to hold off generic entry until well after the expiration of both patents, more than it could have obtained had it won all counts in the lawsuit.

The parties justified the result in the following fashion. Shortly before the settlement, Pfizer filed a separate suit against the generic, claiming infringement on two minor patents that had not appeared on Pfizer's Orange Book listing of patents related to the drug.[82] These patents will expire in 2016. As a result, the parties were able to secure court approval of the settlement by settling all claims together and pointing to the 2016 expiration date.

The Federal Trade Commission and various private parties have filed antitrust actions alleging that such reverse payments violate antitrust law. The reverse payment cases allege that by paying potential competitors to stay out of the market, patent holders are engaging in behavior that unreasonably restrains trade in violation of section 1 of the Sherman Act, 15 U.S.C. § 1. In the alternative they allege that patent holders are attempting to create unlawful monopolies in violation of section 2 of the Act, 15 U.S.C. § 2.[83]

The Federal Trade Commission has had little success in these cases. Although the circuit courts disagree on the precise test that should be applied, the outcome has generally been the same. With one exception the circuit courts have found that the reverse payment agreement at issue in the case did not violate antitrust law.[84]

One could argue that an understanding of the bargain aspect of patents would make one more sympathetic to reverse payments. After all, if one cannot know the boundaries of a patent with certainty, then a settlement may be a rational choice for a patent holder under these circumstances. It could reflect an understandable effort to limit risk and uncertainty—always a goal in litigation settlement—even when a patent holder believes that the case is quite strong.

Hatch-Waxman, however, is intended to bring forth patent challenges in the interest of freeing drugs from the burdens of any patents that are inappropriately binding them. In other words, the legislation is designed to bring issues to the sovereign so that the sovereign may explore these very issues in precisely the way that the patent holders are trying to avoid. From this perspective the settlements are a bargain that undermines the patent system as modified by the act.

From another perspective the goal, if not the execution, of Hatch-Waxman is consistent with principles one might prefer in the interest of efficient patent bargaining. One with a deep appreciation of the bargain aspect of patents might choose an approach that is less complex and less inherently subject to manipulation than the Hatch-Waxman regulatory plan. Nevertheless, the initial aims of Hatch-Waxman are in sympathy with efficient bargaining principles from the following perspective. The bargain aspect suggests that, given the lack of a shared understanding at the invention of something new, the limitations of language, and the weakness of fixing a concept in time, a patent's definition cannot be known at the time of the grant. Thus, we do not know precisely what the patent is, and we will have to develop that definition over time. Processes that block the evolutionary progress of that definition by cutting off challenges or blocking access to the sovereign are likely to hinder the efficient development of the legal definition and thus should be disfavored under the law.

This is not to suggest that all challenges under all circumstances are good. Processes may be abused by those who wish to unseat patents, as well as by those who hold patents. Nevertheless, strategies that allow parties to block testing or exploration of their patent rights are likely to undermine the natural process of definition—to the detriment of an optimal process.

## Staggered and Multiple Suits

As the topic of reverse payments winds its way slowly through the courts, patent holders have long since moved past and developed ever more subtle and sophisticated ways of manipulating the system. As quickly as regulators move to correct practices and provisions that allow such manipulation, the parties invent a new approach. This section looks at three examples involving the cholesterol drug TriCor, the birth-control pill Yasmin, and the arthritis drug Arava. I should note that some of the materials described here represent only allegations of behavior by the companies. Even if the allegations are not accurate, however, the descriptions provide a roadmap for behavior that one can engage in by manipulating the patent, antitrust, and Hatch-Waxman systems.

The first example concerns the birth-control pill Yasmin, which is made by the Bayer pharmaceutical company.[85] Bayer holds patents on the chemical formulation of Yasmin and on the process of using that chemical formulation for birth control. A second company filed for approval of a generic version under Hatch-Waxman, alleging that Bayer's patents were invalid and should not be applied to Yasmin. Following the Hatch-Waxman procedures, Bayer filed suit against the generic. In doing so, however, Bayer alleged that the generic would infringe its patent on the chemical formula and did not include any claims related to the process patent. The parties settled their claims, with the generic receiving the right to produce a generic version of Yasmin in return for payments to Bayer.[86] Under the Hatch-Waxman structure, the generic would then enjoy a six-month period as the only generic on the market, after which time other generics could enter the market.[87] During this six-month period the price of Yasmin for both companies is likely to drop around 10%.[88] More dramatic price drops are likely to occur when additional generics enter the market.[89]

Eyeing the end of the six-month period of exclusivity, a second generic hopeful, Sandoz, filed for approval under Hatch-Waxman. Following the procedure, Bayer sued Sandoz. This time, however, Bayer alleged only infringement of the process patent for using the drug for birth control.[90] Under the Hatch-Waxman structure, when a patent holder responds to a filing request with an infringement claim, an automatic thirty-month stay goes into effect, and the generic in the suit cannot go to market during this period unless the litigation has been resolved.[91]

Under ordinary circumstances, the patent holder and the generic should have enjoyed six months of higher drug prices before later generics could enter and drive the prices down another 20–40%.[92] As a result of using the Hatch-Waxman automatic stay rules against subsequent generic companies, the patent holder and the first generic get to enjoy higher prices on the market for thirty months—five times the length of time that exclusivity is supposed to last under the six-month provision.[93]

Recent reforms may have blunted the appeal of the particular approach taken by Sandoz. A patent holder is now allowed only one thirty-month litigation stay, which reduces the incentive to file multiple suits in this manner. The Sandoz case, however, is instructive as an illustration of the persistence and ingenuity of patent holders who would manipulate the provisions intended to encourage generic entry, as well as the way in which the complexity of the Hatch-Waxman system provides numerous tempting opportunities.

More subtle manipulation of the systems can bring more limited, although still lucrative, rewards. Consider the arthritis drug Arava. At the time that generics were filing for FDA approval of Arava, the FDA had a practice of delaying regulatory approval if it received a citizen's petition filing. Around the time that would have been expected for approval of the generic version, the manufacturer of Arava filed a citizen's petition. Although filed at the eleventh hour, the FDA noted with disapproval that most of the citations and arguments were actually available years before. The agency concluded that the petition appeared, at least in part, to be a simple attempt to delay generic entry.[94]

Among other things, the petition asked that the generic applicants be required to prove that their generic tablets were bioequivalent to the original manufacturer's 100-mg tablets, although the generic applications sought approval to sell only 10-mg and 20-mg tablets. In response, the FDA noted that it could find "no explanation" for the requested requirement and "no reasoned basis" to demand it.

Not surprisingly, the FDA rejected the citizen's petition. Nevertheless, the filing of the petition delayed approval of the generic for five months, presumably allowing the original manufacturer to enjoy greater profits during that time.

The generic company sued the original manufacturer in the Southern District of New York, alleging violation of §2 of the Sherman Act on the grounds that the citizen's petition was an objectively baseless sham designed to delay approval of generics.[95] The generic company, however, could not meet the high standards required for such a case.[96]

Federal and state antitrust authorities have filed antitrust actions in cases such as these, but they have also met with little success. The problem can be traced to the application of what is known in antitrust law as the Noerr-Pennington doctrine.[97] Noerr-Pennington is a doctrine that protects the rights of citizens to petition the government. The doctrine arose in a series of cases in the 1960s, and it is operating as a brake on the antitrust cases here.

The doctrine has roots in the First Amendment's right to petition government for the redress of grievances. In light of this core principle, Noerr-Pennington allows citizens to petition the government without fear of antitrust liability.[98] In reductionist form, the original Noerr-Pennington cases concluded that it is perfectly acceptable for the government to do something that harms competition and that it is perfectly acceptable for a company to beg the government to do something that will harm its competitors even in very unsavory ways. For example, in one of the seminal cases, *Eastern R. Presidents Conference v. Noerr Motor Freight Inc.,* the Supreme Court held that the defendant railroad's campaign for legislation that was intended to ruin the trucking industry was exempt from antitrust laws.[99]

The doctrine originally applied to attempts to persuade the legislative or executive branch to take an action or enforce a law that would have an anticompetitive effect.[100] The doctrine was later expanded to include the right to petition the courts. Thus, the act of filing a lawsuit is protected against an antitrust claim.[101]

Noerr-Pennington is not an absolute doctrine, and it includes several exceptions. Under one of them, parties will lose the protection of the doctrine if they have engaged in sham litigation. Sham litigation occurs when a party files a suit that is no more than an attempt to interfere with a competitor's business relationships.[102]

Many lawsuits may have the effect of damaging a competitor's business, but the sham litigation exception has a different objective. It takes aim at those who are trying to use the governmental process as an anticompetitive weapon.[103] For example, if a company had no genuine interest in the outcome of an action and was merely litigating the action to delay or frustrate competition, its action would be considered sham litigation under the Noerr-Pennington doctrine.

Sham litigation looks as if it should be a very good fit for some of the machinations that patent holders are engaging in under the Hatch-Waxman framework. Patent holders in these suits appear to be using the details of the process to prevent or delay the competition that would result from generic entry. Using the process to damage one's competitors is, in theory, what sham litigation aims to control. Proving sham litigation, however, requires satisfaction of a remarkably high burden—one that may not be well suited to the patent/antitrust/Hatch-Waxman setting.

The modern difficulty flows from a 1993 Supreme Court case, *Professional Real Estate Investors Inc. v. Columbia Pictures Industries*.[104] In *Professional Real Estate* the Supreme Court held that in order to prove that legal actions constitute sham litigation, the actions must be both objectively baseless in the sense that no reasonable litigant can realistically expect success on the merits *and* subjectively baseless such that the lawsuit conceals an actual attempt to use the administrative or judicial processes to interfere with a competitor's business relationships.[105]

With the structure established in *Professional Real Estate,* a court can examine the subjective motives and behavior in a particular suit only if it first concludes that no reasonable litigant could expect success.[106] In the wild world of patents, however, there is always something to say. Given the types of uncertainties described in the opening chapters of the book, patent holders will almost always be able to find some uncertainty they can cite as evidence that a particular filing was not entirely baseless. The key to understanding what is inappropriate about behavior in these particular cases, however, lies in connecting the dots in the complex interaction among the different legal and regulatory regimes as they apply to a particular case. Such an analysis is likely to come in the "subjective" portion of the case, a portion that the court may never reach.

Overcoming the burden of proving sham litigation, however, is even more difficult than the preceding discussion suggests. The Federal Circuit has decided that the standard for proving each of these prongs is the very high "clear and convincing" standard rather than the "preponderance of the evidence" standard that applies in many civil litigation doctrines.[107] The heightened evidence standard makes the barrier to proving sham litigation almost insurmountable. Without being able to show sham litigation, federal and state antitrust authorities cannot successfully bring suit against patent holders for the types of behaviors described earlier.

The higher evidence standard for sham litigation in these antitrust cases has a particularly disturbing aspect. Sham litigation, of course, is an issue that can arise in contexts other than patents, and antitrust authorities may be concerned about sham litigation where no patents are involved. Some courts have suggested that a higher evidence burden is particularly appropriate for sham litigation cases involving patents. Their logic rests on the fact that patents are presumptively valid, once they are issued by the PTO. If patents are presumptively valid, the argument goes, lawsuits to enforce those patents are presumptively valid as well.[108]

The logic is extremely problematic. A patent has a presumption of validity because the government, in the form of the PTO, has already spent a considerable amount of time reviewing it. This is not true of a patent holder's decision to sue someone. I could have a perfectly valid patent on Gummi Bears but choose to go after Microsoft with it. In other words, the validity of my patent does not necessarily relate to the validity of my choice of target. Nor does the validity of my patent necessarily relate to the validity of my use of that patent, and it is the use, or rather the abuse, of the patent that is at issue here.

The logical fallacy is a classic example of the dangers inherent in failing to understand how the pieces of the system work together. Patent holders who have advanced the argument are trying to use patent law to prevent the application of antitrust law in a way that is inappropriate to both. It is an easy trap for courts to fall into.

Bright spots occasionally appear on the horizon for antitrust authorities. In particular, the lower courts disagree somewhat about the proper interpretation of the Supreme Court's test in *Professional Real Estate* and about whether the heightened standard of proof should apply. The Ninth Circuit, for example, has argued that the two-prong test applies only to single lawsuits and that authorities do not have to follow that test when the patent holder files multiple actions. In what I would call "multiplicity" cases, the

Ninth Circuit argued that one should reach back to the language of a Supreme Court case in 1972, the case of *California Motor Transport*.[109] In that case the Supreme Court spoke of looking for "a pattern of baseless, repetitive claims . . . which leads the fact finder to conclude that the administrative and judicial processes have been abused."[110] Some other courts have followed the same path.[111] A multiplicity test might offer more promise for analyzing the dynamic and interactive effects of patent holder actions, particularly in the context of the Hatch-Waxman regulatory scheme.

The Ninth Circuit hedged its bets more recently, however, in the 2009 case of *Kaiser v. Abbott Labs*.[112] In *Kaiser* the Ninth Circuit decided that it did not need to choose between the two-prong test and the alternative pattern of the repetitive-claims approach because the lower court had determined that the infringer could not prove sham litigation under either test.[113] This suggests that the Ninth Circuit has some concern about whether its interpretation of *Professional Real Estate* could withstand Supreme Court scrutiny and thus is covering all possible bases. In addition, in a case decided on other grounds the Federal Circuit has signaled that it does not agree with the Ninth Circuit's approach.[114]

In implementing the two-prong test in *Professional Real Estate*, the Supreme Court did not directly address burdens of proof, and the Court has not clarified questions related to the appropriate burden of proof in the interim. The Federal Circuit, however, has ruled that the burden of proof in patent sham litigation arising in antitrust cases is the higher "clear and convincing" standard.[115] In addition, the Federal Circuit has held that, although for some aspects of antitrust law, it will follow the law of the circuit in which the trial court resided, for *this* aspect of antitrust law the Federal Circuit will ignore circuit law and follow its own holdings.[116] This controversial holding adds further complexity to an already unclear area. Finally, the court decisions in antitrust sham-litigation cases *not* involving patents are not of one mind, either, on the burden of proof required.[117]

In short, the question of the appropriate standards and burdens of proof for parties and antitrust authorities remains murky. As the courts, particularly the Supreme Court, move to clarify the issue, it will be critical to take into account both the uncertain nature of patents and the complex interplay between the Hatch-Waxman Act, patent law, and antitrust law. An appreciation of the bargaining that is occurring and the manipulation that such fast-paced navigating can invite may help us to understand how the rules should be drawn.

In particular, establishing and enforcing rules for the process are crucial for ensuring an appropriate bargain. Courts must be as nimble in their thinking as the patent holders themselves, and they must be sensitive to the fact that allowing patent holders to leverage the power of different legal and regulatory regimes to obtain more bargaining power or a different outcome undermines the design and operation of the patent system.

## May Your Patent Be Ever Green

The end of the life of a patent can be a traumatic time for a pharmaceutical company. The process of drug discovery, approval, and market acceptance is long and expensive, and it can be difficult for a pharmaceutical company to repeat the process successfully for one drug after another. Moreover, a successful drug can generate an extraordinary revenue stream, and companies look to a future bereft of that revenue stream with great trepidation.

The impending loss of revenue places tremendous pressure on company executives to extend that stream for as long as possible and in any way possible. The bargain aspect of patents, combined with the complexity of the regulatory regimes and the intricacies of the surrounding legal doctrines, offers tantalizing opportunities to manipulate the system. Given the temptations, courts and agencies must be particularly sensitive to crafting rules that will block off avenues of abuse.

A variety of techniques to extend the life of a pharmaceutical patent have become known as *evergreening*. The word refers to the notion of trying to keep a dying patent alive by refreshing it as long as possible. This section of the chapter focuses on one particular form of evergreening known as "product hopping." The product-hopping behaviors described here should provide some sense of the types of challenges that courts and regulators face in setting appropriate rules of the game.

### Shifting the Market for Prilosec

Most of today's pharmaceuticals, colloquially called "drugs," are organic compounds composed of rings and chains of molecules that adopt specific formations in space, called "chiral" compounds. When these drugs are synthesized, they are often made in what is known as racemic mixtures, where half of the compounds have one conformation in space, and the other half have a mirror-image conformation. These compounds are analogous to your right hand and your left hand. "Enantiomer" is the term that is used to refer to a specific conformation, or one "hand," of a molecule. Although the two sides have an identical chemical formula, they often do not have equal functionality. Just like a right-handed glove fits only a right hand, one enantiomer may "fit" better with a protein or compound it is intended to affect than its counterpart.

Although it is far cheaper and easier to synthesize a drug as a racemic mixture,[118] many of the drugs in today's market are enantiomers; that is, they have only a right hand or a left hand. This could be due in part to the increased efficacy of one enantiomer over the other. However, not all enantiomers are significantly more efficient or better than their mirror images.

In addition, some of the single enantiomer drugs have been introduced to the market as an improvement over a previously marketed racemic mixture. The practice of replacing a racemic drug with a single enantiomer drug is commonly used in the pharmaceutical industry and is referred to in the industry as a "racemic switch." In many cases the racemic switch has coincided with the expiration of the patent for the original drug. For example, AstraZeneca introduced Nexium, the single-enantiomer version of Prilosec, a mere two years before the patent for Prilosec expired.

AstraZeneca's story is a remarkable one. The company's racemic switch was the brainchild of a group of marketers, scientists, and lawyers that the company convened in the mid-1990s to collectively strategize methods by which the company could frustrate generic competition. This endeavor was named the "Shark Fin Project," borrowing its name from the downward slope of the Prilosec sales graph that AstraZeneca anticipated if the company took no action to ward off generic competition.[119] To avoid this disaster, the company launched an aggressive marketing campaign keyed to the introduction of Nexium, the next-generation version of the product. A chart outlining the success of this campaign over a year-long period was included in a *Wall Street Journal* article and is reproduced here.

By the time Prilosec's patent exclusivity ended, ten million units of annual sales had been switched from Prilosec to Nexium.

A number of aspects of AstraZeneca's strategy are troubling. For example, AstraZeneca applied for incidental patents on Prilosec, such as patents on the chemical form Prilosec takes as it is broken down in the patient's system and patents for coatings to optimize the drug's absorption. One could easily argue that such patents are of questionable validity.[120] In particular, courts and commentators have been quite critical of patents on the chemical forms of absorbed drugs, known as metabolites. Nevertheless, these types of patents can help branded manufacturers delay the entry of generic competition by engaging in litigation to slow down generic entry.

The patent on Nexium itself is troubling. One could argue that a patent on the single enantiomer is invalid given the prior art already included the mixture. Commentators have suggested that such patents should be invalid on the grounds that a single enantiomer would be obvious to those skilled in the art when the prior patent has already claimed the mixture.[121] In fact, when claiming a newly discovered mixture, it is common practice to claim not only the mixture itself but also any "enantiomer thereof" simply on the basis of having developed the compound form.[122]

In addition, some evidence suggests that in the case of Prilosec and Nexium, replacing the racemic mixture with a single one of its enantiomers

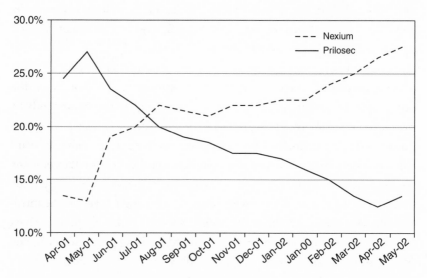

*Figure 4:* Gardiner Harris, "Prilosec's Maker Switches Users to Nexium, Thwarting Generics," *Wall Street Journal*, June 6, 2002, p. A1.

may not have provided increased efficacy. AstraZeneca had conducted several studies to demonstrate the efficacy of Nexium over Prilosec. According to the *Wall Street Journal*, however, the company released only positive studies.[123] Even the positive results have been criticized by notable physicians, including Dr. Maria Angell, the former editor in chief of the *New England Journal of Medicine*.[124]

Most troubling is the way in which AstraZeneca engineered the product switch. This final piece of AstraZeneca's strategy required an intimate knowledge of how and when patients are reimbursed for medication by insurance companies and HMOs. In particular, HMOs and insurers reimburse their patients according to a list of medications known as a formulary. In order to encourage patients to choose cheaper drugs, patients will be charged higher co-pays if they purchase a branded drug rather than a generic. In addition, purchases of over-the-counter drugs are generally not reimbursed at all, and insurers will not reimburse for a prescription medication if an over-the-counter version is available.[125]

Mindful of this structure, AstraZeneca convinced the FDA to change the original branded drug, Prilosec, from a prescription medication to an over-the-counter medication. Physicians could choose the generic versions of Prilosec, but the insurers would not provide any reimbursement at all.[126] In contrast, the newly patented replacement drug, for which no generic could exist, would be fully reimbursable. Economic logic should, therefore, lead patients and their physicians to the new drug, Nexium.

A group of companies led by Walgreens filed an antitrust complaint against AstraZeneca under § 2 of the Sherman Act, which prohibits monopolization.[127] Walgreens argued that the patent holder had tried to improperly maintain its monopoly in Prilosec by switching the market once the Prilosec patent expired. Walgreens tried to compare the behavior to other cases of defensive leveraging, in which a company manipulates the market in an attempt to shore up a naturally fading monopoly.[128] The court declined to find an antitrust violation, however, focusing on the issue of consumer choice. According to the court, the other examples cited in the briefs involved efforts to manipulate the market by eliminating consumer choice, while AstraZeneca had merely introduced a competing drug to the marketplace.[129] In particular, the court distinguished *AstraZeneca* from the other cases cited by using the following logic: Unlike a case involving Abbott, a company that took away the consumer's ability to choose between drug formulations by discontinuing manufacture of a drug, or a case involving Microsoft, a company that took away the consumer's ability to select from different Internet browsers, AstraZeneca had merely introduced *another* drug into the marketplace to compete with their pioneer drug Prilosec and its generics.[130] The court concluded that additional market choices are a good result under an antitrust analysis.

The court's analysis of consumer choice, however, fails to properly account for the role that insurance reimbursement plays. Consumer choice is a hollow concept if the choice is between something for which no reimbursement exists and something that is largely reimbursed.

The logic also does not fully take into account the influence of the prescribing physician and the interactions among all of the parties involved in what the court seemed to view as the consumer's free decision. The choice of a drug to purchase is a delicate dance involving what the physician recommends, what the patient asks for, and what the pharmacist is permitted to suggest as a substitute.[131] None of these parties is a specialist in drug development and testing, nor are they statisticians—although most physicians would likely cast a critical eye to studies whose results are nil. The simple problem is that, given the limitations of time and training, all of the parties are to some extent forced to rely on drug-company promotional representations.[132]

In declining to find an antitrust violation, the court seemed almost mesmerized by the power of a patent as an instrument of exclusion. Concluding that the plaintiffs could not support a claim of antitrust violation, the court cited the following language from the seminal antitrust treatise:

> [A] patent . . . is no different than [*sic*] any other property right . . . [such as] ownership of an airplane or pipeline [that] exclude[s] others from using them. . . . Further, the Patent Act creates a federal right to exclude others from practicing the patent. . . . As a result, antitrust must tread lightly.[133]

Citing the language in this context focuses on the wrong patent and ignores the dynamic effects of the behavior as a whole. The comment may be applicable to the patent on the original drug, Prilosec, which may have enjoyed a well-deserved monopoly. Any monopoly power attained during the term of the Prilosec patent, however, should end when the Prilosec patent ends. The case at hand concerns not the Prilosec patent but the Nexium patent, and the operative question is whether a follow-on patent is being used in combination with insurance and regulatory structures to extend the monopoly power gained during the term of the Prilosec patent.

## SHIFTING THE MARKET FOR TRICOR

A similar process of market manipulation occurred with the cholesterol drug TriCor. TriCor's manufacturer, Abbott, used a different version of product hopping and formulary manipulation in a highly successful maneuver to block generic competition.[134]

The blocking process began after a generic pharmaceutical filed for approval under Hatch-Waxman, alleging that the claimed patent did not infringe the new generic. Abbott filed suit, alleging that the generic would indeed infringe. Abbott, the patent holder, lost.[135] At this point Abbott started hopping.

The original branded drug was produced in the form of a capsule. After a generic capsule gained approval, Abbott switched the formulation to a tablet form, which it acknowledged was the bioequivalent of the capsule.[136] The first generic and then another generic followed, filing applications for generic versions of the tablet under the Hatch-Waxman framework. Abbott again filed suit, alleging infringement, which triggered a thirty-month stay. Abbott then hopped to a different tablet formulation. Again the generics followed, and Abbott filed for infringement, triggering another thirty-month stay.

While the generics were filing their applications and suffering successive stays, Abbott was busy ensuring that the original capsule generic that had already received approval would be unable to generate significant sales. Abbott announced that it would stop selling the capsule, bought back any excess stock on pharmacy shelves, and had the capsule form listed as obsolete in the National Drug Data File. These actions took place shortly before the generic made it to the pharmacy shelves and caused two insurmountable problems for the generic.

First, the generic business model depends largely on the fact that, when faced with a prescription for a branded drug for which a generic alternative exists, pharmacists may substitute the cheaper generic with little difficulty. With the branded drug no longer available, doctors would stop writing prescriptions for it and begin writing for the new tablet form. By the time the generic capsule made it to the shelves, physicians would have stopped writing prescriptions for the capsule and begun writing for the tablet instead. Thus, pharmacists who received a prescription for the tablets could not, on their own, fill the prescription with the generic capsules. This would limit the sales of the generic capsules, the only generic form available on the market.

It is always possible, however, that a physician might write a prescription directly for the generic capsule. Abbott's strategy limited that route as well. By listing the Abbott capsule as obsolete, the new generic capsule became the only drug on the market in its category. Under insurance formulary definitions, when only one drug in a category is on the market, that drug is considered the branded form and is not subject to the copay discounts offered for the generic version. Thus, rather than receiving the expected copay discount, patients who ordered the generic version would be hit with a higher copayment. This further discouraged purchase of the generic capsule. It also discouraged any enterprising pharmacist who might be tempted to call a physician to ask for permission to substitute generic capsules for the branded tablet because, under pharmacy practice, the pharmacy will not call to request a substitution unless the patient will save money.[137] Given that patients would have to pay the higher copay amount for either the branded capsule or the generic tablet, pharmacists would not make the call.

Abbott's internal documents estimated that the company would make ten times the profit if it could get a reformulated product to market before the original generic made it to the shelves.[138] That type of dramatic profit response is echoed in other industry comments on the effects of reformulation prior to generic entry.

One academic article cites several interesting internal documents from other companies related to their reformulation efforts. These include a manufacturer's estimating that post-generic sales would be three times greater if it could get a reformulated product to market well before the generic version arrived and another manufacturer's acknowledging that its reformulation was a gimmick from a medical standpoint but that switching the market before general entry was the cardinal determinant of success.[139] The documents mentioned in the article are sealed under protective order and thus cannot be confirmed.

The result of all of Abbott's tactics was the following. First, Abbott was able to shift the market from the capsule to the tablet form. By the time the generic capsule made it to the shelves, it was unable to generate significant sales. Second, Abbott was able to substantially delay generic versions of the new tablet form through the automatic stays generated in the Hatch-Waxman process. With the tremendous profits generated by successful drugs, delays of this kind can be highly profitable. In short, Abbott managed to manipulate the patent, antitrust, and regulatory regimes in a way that maintained the benefits of its patent long after the patent had expired.

The original generic company, joined by two major drugstore chains and others, filed suit alleging that Abbott had engaged in attempted monopolization under § 2 of the Sherman Act and had violated other state and federal competition doctrines as well. The case survived a motion to dismiss but settled after one week of trial.[140]

In the highly charged, fast-paced bargaining environment that characterizes the patent system, one might be tempted to argue that product hopping and other forms of manipulation described earlier should be acceptable. After all, if patent holders are constantly bargaining to affect the definition of a patent and that activity is expected, why should one condemn the type of maneuvering identified here? The answer again lies in understanding the difference between bargaining within the process and bargaining to avoid the process. The behaviors described earlier do not relate to exploring and defining an invention. They relate to preventing that exploration by blocking competitive entry or preventing others from initiating challenges to the patent. Even a system characterized by intense bargaining must ward off efforts to alter the rules such that parties can obtain more than would be allowed under any bargain.

## Summary

This chapter has explored different types of approaches that patent holders use when interacting with various legal systems, including contract, patent, antitrust, and even regulatory, to avoid the limitations each one imposes. Solutions to these problems may turn on the proper granting of patents and interpretation of patent law, proper application of antitrust laws, proper analysis of contract law related to patents, or the proper development of regulatory processes. Nevertheless, in all of these circumstances, courts must be attuned the parties' efforts to use the dynamic effects of the interactions among the various legal regimes to undermine the restrictions of each. It is the broader view of the dynamic effect that tells the story. Particularly in an intense bargaining environment, we should be sensitive to circumstances that allow parties to bring improper weapons to the table.

# 6

## Beyond the State of the Art

From the perspective of the bargain aspect of patents, not all inventions are created equal.[1] An improvement on a simple mechanical device may have a narrow range of uncertainty. In contrast, an organic substance created by genetic engineering may have a far broader range of potential definition. The difference flows from the newness of the field of genetics and from the vast range of things we do not know about the workings of biology. The breadth of our ignorance, however, is not unique to the field of genetics but pertains to many fields, ranging from nanotechnology to inventions that utilize the more complex laws of physics.

Although the extent of what is unknown may be greater in some fields than in others, it would be difficult to eliminate uncertainty from any field. Factors such as the lack of shared understanding, the limitations of language, and the problems of time fixation ensure that uncertainty, as well as the bargaining that results, will plague all patents to some extent. Fields with the greatest uncertainty and fluidity, however, dramatically demonstrate the danger of approaching patent doctrines as if the boundaries of a patent can be delineated at the outset.

With this in mind, the following chapter offers an example from the biologic arts in which failure to properly acknowledge limitations at the time of a patent grant is wreaking havoc in the substantive doctrines. The example also demonstrates a key issue to keep in mind when approaching a problem from the perspective of the bargain aspect of patents. Even if it is not possible to clearly delineate the boundaries of a patent at the time of the grant, the law is capable of cabining both the reach of an individual invention and the range of the bargaining. Failure to do so can lead to uncomfortable results.

In this chapter I focus on a single problem threaded through five disparate doctrines. With each of the doctrines, the courts must grapple with the question of whether the definition of an invention should extend to things that are beyond the state of the art at the time of the invention. It is the perfect question to highlight how little we know at the time of the patent grant and how strange the results can be if we fail to take this into account.

## Overview of the Problem

Thirty years ago the Supreme Court opened the door to the biotechnology revolution when it granted inventors the right to hold patents on genetically engineered organisms. In the seminal case of *Diamond v. Chakrabarty,* the Court ruled that inventors can patent an organism itself, not just the process of creating it.[2] Although the outcome was revolutionary, the resulting legal doctrines were familiar. The case and its progeny would treat biologic inventions, such as genetically engineered organisms and laboratory-crafted genes, the way patent law treats any other newly invented product.

In patent law, we define a product by identifying its structure. Once the structure is identified, the inventor then controls the product, no matter what method or materials are used to make it. For example, suppose our simple mechanical invention is a doorknob. Once the patent holder identifies the "doorknob" invention by describing the structure of a doorknob, the patent holder controls all doorknobs. This is true regardless of whether the other doorknobs are made of wood, glass, or plastic. The rule is intended to protect inventors from those who would make minor alterations and claim "a new product."

The rule has created chaos, however, in the realm of biotechnology. For example, suppose the invention is an antibody. The inventor begins by isolating and identifying a harmful agent, perhaps something that causes cancer in humans. Next, the inventor isolates and identifies a single antibody that binds with the harmful agent. Based on identifying the single antibody, the inventor then claims the right to all antibodies that bind with the harmful agent. In simplified terms the inventor wishes to claim the class of things created by the immune system that bind with the relevant agent. Analogous to claiming the class of doorknobs, the inventor claims the class of relevant antibodies, no matter what materials are used to make the antibodies or how they are constructed.

Suppose that at the time of the antibody invention, antibodies were made in the lab using DNA-encoding materials from mice. At that time, no one in the field of science knew how to do much more than that. Suppose that a later inventor constructs the relevant antibody using DNA-encoding materials from a combination of different species, perhaps one section from human materials and another section from mouse materials. Better yet, suppose an inventor creates an appropriate antibody using materials almost entirely from the human body so that the antibody could be administered to human patients without the risk of rejection. Suppose further that the development of a humanized antibody that binds to a specific antigen would be quite difficult to accomplish and that humanized antibodies were entirely unknown when the mouse-based antibody was created. Should we nevertheless grant the inventor of the relevant mouse antibody control of all relevant humanized ones?

Can we really say that an antibody is an antibody no matter how it works or what materials it is made out of? Moreover, are we prepared to say that an antibody is an antibody given that our knowledge of why particular antibodies arise in the body and how they fit into the body's overall organic processes is limited? Finally, can we ever say that an antibody is an antibody when the definition of each antibody invention will be developed over time after the patent has been granted?

This issue goes to the heart of defining the footprint of an invention—in other words, how far an inventor can reach against inventions that existed before and how far an inventor can reach against those that will come after. Modern case law reflects confusion over whether this footprint includes things unknown at the time of the invention. Despite precedent from cases related to mechanical inventions, courts have increasingly shied away from permitting biotechnology inventors to reach embodiments and characteristics unknown at the time of the invention. They have done so, however, without a comprehensive vision of the problem or how to solve it. The result is a wealth of contradictory opinions and unworkable doctrines.

For example, cases concerning the limits that should be placed on a biotechnology inventor's reach toward future inventions stand in contradiction to each other. Some opinions conclude broadly that the definition of an invention includes all embodiments, even those that could not have existed at the time of the invention. Others use claim construction doctrines to limit a patent holder's reach only to embodiments known at the time of the invention. Still others use a different set of doctrines to conclude that a patent holder's reach sometimes—but not always—includes things that were unknown at the time of the invention. These opinions, which pull in different directions, make it difficult to predict how far an inventor can reach toward later inventions.

Similar confusion exists in the doctrines that spell out how far an inventor can reach toward earlier inventions. In general, a new invention cannot be defined to include someone else's prior invention, called "prior art." Some opinions find that prior art includes things that were inherent in a prior invention but that no one knew about. Other courts decline to read prior art in that manner. Still other courts answer the question of how far an inventor can reach toward prior inventions by referencing doctrines that explain how far an inventor can reach toward later inventions. As described earlier, doctrines that define earlier inventions are remarkably confused about whether an invention includes things unknown at the time of the invention. Most important, the convergence of these areas demonstrates the futility of addressing piecemeal the question of whether the definition of an invention includes things unknown at the time of the invention.

One could argue that we should live with the inconsistencies. In fact, some scholars suggest that we define an invention one way for one set of doctrines and another way for another set of doctrines.[3] Such an approach, however, inevitably leads to the type of chaos we are now experiencing. We would not want to hold up a sphere and say, "When we look at it from one direction it is an apple, and when we look at it from another direction it is an orange." Such an approach is an invitation for clever manipulations, which result in an unworkable body of law.

Granting rights beyond the state of knowledge at the time of the invention can project an enormous shadow of rights across the future and lead to untenable results. The temptation to restrain that reach is leading to strange doctrinal twists and an ineffectual body of law. An appreciation of the way in which the doctrines fit together and of the uncertainty in patent definitions would suggest that we need to make a change in approach.

The problem can be viewed most prominently in the context of biologic inventions. Nevertheless, it is a concept that should be applied more broadly.[4] In light of the lack of shared conception, the limitations of language, and the problems of time fixation, a patent will never clearly delineate the boundaries of an invention regardless of whether the invention is an antibody or a doorknob. We should always be wary of granting rights to embodiments beyond the state of the art at the time of the invention.

## The State of Knowledge in Biologic Inventions

### PATENTING LIVING ORGANISMS

In 1972 microbiologist Ananda Chakrabarty filed a patent application for a genetically engineered bacterium capable of breaking down multiple components of crude oil.[5] Although bacteria found in nature could degrade individual components of oil, no natural bacteria could degrade a combination of oil components. This made Chakrabarty's invention particularly promising for cleaning up oil spills.[6]

Chakrabarty's application included claims related to the process for manufacturing the organism, claims that were approved without much consternation.[7] The more difficult claims concerned rights to the living organism itself.

The patent examiner rejected Chakrabarty's claims involving the organism itself on the grounds that living things are not patentable subject matter because they are nature's creation rather than humankind's.[8] The case reached the Supreme Court on the question of whether living things may be patentable subject matter.[9]

Patentable subject matter is governed by section 101 of the Patent Act.[10] The section states that "whoever invents or discovers any new and useful process, machine, manufacture, or composition of matter, or any new and useful improvement thereof, may obtain a patent."[11] The Supreme Court, noting the expansive language of this section, concluded that Congress intended to provide a wide scope for patentable subject matter, one that would include the types of laboratory-created matter claimed by Chakrabarty.[12] As the Court explained, "Congress thus recognized that the relevant distinction was not between living and inanimate things, but between products of nature, whether living or not, and human-made inventions. Here, respondent's micro-organism is the result of human ingenuity and research."[13]

After *Chakrabarty* it was clear that laboratory-created inventions with characteristics markedly different from those found in nature are patentable subject matter, assuming, of course, that the inventor can identify the potential for significant utility. The decision, therefore, announced clearly that inventors could protect the organism itself, not just the process of creating it.

To create his invention, Chakrabarty used a process that can be classified as genetic engineering but did not involve recombinant DNA. Many modern biologic inventions are invented using recombinant DNA. Others are created by the use of techniques that involve recombinant materials or bioengineering. For the remainder of the chapter I use the term "biospace," which one can think of as the commercial space that includes things such as biotech creations and inventions produced by using techniques that involve bioengineering or biotechnology.

### From Patenting Whole Organisms to Patenting the Components of Life

In a 1987 ruling the Patent and Trademark Office extended the doctrine announced in *Chakrabarty* to grant rights in more complex organisms such as oysters.[14] The PTO, however, carefully excluded the possibility of granting rights in human beings.[15] Despite this limitation, courts and the PTO have extended patent protection to components of human life, such as genes, proteins, and antibodies, as they exist in laboratory form.[16]

### The One Embodiment Doctrine

As mentioned in chapter 3, custom and practice in the courts and the patent industry separate patentable subject matter into two broad types of patents: products and processes.[17] The Patent Act itself does not employ such a neat, bipolar categorization. Rather, it lists the categories of patentable subject matter as processes, machines, manufactures, compositions of matter, and improvements thereof.[18] Nevertheless, the two general categories and the distinction between them have profound implications for patent rights.

Traditionally, a product claim is defined in terms of structural characteristics.[19] In other words, an inventor will claim rights to a particular machine, which can be described by its structural design. For the product to qualify as patentable subject matter, however, the inventor must demonstrate that it has a use beyond mere academic curiosity.[20] Once the inventor identifies a single use for the product, the inventor may exclude others from the full spectrum of the product, including any use of it and other embodiments of it.[21] Thus, one embodiment provides an inventor with a broad range of rights.

The same is not true for a process claim.[22] For example, if Chakrabarty had received a patent on the process of making the microorganism, he would have controlled only microorganisms made using the process he had invented, not those made in any other way. By securing product rights, however, Chakrabarty was protected by the "one embodiment" doctrine. He could control all manifestations of the microorganism, no matter what process was used to produce it.

The one embodiment notion has particularly troubling implications in the context of biospace inventions that highlight the problem with this rule. With biospace inventions, we grant rights in the face of extraordinary unknowns. Consider patent rights to genes isolated or manipulated in ways distinguishable from genes undisturbed in the human body. Genes are segments of the DNA double helix that exists inside the cells of a living creature.[23] Genes are made up of nucleotide building blocks.[24] These building blocks not only form the structure of the gene but also serve as blueprints by providing the information necessary for the cell to conduct activities such as reproducing itself and constructing proteins.[25]

Although the sequence of the nucleotide building blocks forms the structure of the gene, this structure does not contain anything new. It already exists in nature and is not a new design of human ingenuity.[26] The problem for human ingenuity is to identify the potentially useful sequences, separate them from their natural forms, recombine them in more useful forms, and, finally, determine what to do with those new configurations.[27]

In many genetic experiments that lead to patents, scientists begin by identifying and separating the DNA sequence that carries the coding information needed. For example, scientists might be trying to create large amounts of a particular protein that could be administered to human patients. Having identified and separated the relevant sequence, the scientists prepare a piece of carrier DNA into which they can splice the relevant sequence. This carrier DNA is called a vector, and when the relevant DNA sequence has been successfully spliced into the vector, the resulting product is called recombinant DNA. In the final steps the scientists cultivate a host cell capable of incorporating the recombinant DNA. The host cell is primed with the proper materials so that the cell can create the desired protein using the coding information from the relevant DNA sequence.

Out of this enterprise, scientists might claim rights to the following products: the isolated and purified DNA sequence, the recombinant DNA that holds the sequence, and the transformed host cell that has incorporated the recombinant DNA and produced the protein.[28] Scientists who are hoping to publish their work in a respected journal would recognize that the publication could claim no more than the narrow task that had been accomplished. For example, they could claim as their own work no more than the achievement of getting a particular carrier DNA to include the sequence in a particular type of cell. One could publish that and no more. The question for patent rights, however, is more expansive. Rights to the invention described earlier, for example, would have little value if a second comer could alter the vector slightly and escape the prior inventor's work and the reach of the patent. Thus, patent rights to this type of recombinant invention have been defined to include the isolated and purified sequence in any vector and in any host cell that includes the vector.[29] Once again, analogous to the class of doorknobs, we are granting rights to the class of carrier DNA segments regardless of what materials the carrier DNA is made up of. We grant these rights, however, in the face of significant unknowns.

Consider, for example, noncoding regions of DNA. As described earlier, the nucleotide building blocks of genes serve as blueprints for constructing proteins or for starting and stopping the process of protein production. Vast sequences of these nucleotide building blocks, however, do not appear to serve any such purpose. Although these sequences exist in the DNA, they drop out as DNA information is transferred through different forms to create proteins. Scientists have dubbed these stretches "noncoding" regions or "junk DNA."[30] For a quarter of a century they were considered irrelevant or evolutionary junk.[31]

In the last few years, however, researchers have uncovered striking evidence that noncoding regions perform different but essential functions in the human biologic process.[32] For example, scientists have determined that changes in just two noncoding nucleotides determine whether a person is lactose intolerant after weaning.[33]

More important, many so-called noncoding regions actually code for RNA[34] rather than proteins. Scientists are discovering that RNA performs essential functions either alone or in conjunction with proteins, making these noncoding regions essential to human function.[35]

These discoveries will have little effect on patent rights granted under many of the first-generation gene patents. Such patents described the sequences in the form of a later translation after the noncoding regions drop out. Nevertheless, where patents have been granted for something that encompasses the entire DNA sequence, including coding and noncoding regions, the inventor may now control far more than imagined at the time of the invention. Similarly, patents that grant control of a gene sequence and a vector (that is, a host cell that encompasses the gene in a form that allows it to continue to function) may be granting control of many hidden substances and operations that we have yet to decipher.

Consider further patents related to antibodies. Antibodies defend against infection by binding to viruses and toxins in our system and interacting with such harmful agents to inactivate them.[36] Antibodies are proteins produced by immune cells in response to instructions from the active genes in those cells.[37] Knowing which antibodies bind to a particular disease agent, as well as manufacturing and manipulating them, can be important in treating diseases ranging from AIDS to cancer to the common cold.

Suppose that an inventor has isolated a particular disease-causing agent, and we know that antibodies will bind to that agent in the human system. Having isolated the harmful agent, the inventor can then claim rights in all antibodies that will bind with the harmful agent. This is true even if the inventor has not isolated and identified any of those antibodies.[38]

The logic of granting these rights rests on combining the antibody information we already have with the information gained once we identify the harmful agent. We know much about the structure of antibodies. For example, a typical antibody has a Y-shaped structure made up of four chains of amino acids—two identical heavy chains and two identical light chains.[39]

Ordinarily we would not allow an applicant to claim something by its function.[40] Thus, in the antibodies example, we would not allow a claim to a group of things based on their propensity to bind with a particular agent. Rather, we would require structural identification.[41] The PTO will allow this claim, however, on the basis of the functional information combined with the structural information that we already have about antibodies in general.[42]

The problem with granting rights in this area lies with the information we do not have. Although the general structural features of antibodies were realized nearly four decades ago, slight differences among antibodies account for their ability to discriminate among targets. The rules governing the development of these slight differences remain elusive.

More important, different antibodies bind to different places on the harmful agent and disarm it in different ways.[43] In addition, some antibodies may be more useful than others. For example, some may bind with the harmful agent but fail to turn off its damaging activity. Claims to the class of antibodies generally are not limited to those that bind to the same place or perform in the same way.

Antibodies may also cross-react with harmful agents other than the one identified in the invention.[44] Suppose that, based on isolating and identifying a harmful agent, an inventor claims all antibodies that bind with that agent. Later it turns out that one of these antibodies also binds with something else or performs some other function unrelated to the harmful agent. The inventor still holds rights to that antibody for any operation and in any context.

The notion that later research may yield new information about biological elements and processes is not merely theoretical. Consider the case of *Schering Corp. v. Amgen Inc.*[45] The case concerned patent rights related to a particular leukocyte interferon. Leukocytes are white blood cells, and interferons are proteins that play important roles in fighting viruses and tumors.[46] When the patent application was filed, scientists viewed leukocyte interferons as a single category.[47] While the application was pending, however, scientists determined that different species of interferons exist.[48] This revelation led to a change in the scientific terminology and to questions for the Federal Circuit concerning how to treat the patent.[49]

The preceding examples highlight the problems of granting rights in the face of unknowns. As the opening chapters explain, these problems run throughout every field of patenting. At times we know there are things we do not know. At other times experience suggests that science will show us things we never dreamed we did not know. Whether we are talking about known unknowns or unknown unknowns, the patent system is faced with the problem of granting rights in the face of incomplete information. This is particularly true of biospace inventions, in which we may never fully solve the mystery of the human body and the intricate interactions of its myriad parts and functions. The challenge is to craft rights in a way that has some economic vitality and reflects the inventor's contribution without reaching into unknown territory and hindering downstream innovation.

## Doctrinal Chaos

Applying the one embodiment notion has led to uncomfortable results in the field of biologic invention.[50] Struggling with the implications of the rule, courts have introduced a variety of doctrinal rules that contradict each other and point in different theoretical directions. In particular, courts have failed to establish a consistent vision of whether the definition of an invention includes anything beyond the state of the art at the time of the invention. The tension appears both in doctrines that spell out how far a patent holder can reach toward later inventions and in doctrines that spell out how far a patent holder can reach toward prior inventions.

### How Far Can a Patent Holder Reach toward Later Inventions?

On the question of whether the definition of an invention reaches beyond the state of the art at the time of the invention, the contradictions are most striking in the doctrines concerning how far a patent holder can reach toward later inventions. In this arena some opinions conclude broadly that one embodiment grants rights to all embodiments, even those that could not have existed at the time of the invention. Other opinions apply claim construction doctrines to limit a patent holder's reach only to embodiments that could have existed at the time of the invention. Still others use a different set of doctrines to conclude that a patent holder's reach can sometimes include things beyond the state of the art at the time of the invention.

*The One Embodiment Doctrine Applied Broadly:* For example, the *Amgen Inc. v. Hoechst Marion Roussel Inc.* decision in 2002 held broadly that one embodiment of an invention brings rights to all embodiments of the invention, even those beyond the state of the art at the time of the invention. The *Hoechst* case concerned erythropoietin (EPO), a hormone that occurs naturally in the body and controls the formation of red blood cells, which transport oxygen from the lungs to other parts of the body.[51] An insufficient number of red blood cells in the blood can occur as a result of chronic kidney disease or heart disease, the effects of chemotherapy to treat cancer, and other causes.[52] Increasing EPO in a patient's system can help raise the level of red blood cells.[53] Early attempts to obtain EPO for treating patients involved recovering EPO from surplus human blood or urine. The approach was complicated and yielded only small amounts of EPO that were very impure and highly unstable.[54]

Instead of purifying EPO from blood and urine, the patent holder in *Hoechst* used genetic engineering techniques to produce large amounts of the hormone.[55] The patent holder used information from the relevant protein—the hormone EPO—to predict and create small DNA pieces that could be used to fish out the entire DNA sequence necessary to produce EPO.[56] Having isolated the full sequence, the patent holder transferred it into a circular piece of carrier DNA. The carrier DNA was then transferred into Chinese hamster ovary cells, which could churn out large amounts of EPO.[57] The patent holder received a patent covering a variety of claims, including a claim to "non-naturally occurring" EPO.[58]

Rather than the traditional recombinant techniques used by the patent holder, the second inventor in *Hoechst* used a different approach to obtain large amounts of EPO. The second inventor, in essence, figured out how to spike the start and stop mechanisms that control the production of EPO in human cells.[59] The inventor then used human cells in the lab to produce large amounts of EPO that could be administered to patients.[60]

The Federal Circuit considered whether the second inventor infringed the first inventor's patent, which had been based on recombinant DNA techniques. The court found infringement, choosing the broad notion of one embodiment.[61] In particular, the court held that the first inventor's claims covered any EPO other than the way nature intended it and were not limited to EPO produced from any particular source or by any particular method.[62] The court held further that for such product claims the inventor did not need to describe or enable technology that arises after the patent application.[63] The court cited with approval the lower court's conclusion that "the specification's failure to disclose the later-developed . . . technology cannot invalidate the patent. . . . 'The law makes clear that the specification need teach only one mode of making and using a claimed composition.'"[64] In short, the *Hoechst* court allowed the footprint of the invention to cover things beyond the state of the art at the time of the invention.

*Claim Construction:* In contrast to the approach embraced by the Federal Circuit in *Hoechst,* other Federal Circuit opinions have limited the forward reach of the patent. For example, the Federal Circuit in *Schering Corp. v. Amgen Inc.* used claim construction to limit the footprint of the patent to things known at the time of the patent application.[65]

The *Schering* case concerned proteins known as interferons, which occur naturally in the body and play an important role in fighting viruses and tumors.[66] At the time of the invention, scientists knew of only two types of interferons, those produced by leukocytes and those produced by fibroblasts.[67] Leukocytes are white blood cells, while fibroblasts are a common cell type found in connective tissue.[68] The patent holder filed claims related broadly to leukocyte interferons, that is, any interferon produced by white cells.[69]

Interferons, however, turned out to have many more subtypes than originally known and vary according to the strength and type of the activity they engage in, as well as the type of receptors to which they bind.[70] Thus, the term "leukocyte interferon" covered many subtypes beyond the one that the patent holder had manipulated in his experiments.

As information about the various subtypes came to light, a committee of scientists adopted new terminology to describe interferons according to factors such as the type of cell that produces them, their binding affinity, and certain physical properties.[71] Following the nomenclature change, the inventor amended his patent application to remove the term "leukocyte interferons" and substitute the term interferons of the "IFN-a type."[72] At the time of the amendment, however, even the term "IFN-a" included numerous subtypes of interferons that differed from the one that the inventor had successfully isolated and manipulated.[73]

The Federal Circuit panel in *Schering* expressed admiration for the patent holder's invention, describing the experiments as "elegant" and the work as "pioneering."[74] Nevertheless, the court limited the reach of the invention by confining it to the limits of scientific knowledge at the time of the patent application.[75]

To reach its limiting result, the Federal Circuit panel used doctrines related to claim construction. Traditionally, patent cases begin with an examination of the meaning of the terms in the patent. Words in the patent are studied to try to divine their precise definition in the context of the patent. This determination, known as claim construction, proceeds as a matter of law.[76] The relevant hearings are called "Markman hearings," after the 1996 Supreme Court case holding that claim construction does not reside within the purview of the jury.[77] Thus, claim construction issues are decided by the trial judge, and appellate courts review such issues de novo without deference to the trial court's decision.[78] Once the patent claims have been construed, those accused of infringing the patent generally defend along two lines of argument: that the claims are invalid or that the accused product does not infringe the claims as interpreted.

Claim construction was the sole issue on appeal in *Schering*. In the process of defining the claim terms, the court declared that claim terms are not permitted to embrace technology arising after the patent application.[79] The court found that "the term as used in the . . . patent . . . did not and could not enlarge the scope of the patent to embrace technology arising after its filing."[80] With this simple declaration the court limited the footprint of the invention to the state of the art at the time of the application. In essence, the court limited the reach of the invention, freezing it to include only scientific knowledge available when the application was filed.

The *Schering* court did not directly address the theoretical question of how far the footprint of the patent should extend and why we might make that choice. Rather, it accomplished the limitation indirectly in its application of the rules of claim construction. Having declared that claim terms cannot reach forward to things arising after the application, the court proceeded to save the claim by reading limitations into it, adopting an inspired interpretation.

The terms used in both the original and the amended claim appeared to include subtypes discovered after the time of the invention, which the court had suggested was problematic. Normally, words in a claim should be interpreted according to their ordinary meaning in the art at the time.[81] A court may overlook the ordinary meaning of a term, however, if the patent applicant expressly designates a particular definition of the term.[82] In amending his patent, the *Schering* applicant stated that "in this application the interferon nomenclature announced in *Nature* . . . is used. E.g., leukocyte interferon is designated IFN-a."[83] The court read this sentence from the amendment as expressing a broad intent to limit the claim to what was known at the time of the invention.[84]

This interpretation is somewhat strained. The declaration in the amendment stops far short of declaring a limitation on the ordinary meaning of terms. It is a substantial leap to conclude that the act of narrowing the size of a group is the same as expressly limiting the claim to what could have been known at the time of the invention. More important, although the applicant narrowed the group, he still chose a group larger than what was known at the time of the invention.[85] Thus, it is difficult to understand how choosing a group that reaches beyond what was known at the time of the invention evidences an intent to limit the claim to what was known at the time of the invention.

Nevertheless, the court interpreted that sentence as expressly limiting the claims to the specific science and knowledge at the time of the invention. The court, therefore, found a way to declare that the terms did not mean what they said and that the claim was limited only to subtypes that could have been known at the time of the invention. In the process the court suggested something about the proper footprint of the patent. The opinion suggested that as scientists discover and distinguish variations of the product, the footprint should be limited to the science at the time of the invention. This approach stands in contrast to the opinion delivered three years later in *Hoechst,* which embraces the broad notion of one embodiment and allows the patent holder to reach embodiments and variations beyond the state of the art at the time of the invention.

*Disclosure Doctrines:* In contrast to both *Hoechst* and *Schering,* the decision in *Chiron Corp. v. Genentech Inc.*[86] used a different set of doctrines to address a patent holder's ability to reach embodiments that could not have been known at the time of the invention. Applying these doctrines, *Chiron* suggested a definition of the footprint of the invention that is inconsistent with both of the prior cases.

The *Chiron* case concerned claims to monoclonal antibodies used in the treatment and diagnosis of breast cancer.[87] As described earlier, antibodies are Y-shaped proteins that defend the human body against harmful agents, such as viruses and toxins, by binding to such agents and interfering with their activity.[88] We generally refer to such harmful agents as antigens.[89]

About 25% of breast cancer tumors express unusually high levels of a protein named Her2.[90] This fact suggests that Her2 plays a role in sustaining the development of the cancerous cells.[91] By blocking the activity of Her2, scientists hope to prevent the growth of the cancerous cells that may depend on it.[92] In particular, breast cancer patients may benefit from doses of antibodies that bind to and interfere with Her2.[93]

The challenge for scientists is to produce a sufficient supply of stable antibodies that the human body can accept. As described earlier, antibodies vary in terms of where they bind to an agent, the way in which they interact with the agent, and the effectiveness of that interaction. Monoclonal antibodies, however, are created by using populations of identical cells that are developed to secrete a single type of antibody.[94] Given that a single antibody is produced, the antibody will bind to a specific site on an antigen and interact with the antigen in a consistent manner.[95]

The science of producing antibodies advanced dramatically in 1975 with the development of hybridomas.[96] Ordinarily, the immune system cells that produce antibodies have a limited life span in the lab. Thus, although a population of homogenous cells that produce a single antibody could be developed, the cells would die out, making it difficult to produce large amounts of a single, consistent antibody. Hybridoma technology, which involves fusing the desired immune cells with tumor cells, creates the capacity to replicate indefinitely.[97]

Early antibody populations were produced from hybridomas using mouse cells.[98] Such antibodies could not be administered long-term to humans because the patient's immune system would eventually attack the mouse antibodies, risking toxic shock or death.[99] In response, scientists turned to antibodies created from DNA-encoding materials combined from different species.[100] In other words, the arms of the Y antibody may be created by genetic coding regions from a mouse while the tail of the Y may be created by genetic coding regions from a human. Antibodies created in this combined fashion are called "chimeric" antibodies.[101] "Humanized" antibodies are created predominantly from human genetic-coding materials, although they may contain some nonhuman portions.[102]

The patent holder in *Chiron* produced monoclonal antibodies that bind to the human breast cancer antigen Her2.[103] The original application disclosed one antibody, which was prepared using a hybridoma developed from mice.[104] Later versions of the application disclosed additional monoclonal antibodies that also bind to Her2, again produced by other hybridomas developed from mice.[105] Some of the variations revealed in the later versions of the application had binding affinities for different locations on Her2.[106]

Claiming all monoclonal antibodies that bind to Her2,[107] the patent defined "monoclonal antibody" in the application as not limited with regard to the source or manner in which it is made.[108] In other words, the product of the patent application was defined as all antibodies that bind to the Her2 target, no matter how the antibody is derived, as long as it is derived differently from the way that nature creates it.[109]

The patent holder sued a company making a product called Herceptin, a humanized antibody used in the long-term treatment of breast cancer.[110] Neither chimeric nor humanized antibodies existed at the time of the original patent application.[111] Thus, the patent holder was attempting to extend the patent's footprint to embodiments beyond the state of the art when the patent application was filed.

In analyzing the claim, the Federal Circuit chose an entirely different path than either of the paths taken before. The *Hoechst* court refused to limit a patent holder's reach to embodiments that could have existed at the time of the patent, thereby remaining faithful to the one embodiment notion. The *Schering* court did limit a patent holder's reach and used claim construction doctrines to accomplish that limitation. The *Chiron* court also limited a patent holder's reach but not by claim construction. Rather, it used disclosure doctrines.

As described earlier, patent cases begin with an inquiry into the meaning of the words in the claims. Once claim construction is completed, an accused infringer generally proceeds by claiming that the patent is invalid and that the accused product does not infringe. To establish invalidity, the accused infringer traditionally must show that the patent is deficient in one of the five elements of patentability: proper subject matter, utility, novelty, nonobviousness, and proper disclosure.[112] The *Chiron* court chose to limit the footprint of the patent using doctrines related to proper disclosure.

Disclosure is governed by section 112 of the Patent Act. This section stipulates that the patent contain "a written description of the invention . . . in such full, clear, concise, and exact terms as to enable any person skilled in the art to which it pertains, or with which it is most nearly connected, to make and use the same."[113] The disclosure requirement is the patent holder's payment in the bargain of granting a patent. The government confers patent rights for a limited time in anticipation that society will later receive the full benefit of the knowledge of those inventions.[114] Disclosure guarantees that society will receive the benefit of the patent holder's knowledge.

In addition, early cases suggested that the disclosure requirements of section 112 and its predecessors not only guaranteed society's proper reward but also served to notify others of the rights claimed.[115] More recent cases have expanded the role of section 112 from explanation and notice to determining whether the inventor possessed the invention claimed.[116] To accomplish this expansion, the Federal Circuit in 1997 in Regents of the *University of California v. Eli Lilly & Co.*[117] identified within the disclosure language of section 112 two separate requirements, one for enablement and one for written description.[118] Enablement would continue to ensure that the public has sufficient information to understand and practice the invention, while written description would ensure that patent applicants possessed what they wished to claim.[119]

The new written description test is couched in terms of performing an accurate accounting of what the inventor actually possessed and when.[120] A court, however, cannot determine what an inventor possessed at a given time without making assumptions about how far a particular invention can reach. The new written description jurisprudence, therefore, has become a battleground for indirect struggles over how far a patent holder can reach.[121] It is within this context that the *Chiron* court uses written description to reduce the footprint of the patent for biotechnology inventions.

In *Chiron* the patent holder tried to reach embodiments of the invention that could not have been accomplished at the time of the patent application.[122] The appeal centered on whether the patent holder's original application satisfied section 112.[123] On this question the court faced precedent from the cases of *In re Hogan*[124] and *Plant Genetic Systems, N.V. v. DeKalb Genetics Corp.*[125]

*Hogan,* which was decided by the predecessor court to the Federal Circuit, concerned an invention in the field of chemistry.[126] Although the original patent application in *Hogan* was filed in 1953, amendments and continuations lasted for two decades, with the PTO finally rejecting the version of the application submitted in 1971.[127] Under the Patent Act an applicant can amend its patent but may not add any new matter to the application.[128]

In its rejection the PTO objected that later incarnations of the application included versions of the original chemical that could not have existed decades before, when the original application was filed.[129] Thus, the PTO objected on the ground that the rights sought reached far beyond the invention as defined in the original disclosure of the patent.[130]

In reversing the PTO, the *Hogan* court held that a patent applicant need not enable later-developed technology, arguing that such a limitation would place an intolerable burden on a patent holder's ability to claim broadly.[131] With this approach the *Hogan* court embraced a broad view of the footprint of a patent by allowing the reach to extend to embodiments beyond the state of the art at the time of the invention.

Grappling with the *Hogan* language twenty-five years later, a Federal Circuit panel in *Plant Genetic Systems* suggested that *Hogan* itself could be limited.[132] As the court explained, "We do not read *Hogan* as allowing an inventor to claim what was specifically desired but difficult to obtain at the time the application was filed, unless the patent discloses how to make and use it."[133] Under the approach outlined in *Plant Genetic Systems* patent holders do not have to enable embodiments completely unknown at the time of the patent but must enable embodiments that were desired but difficult to obtain at the time of the patent.[134]

This reading of *Hogan* attempts to rein in a broad footprint that would allow patent holders to reach forward to embodiments that could not have been known at the time of the invention. After all, by reading *Hogan* in this fashion, the court changed the law from allowing patent holders to reach all embodiments beyond the state of the art to reaching only some of them. The limitation, however, has a perverse effect. In designing a coherent vision of the footprint of the invention, one would expect to reduce a patent holder's reach as technology advances beyond what was known at the time of the patent. The more the science advances, the more we would anticipate new products to be substantially different from what the patent holder accomplished and, therefore, should not be covered by the patent. Thus, we would expect to create the strongest limits on a patent holder's reach for embodiments that are the farthest from the state of the art at the time of the invention.

The *Plant Genetic Systems* limitation, however, has the opposite effect. A patent holder's reach is most clearly protected in the case of advancements that are beyond anyone's imagination at the time of the invention. The patent holder's reach is denied for technology that is closer to the art at the time. Thus, the patent holder has more control over things vastly beyond the state of the art and less control over things close to the state of the art. This is the opposite of the effect that one would logically impose because courts again are looking for stopgap measures to limit a patent holder's reach rather than developing a comprehensive view of what should be protected.

*Plant Genetic Systems* suggested that a patent holder's ability to reach beyond the state of the art at the time of the invention could be limited by the enablement doctrine. Two months later the *Chiron* court followed *Plant Genetic Systems,* finding that patent holders are required to enable some, but not all, embodiments beyond the state of the art at the time of the invention.[135]

The *Chiron* court went farther, however, in its application of the written description doctrine. Regarding written description, the *Chiron* court ruled that the patent holder could not possibly have described what did not exist in the art at the time of the invention.[136] Thus, the *Chiron* court ruled that patent holders who try to reach to embodiments beyond the state of the art at the time of the invention will fail on written description grounds even if they survive enablement. At the end of the day in *Chiron,* therefore, patent holders can never reach embodiments beyond the state of the art at the time of the invention. The case, however, adopts a number of strange twists to reach that result and stands in contradiction to other cases.

The author of the *Chiron* opinion, Judge Rader, has railed against the Federal Circuit's elevation of written description to the level of a separate test in section 112 jurisprudence.[137] In fact, Judge Rader continued his strenuous objections a few months after *Chiron* in his dissent from the Federal Circuit's refusal to take a written description case *en banc*.[138] In particular, Judge Rader argued that the Federal Circuit's current separation of written description and enablement leaves juries with the cumbersome task of deciding that "the patent's disclosure can enable a skilled artisan to make and practice the entire invention, but still not inform that same artisan that the inventor was in possession of the invention."[139] Nevertheless, the separation of written description and enablement was a happy circumstance for Judge Rader in *Chiron* inasmuch as it provided a vehicle for blunting the impact of *Hogan*.

Regardless of the technical conflicts over how the written description doctrine operates or how it fits with the enablement doctrine, the more serious conflicts are theoretical. Across a broad range of doctrines, the courts have adopted entirely inconsistent visions of the proper footprint of the invention and how far an inventor can reach toward things that come after the invention. The *Hoechst* court suggested broadly that a patent holder can reach to all embodiments, including those that could not have existed at the time of the invention. The *Schering* court suggested through claim construction that a patent holder cannot reach to things that could not have existed at the time of the invention. The *Hogan* court suggested through enablement that a patent holder can reach to unknown embodiments. The *Plant Genetic Systems* court suggested through enablement that a patent holder could reach some, but not all, embodiments that could not have existed at the time of the invention. Finally, the *Chiron* court suggested through written description that a patent holder cannot reach any embodiments that could not have been known at the time of the invention.

### HOW FAR CAN A PATENT HOLDER REACH TOWARD EARLIER CREATIONS?

The preceding section explains how defining an invention to include things beyond the state of the art at the time of the invention has led to chaos in the doctrines concerning how far a patent holder can reach toward later inventions. The same expansive notion is wreaking havoc in doctrines related to how far a patent holder can reach toward earlier creations, whether created by nature or by other inventors.

Ordinarily, a patent applicant's reach is constrained by prior art. Patents are granted only for new inventions, not for things that are already available in the science.[140] If an invention already exists, it is not novel but rather "anticipated by the prior art."[141]

Traditionally, to argue that a current invention was anticipated by prior art, one had to point to a single piece of prior art and find all of the elements of the current invention within the four corners of that prior art. Courts have broadened the classic definition of anticipation, however, to include references to what a person of ordinary skill in the art would understand. Thus, even when a piece of prior art does not describe a particular element of the claimed invention, the prior art may still anticipate if a person of ordinary skill in the art would have understood the prior art reference to include the element.[142] Therefore, if a person skilled in the art would have understood the element to be included in the prior art, the prior art anticipates.[143]

Some opinions broaden the anticipation standard even further by finding that a prior art reference can anticipate if the necessary element is inherent in the prior invention even if those of ordinary skill in the art could not have recognized the element.[144] This interpretation expands the definition of anticipation beyond what one skilled in the art would know to things that are entirely unknown but contained in the invention.

For example, in *Schering Corp. v. Geneva Pharmaceuticals Inc.*, the court found that anticipation by prior art does not require recognition as long as the necessary element is inherent in the prior invention.[145] *Geneva* concerned a patented antihistamine that is the active ingredient in the popular allergy medicine Claritin.[146] Unlike the other antihistamines that were available at the time of the invention, the Claritin antihistamine did not cause drowsiness.[147]

Six years after receiving the patent on the Claritin antihistamine, the patent holder also received a patent on DCL, a metabolite of its antihistamine.[148] A metabolite is a compound formed in a patient's body. As a patient's body digests, or metabolizes, a medicine, the medicine is chemically converted into a new compound, known as a metabolite.[149]

Scholars have expressed concern over patent holders' attempts to refresh their patents by patenting updated versions, alternative delivery methods, or other variations of the original product. This practice is referred to as "evergreening" (see the discussion in chapter 5),[150] and one could argue that patenting metabolites is a form of evergreening.

When the patent on the Claritin antihistamine expired, generic versions entered the market. The patent holder sued the generics on the grounds that although the antihistamine patent had expired, the generics infringed the metabolite patent, which still had six years to go.[151]

The court had to determine whether the metabolite patent was invalid because of prior art.[152] The relevant prior art was the original Claritin antihistamine.[153] Thus, the key question concerned whether an invention is anticipated by prior art if the element is present in the operation of the prior art despite the fact that those skilled in the prior art would not have recognized it.[154]

The *Geneva* court found that anticipation by prior art does not require recognition.[155] In other words, a prior art reference can anticipate if all of the elements are contained in the prior art even if a person of ordinary skill in the art would not have been able to recognize the disputed element as part of the invention.[156] Thus, the antihistamine anticipated the metabolite because the metabolite compound was inherently formed during the operation of the antihistamine invention even though those of ordinary skill in the art did not know this at the time of the antihistamine patent.

Another Federal Circuit panel reached a similar conclusion in *In re Cruciferous Sprout Litigation*.[157] *In re Cruciferous* concerned a patent for a method of lowering the risk of developing cancer by selecting for particular vegetable seeds that would grow plants containing high levels of substances thought to reduce the risk of developing cancer.[158] The substances, also known as glucosinolates, encourage the body to produce certain enzymes that are part of the body's mechanism for detoxifying agents that have the potential to cause cancer.[159] The inventors recognized that the amount of the desired substances varies from one broccoli plant to another.[160] The inventors, therefore, suggested sorting through the seeds of particular plants to select those that will produce high levels of the desired substances and assembling them into a food product to reduce cancer in humans and animals.[161] The patent claimed a new method for treating cancer, not a new method for growing or harvesting sprouts.[162]

The Federal Circuit panel found that the invention was anticipated by the prior art of harvesting this class of vegetables for general human consumption.[163] The patent holder tried to argue that even if the prior art included eating one's vegetables, nothing in the art identified the particular

vegetables with the desired substances or suggested assembling a food product from the cultivated seeds that contained particularly high quantities of
the substance.[164]

The court, however, concluded that all of the invention was inherent
in the prior art.[165] A person eating vegetables would have eaten some vegetables with high quantities of the desired substances. Thus, there was nothing
new in directing people to do something that had been done before. As the
court explained, "[The patent holder] cannot credibly maintain that no one
has heretofore grown and eaten one of the many suitable [particular seeds]
identified by its patents."[166]

The court ruled, therefore, that prior art can anticipate even if those of
ordinary skill in the art would not have recognized the inherent characteristics or functions.[167] "Stated differently, a sprout's glucosinolate content and
Phase 2 enzyme-inducing potential are inherent characteristics of the sprout.
It matters not that those of ordinary skill heretofore may not have recognized these inherent characteristics of the sprouts."[168]

As described earlier, the classic test for finding that an invention is anticipated by the prior art requires that a single piece of art contain all of the elements of the claimed invention. Courts have eased this requirement by considering what a person skilled in the art would have understood as inherent
in the invention. The *Geneva* and *Cruciferous* cases ease the requirement even
further by finding that a prior art reference can anticipate if the necessary
elements are inherent in the invention even if one skilled in the art would not
have recognized or appreciated those elements.

Not all Federal Circuit panels, however, embrace the view that prior art
can anticipate even if those skilled in the art would not have recognized the
elements. Some Federal Circuit decisions have held, to the contrary, that
prior art can anticipate only if the element or characteristic would have
been recognized by those skilled in the art.[169]

The notion that an invention encompasses things inherent but unknown
is consistent with the one embodiment concept. In both concepts, the footprint of the invention is defined broadly to include things beyond the state of
knowledge at the time of the invention. With the inherency cases, Federal
Circuit opinions again struggle with the implications of applying such a wide
footprint, with some cases ruling that prior art includes things unrecognized
in the arts and others declining to do so.

Within the opinions that allow inherency for unknown elements, one can see an instinct to limit what can be patented by expanding the notion of prior art. In *Cruciferous,* for example, the court denied patent coverage by finding that the invention existed inherently in common activities.[170] In *Geneva* the court denied patent coverage by finding that the invention existed inherently in the applicant's own prior inventions.[171] This suggests an effort to limit an inventor's ability to lock up rights by granting a large footprint to what has come before.

This approach, however, eventually expands rather than limits what can be patented. If the definition of a piece of prior art includes unknown elements, then the inventor who holds the patent on that piece of prior art should be able to define the invention to reach those unknown elements as well. After all, an invention is what an invention is. Why define an invention one way for one set of doctrines and another way for another set?

Altering the inherency doctrine so that prior inventions are defined to include elements beyond what those in the art recognize creates an expansive reach for all patent holders. Thus, an effort to rein in patenting in some cases has the perverse effect of expanding the footprint of patents in general.

In short, the inherency doctrine suggests defining an invention to include things beyond the inventor's knowledge or the state of the art at the time of the invention. Although this arises in the context of how far an inventor can reach toward prior inventions, logically it should also apply in the context of how far an inventor can reach toward later inventions. In fact, a recent Federal Circuit opinion made this logical connection.[172] The opinion takes inherency questions, in other words, those related to how far an inventor can reach toward earlier inventions, and links them to the doctrines related to how far an inventor can reach toward later inventions. Thus, the opinion confirms the inextricable link between defining an invention for the purposes of delineating prior art and defining an invention for the purposes of delineating future art.

Specifically, in *Elan Pharmaceuticals Inc. v. Mayo Foundation for Medical Education & Research,* a Federal Circuit panel found that when anticipation is based on inherency, the information must have been known in the art.[173] This opinion, therefore, followed the line of cases denying inherency for unknown elements, in contrast to cases such as *Cruciferous* and

*Geneva.* Following publication of the opinion, the full Federal Circuit initially agreed to rehear the case *en banc.*[174] The court withdrew the *en banc* order, however, when the panel reissued the opinion avoiding the question of whether inherency must be recognizable.[175]

The original panel opinion had upheld the patent, adopting a narrow view of prior art by finding that prior art cannot anticipate unless the elements are recognized.[176] The reissued opinion similarly upheld the patent but avoided all discussion of inherency. Rather, in the reissued opinion, the court found that prior art does not anticipate if the prior art is not enabled.[177]

Although the final *Elan* opinion pursued a perfectly logical connection, the opinion completes the circle of confusion in this area. First, the results in *Elan* conflict with the cases finding that anticipation does not require recognition. Under those cases, prior art with unrecognized qualities anticipates, whereas under *Elan,* prior art with unrecognized qualities does not. The Federal Circuit cannot solve the conflicts in the inherency doctrine by deflecting questions into another doctrine. The results are still in conflict in terms of whether the footprint of an invention can reach back to cover prior unrecognized elements.

Second, current conflicts within the enablement doctrine itself will lead to further confusion on the question of whether an inventor can reach back toward unrecognized elements. As explained earlier, the enablement doctrine is itself in disarray in terms of whether an inventor can reach things that could not have been known at the time of the invention. *Hoechst* and *Hogan* hold that an inventor need not enable information that could not have been known at the time of the invention, while *Chiron* and *Plant Genetic Systems* hold that an inventor must enable some but not all of such information. Tossing the inherency question into that realm places it at the center of opinions that point in different directions and guarantees further confusion.

Finally, if a prior art reference must satisfy the enablement doctrine in order to anticipate, then it must also satisfy written description. If a prior art reference must be described to anticipate, then the conflicts throughout both sets of doctrines will be complete. The same question of whether an inventor can reach back to unrecognized elements would be decided in a variety of ways depending upon which doctrinal box the court uses to frame the question and which line of cases the court follows. If decided based on inherency, some cases would find that the prior art anticipated even though there was no recognition in the art, and some would find the opposite. If decided based on enablement, some cases would suggest that the prior art may anticipate despite lack of knowledge by those skilled in the art, and others would disagree with this proposition. Still others would suggest that the prior art may anticipate only if those skilled in the art have a total lack of knowledge but not if the level of knowledge is such that the element was desired but difficult to obtain.

If decided based on written description, some cases would suggest that the prior art may anticipate despite lack of knowledge by those skilled in the art,[178] while others would suggest that this is not the case.[179] Again, one case would suggest that prior art may anticipate only if those skilled in the art have a total lack of knowledge but not if the level of knowledge is such that the element was desired but difficult to obtain.[180] Those who hold patents or challenge them could be assured only of a complete inability to predict the answer to the question.

Most important, the convergence of these areas demonstrates the futility of addressing the issue piecemeal. The courts cannot simply resolve the question, for example, of whether inherency includes unrecognized elements. Any decision there, no matter what, leaves conflicts in the areas of written description, claim construction, and enablement that will wrap back around into the inherency inquiry.

The temptation to define prior art as including inherent elements is strong. It provides the instant gratification of shutting down certain types of evergreening such as metabolite claims.[181] That satisfaction, however, comes at the cost of exacerbating chaos across the doctrines. In addition, other approaches are available for reining in those who would extend their patents through metabolite claims.[182]

From another perspective, Dan Burk and Mark Lemley suggest that the inherency cases can be understood differently from the way in which they are currently interpreted in the field.[183] According to Burk and Lemley, the cases actually turn on whether society is already using and receiving the benefit of an element, not whether the element was unrecognized.[184] In other words, the rule should be that if the public already benefits from an invention even if they do not know about it, that invention is inherent in the prior art.[185]

The public use and benefit rule has the advantage of carefully threading a line through some of the trickier inherency cases.[186] Problems with the approach emerge, however, when doctrines throughout the area are considered as a whole.

For example, recall that in *Geneva,* a pharmaceutical company tried to extend its patent on a drug by patenting the compound formed by the patient's body when the drug was digested.[187] The public use and benefit rule would deny a patent on the compound. The theory would be that the compound was already being formed in the body, and the public, at least those taking the drug, already had the benefit of it.

The pharmaceutical company's invention, however, looks very much like many of the gene and protein inventions that commonly receive patents. For example, the pharmaceutical company determined that the body formed a substance. The company isolated and purified the substance, identified its structure and biologic properties, and then applied for a patent on the substance.[188] Many patents for genes and proteins are based on the same type of work. An inventor determines that the body forms a substance, a protein, for example. The inventor isolates and purifies the substance, identifies its structure, determines a use, and then applies for a patent on the substance.

Although such protein patents are routinely granted, the logic of the public use and benefit rule would deny patenting under the circumstances. After all, the production of the protein is inherent in the prior art of the human body. People are already making, using, and receiving the benefit of the protein in their bodies even if no one skilled in the art knows about it. If the body's formation of the *Schering* metabolite leads to inherency, so should the body's formation of the protein. From the logic of the proposed rule, therefore, the protein, as well as an astounding array of other biospace inventions, would be unpatentable.[189]

The public use and benefit rule also suffers from the same problem as the broader inherency rule. Although that rule offers the prospect of reining in patent holders by limiting their ability to reach backward, it has the perverse effect of increasing their ability to reach forward.

Specifically, when examining a piece of prior art to decide whether a later invention is anticipated, the proposed rule would hold that the piece of art includes things inherently in use even if no one knows about those things. If that piece of prior art is something on which another inventor holds a patent, however, the inventor of that piece of prior art should also be able to claim that the invention includes things inherently in use. After all, how can we hold up a sphere and say, "When we look at it from one direction it is an apple, and when we look at it from another direction it is an orange"? Either the invention includes the unknown element, or it does not.

Following the logic of the proposed rule, therefore, all inventions would reach to things inherently in use—even if those elements could not be recognized by anyone in the field and were not described or enabled by the inventor. This is a remarkably expansive view of the footprint of an invention.

We could, of course, draw artificial lines. We could declare that, on the one hand, when an inventor creates something with unknown qualities and we are trying to determine the inventor's rights, then the invention does not reach those qualities. On the other hand, when an inventor creates something with unknown qualities and we are trying to determine the rights of other inventors, then the invention does reach those qualities. This approach is offered by Burk and Lemley to rationalize the asymmetries created by the proposed rule.[190] The Federal Circuit has taken the same path on the related question of filings that fully disclose a new compound but fail to properly identify how the compound may be used. In those circumstances, the Federal Circuit has ruled that the information in the patent filing is insufficient to give the inventor a valid patent but sufficient to serve as prior art that would prevent others from patenting future uses of the compound even if those of ordinary skill in the art would not have expected the compound to work for those purposes.[191] Thus, the court has decided that terms like "enablement" should have different meanings in different circumstances.

If we create different definitions that are to be applied when looking from different directions, however, these definitions are likely to wrap around and collide with each other. In fact, that is precisely what is happening now in the Federal Circuit as doctrines established in isolation expand and collide. Such collisions are bound to occur because, conceptually, we are asking the same question: Does the footprint of something that exists reach to things beyond the state of the art at the time of the invention? If we simply add greater twists and turns of complexity without resolving the conceptual question, we will do no more than exacerbate the current chaos in the doctrines. In a bargaining environment, doctrinal chaos breeds opportunity.

## Defining the Footprint

As described earlier, the Federal Circuit starts out on the path to chaos with cases like *Hoechst* and *Hogan,* which allow patent holders to reach broadly into the unknown. *Hoechst* does this through general pronouncements of the reach of an invention and through specific applications of the enablement and written description rules.[192] *Hogan* does this simply through application of the enablement rule.[193]

In later opinions judges bob and weave, trying to avoid the implications of doctrines that lead to puzzling and uncomfortable results. *Schering* adopts a highly strained reading of the claims.[194] *Plant Genetic Systems* crafts a strange line in which a patent holder can reach some, but not all, things unknown.[195] The *Chiron* court echoes *Plant Genetic Systems* but then uses another doctrine to completely eliminate a patent holder's ability to reach anything unknown.[196]

Similar patterns emerge in the inherency cases concerning whether new inventions should be blocked by interpreting prior art to include things unknown. Some cases hold that prior art includes things unknown. Others disagree. Finally, the *Elan* court tries to avoid the conflict by throwing prior art questions into the enablement doctrine.[197]

The better path is to acknowledge that cases like *Hoechst* and *Hogan* are grounded in theories that are incompatible with the uncertainty in patent law. Given how little we know about each biospace invention, granting rights to all embodiments and everything contained therein projects an enormous shadow across the future, one whose size cannot even be contemplated at the time of an invention. We should discard the notion that the basic definition of an invention includes things that could not have been known at the time it was invented. Rather, an invention should be defined in light of the art at the time.

Framing the inquiry in this way not only makes sense theoretically but also enhances doctrinal coherence. After all, much of the current disarray has developed as courts strain against the sweeping implications of allowing biospace inventions to reach into unknown territory. Establishing that the basic definition of an invention arises in light of the art at the time of the invention can resolve both the overt doctrinal conflicts and the more subtle inconsistencies.

This theoretical perspective would play out across the doctrines in the following manner: In claim construction, claims would be interpreted in light of the art at the time of the invention, and the type of strained interpretation applied in *Schering* would be unnecessary. Under the enablement and written description doctrines, a patent holder could not reach embodiments unknown at the time of the patent. This would eliminate the strange enablement rules in which a patent holder can reach to some but not all things unknown, rules that are then completely undone by certain versions of the written description doctrine. Finally, in the doctrine of inherency, a prior art reference could not anticipate if the element could not have been recognized by those skilled in the art at the time of the invention.[198] In short, defining inventions in light of the state of the art at the time would resolve both the surface inconsistencies and the conflicting undercurrents described earlier.

This approach would not necessarily confine an inventor's rights precisely to what was done by the inventor but rather would suggest that patents should be interpreted in light of the art at the time.[199] Thus, an inventor could potentially reach beyond the precise work completed to what could be accomplished given what scientists knew at the time of the invention. An inventor, however, could not reach to things that could not have been accomplished or were unknown in the art at the time.

## Conclusion

Basic doctrines would define an invention broadly to include embodiments and aspects of the invention that were unknown at the time of the invention. In light of uncertainty in patent law, however, we cannot define an invention to include the unknown without granting an extraordinarily expansive reach to inventors, far beyond what they may have contributed. The temptation to restrain that reach has led to strange doctrinal twists and an unworkable body of law.

The problem has emerged with particular intensity in cases related to the biologic arts. In five disparate doctrines, current cases related to the footprint of a biospace invention pull in different theoretical directions and stand in contradiction to each other. Judges are unable to resolve the dilemmas because the basic theory underlining this doctrinal area is unsound.

Defining an invention in light of the art at the time of the invention brings coherence to this area of law and eliminates the need for the contorted doctrines that have developed in the field. More important, it is a reminder of the dangers of assuming that the boundaries of an invention can be clearly delineated at the moment of the patent grant. If boundaries are uncertain, reaching beyond the state of the art at the time of the invention provides a remarkable breadth for patent holders, one that can easily create troubling results.

The example also demonstrates the need for and the importance of properly managing the bargaining. Despite the inherent uncertainty in the definition of an invention, one can use substantive rules to cabin the reach of an individual invention and the range of the bargaining room.

# Conclusion

As judges, academics, and commentators increasingly focus on the role that patents play in our modern society, we have an opportunity to look more deeply at the nature of these strange patent beasts. The conventional wisdom in patent law conceptualizes patents by analogy to land, with the claims forming the metes and bounds of the property lines. This conceptualization, however, misses an important aspect of patents, as well as a critical distinction between rights in relation to land and rights in relation to inventions. With real property, we have at least some shared concept of the core of a piece of land. We may argue about rights in relation to it. Society, nevertheless, begins with some concept of what "it" is. The circumstances are necessarily different when we engage in creating a definition of what is new.

With a true innovation, there is no shared conception upon which a definition can be based. Even if there were a shared conception with which we could all agree, the limitations of language prevent the creation of a solid definition, particularly given that any language chosen at the time of the invention will be used to compare the invention with things created later. Most important, at the time of the patent grant, no one has the information necessary to determine the boundaries of the rights. Those boundaries cannot be known without knowing what applications will develop and what other products and inventions will emerge. These developments will determine what aspects of the definition will be explored and will drive the process of creating a definition during the life of a patent.

Thus, from both a descriptive and a theoretical perspective the law does not and cannot definitively set the boundaries of a patent at the moment the patent is granted. The boundaries of an invention will be formed as applications are created, other innovations emerge, and shared understandings develop.

In this process the patent grants an opportunity to bargain over the contours of the rights that will be developed over the life of the patent. Rather than being a definitive grant, a patent offers a seat at the bargaining table, with certain rules in place. In this intricate set of interactions the grant of the patent is an important moment, but it is only one moment of many. The groundwork for the bargaining begins long before the grant of the patent, the process continues throughout the life of the patent, and the impact of those interactions will echo throughout other bargaining moments long after the patent has expired. Most important, in much of the process in which the contours of the rights are developed, the presence of the sovereign will be indirect at best.

The extensive bargaining and uncertainty do not mean we should abandon any effort to influence the definition of rights that will eventually emerge. Through both procedural and substantive doctrines, patent law can be very effective in limiting the range within which the bargaining will occur and in driving parties toward an optimal outcome. When examining issues within patent law, at least part of the analysis should be framed in terms of whether particular choices will promote the best development of the patent's definition during the life of the patent.

Viewing patent law from this perspective can shed light on some of the most challenging issues facing modern patent law. The chapters have explored the application of insights from the bargain aspect to the question of where the processes of nature end and the processes of invention begin, the interaction of patent law with contracts and antitrust, and whether patent holders should be able to reach beyond the state of the art at the time of the invention. Throughout each of these discussions, the goal of the book has been to prompt readers to view patents with a different eye with the hope that by appreciating the bargain aspect of patents we can move toward a more realistic and workable patent domain.

NOTES

ACKNOWLEDGMENTS

INDEX

# Notes

## Introduction

1. See, e.g., Bilski v. Kappos, 130 S. Ct. 3218 (2010); Quanta Computer Inc. v. LG Elecs. Inc. 553 U.S. 617 (2008); Microsoft Corp. v. AT&T Corp., 550 U.S. 437 (2007); KSR Int'l Co. v. Teleflex Inc., 550 U.S. 398 (2007); MedImmune Inc. v. Genentech Inc., 549 U.S. 118 (2007); Lab. Corp. of Am. Holdings v. Metabolite Labs. Inc., 548 U.S. 124 (2006); eBay Inc. v. MercExchange, L.L.C., 547 U.S. 388 (2006); Ill. Tool Works Inc. v. Indep. Ink Inc., 547 U.S. 28 (2006); Unitherm Food Sys. Inc. v. Swift-Eckrich Inc., 546 U.S. 394 (2006); Merck KGaA v. Integra Lifesciences I Ltd., 545 U.S. 193 (2005); Holmes Group Inc. v. Vornado Air Circulation Sys. Inc., 535 U.S. 826 (2002); Festo Corp. v. Shoketsu Kinzoku Kogyo Kabushiki Co. Ltd., 535 U.S. 722 (2002); J.E.M. Ag Supply Inc. v. Pioneer Hi-Bred Int'l Inc., 534 U.S. 124 (2001).
2. Ass'n for Molecular Pathology v. United States PTO, No. 09 Civ. 4515, 2010 U.S. Dist. LEXIS 35418 (S.D.N.Y. Apr. 2, 2010).
3. See Internet video: "Liberate the Breast Cancer Genes," www.aclu.org (accessed 8/16/10).
4. See "The Pope on Patents," www.patentlyo.com, July 9, 2009 (accessed 8/16/10); "Caritas in Veritate: Encyclical Letter of His Holiness Benedict XVI," www.vatican.va, June 29, 2009 (accessed 8/16/10).
5. In this I echo the approach taken by Edmund Kitch in presenting his prospect theory, although bargain aspect offers a very different perspective from that of prospect theory. See Edmund W. Kitch, "The Nature and Function of the Patent System," 20 *Journal of Law & Economics* 267 (1977) (arguing that all patent

systems will have some prospect elements, the rules of a patent system can be adjusted to highlight the prospect system, and the prospect system is a significant function of how the American system has operated in fact).

6. For a more detailed discussion, see chapter 1 (noting that although courts profess to define the reach of the claims first, without considering the supposedly infringing product, human nature suggests that courts will be unable to operate with such blinders on and that, in fact, they do not).

7. See O'Reilly v. Morse, 56 U.S. (15 How.) 62 (1853).

8. See, e.g., Pamela Samuelson, "Google Books Is Not a Library," *The Huffington Post*, Oct. 13, 2009 (criticizing a proposed settlement in the case).

9. For a critique of modern claim construction rules, see Dan L. Burk and Mark A. Lemley, "Fence Posts or Sign Posts? Rethinking Patent Claim Construction," 157 *University of Pennsylvania Law Review* 1743 (2009). See also Michael S. Connor and John A. Wasleff, "Where Do We Go from Here? A Critical Examination of Existing Claim Construction Doctrine," 86 *Journal of the Patent & Trademark Office Society* 878 (2004); Alan Devlin, "Indeterminism and the Property-Patent Equation," 28 *Yale Law & Policy Review* 61 (2009); David L. Schwartz "Practice Makes Perfect? An Empirical Study of Claim Construction Reversal Rates in Patent Cases," 107 *Michigan Law Review* 223 (2008).

10. See Robin Feldman, *The Role of Science in Law* (Oxford, 2009), pp. 187–193 (arguing that problems at the Federal Circuit are structurally predictable); see also Cybor Corp. v. Fas Techs., 138 F.3d 1476 (Fed. Cir. 1998) (Rader, J., dissenting) (en banc) ("In implementation, a de novo review of claim interpretations has postponed the point of certainty to the end of the litigation process, at which point, of course, every outcome is certain anyway."); John F. Duffy, "On Improving the Legal Process of Claim Interpretation: Administrative Alternatives," 2 *Washington University Journal of Law & Policy* 112–113 (2000) (arguing that although centralization in the Federal Circuit contributes to uniformity in claim interpretation, it may also lead to costly procedural inefficiencies and evaluating possible solutions); Andrew T. Zidel, "Patent Claim Construction in the Trial Courts: A Study Showing the Need for Clear Guidance from the Federal Circuit," 33 *Seton Hall Law Review* 737, 745–746 (2003) (finding that the Federal Circuit reversed 41.5% of trial court claim construction decisions in 2001 and calling for the Federal Circuit to provide clearer guidance to trial judges); Kimberly A. Moore, "Markman Eight Years Later: Is Claim Construction More Predictable?" 9 *Lewis & Clark Law Review* 245–247 (2005) (finding that the Federal Circuit's reversal rates of appealed claim construction decisions is getting worse, not better).

11. See generally Mark A. Lemley, "Rational Ignorance at the Patent Office," 95 *Northwestern University Law Review* 1495 (2001); Jay P. Kesan and Andres A. Gallo,

"Why 'Bad' Patents Survive in the Market and How Should We Change?—The Private and Social Costs of Patents," 55 *Emory Law Journal* 61 (2006); Gregory Mandel, "The Non-Obvious Problem: How the Indeterminate Nonobviousness Standard Produces Excessive Patent Grants," 42 *UC Davis Law Review* 57 (2008).

12. See Hayim Halevy Donin, *To Pray as a Jew* (New York, 1991), p. 17.

13. See Robin Feldman, *The Inventor's Contribution,* 2005 *UCLA Journal of Law & Technology* 6, ¶39 (using the Shakespeare analogy to describe improper disclosure caused by insufficient narrowing).

14. I am indebted to Dr. Garry Nolan, Stanford University Department of Microbiology and Immunology for this wonderful imagery.

15. I am reminded of Charles McCarry's description of a crowd of media correspondents as an amoeba controlled by a single brain, moving as a whole or splitting into separate gelatinous parts, dragging tentacles of cables and wires behind it. See Charles McCarry, *Shelley's Heart* (New York, 1995), pp. 313, 325.

16. See Darien Shanske, *Thucydides and the Philosophical Origins of History* (New York, 2007), pp. 34, 177–187 (describing Wittgenstein's notion of aspect seeing).

17. Ludwig Wittgenstein, *Philosophical Investigations* (Oxford, 1958), p. 194.

18. Shanske, *Thucydides,* p. 34.

## 1. The Bargain Aspect of Patents

1. Phillips v. AWH Corp., 415 F.3d 1312 (Fed. Cir. 2005) (en banc), cert. denied, 546 U.S. 1170 (2005) (citing White v. Dunbar, 119 U.S. 47, 52 (1886)) (internal quotation marks omitted).

2. See, e.g., James v. Campbell, 104 U.S. 357 (1881); In re Papesch, 315 F.2d 391 (C.C.P.A. 1963) (comparing the relationship between claims and patents to that of metes and bounds of property and a deed); Martin J. Adelman et al., *Cases and Materials on Patent Law* (St. Paul, Minn., 2003), p. 583; William Macomber, *The Fixed Law of Patents* (Boston, Mass., 1913), p. 15.

3. Robert P. Merges and Richard R. Nelson, "On the Complex Economies of Patent Scope," 90 *Columbia Law Review* 844 (1990).

4. Charles E. Lipsey and Amy L. Tsui Collins, "Patent Infringement in the Field of Biotechnology," in Gale R. Peterson, ed., *Understanding Biotechnology Law: Protection, Licensing, and Intellectual Property Policies* (New York, 1993), pp. 240–242.

5. Ibid., pp. 241–242.

6. See, e.g., Markman v. Westview Instruments Inc., 517 U.S. 373 (1996); Consol. Elec. Light Co. v. McKeesport Light Co., 159 U.S. 474 (1895).

7. See, e.g., Festo Corp. v. Shoketsu Kinzoku Kogyo Kabushiki Co., 535 U.S. 730 (2002) (the monopoly right granted by a patent "is a property right"); Fla. Prepaid

Postsecondary Educ. Expense Bd. v. Coll. Sav. Bank, 527 U.S. 642 (1999) (finding that patents are protected as property and should be afforded the same due process and taking protections as other property); Patlex Corp. v. Mossinghoff, 758 F.2d 599 (Fed. Cir. 1985) (finding that eminent domain applies to patents vis-à-vis both property rights of licensing and the right to exclude); Blum v. Comm'r, 183 F.2d 287 (3d Cir. 1950) (patents are property and subject to the same rules as other property with regard to transfers and assignment of title).

8. See, e.g., Andrew Beckerman-Rodau, "Patents Are Property: A Fundamental but Important Concept," 4 *Journal of Business & Technology Law* 87 (2009); Sean Flynn, "Legal Strategies for Expanding Access to Medicines," 17 *Emory International Law Review* 545 (2003); Timothy R. Holbrook, "Equivalency and Patent Law's Possession Paradox," 23 *Harvard Journal of Law & Technology* 48 (2009); F. Scott Kieff, "Property Rights and Property Rules for Commercializing Inventions," 85 *Minnesota Law Review* 732–736 (2000); David W. Opderbeck, "Patent Damages Reform and the Shape of Patent Law," 89 *Boston University Law Review* 162 (2009); Henry E. Smith, "Intellectual Property as Property: Delineating Entitlements in Information," 116 *Yale Law Journal* 1797 (2007).

9. William C. Robinson, *The Law of Patents for Useful Inventions* (Boston, Mass., 1890), pp. 39–40.

10. Ibid., p. 114.

11. The examples could fill pages upon pages, and I list a representative few here. Gretchen Ann Bender, "Uncertainty and Unpredictability in Patent Litigation: The Time Is Ripe for a Consistent Claim Construction Methodology," 8 *Journal of Intellectual Property Law* 206–207 (2001) (noting that the Federal Circuit changed lower courts' claim interpretations in about 40% of cases between 1996 and 2001, indicating a large degree of uncertainty for inventors and practitioners); Matthew Sag and Kurt Rohde, "Patent Reform and Differential Impact," 8 *Minnesota Journal of Law, Science & Technology* 33–35 (2007) (noting that the Federal Circuit's failure to adopt a consistent methodology for claim construction has created "significant doctrinal instability and confusion in the lower courts"); R. Polk Wagner and Lee Petherbridge, "Is the Federal Circuit Succeeding? An Empirical Assessment of Judicial Performance," 152 *University of Pennsylvania Law Review* 1161–1163 (2004) (analyzing the Federal Circuit's decisions involving claim interpretation from 1996 to 2002 and finding a pattern of panel-dependent outcomes, as well as variability in the choice of methods used in claim construction by individual judges). But see Doug Lichtman and Mark A. Lemley, "Rethinking Patent Law's Presumption of Validity," 60 *Stanford Law Review* 58 (2007) (pointing out that from a business perspective, patent uncertainty is only one of many uncertainties and should not be overemphasized).

12. See Dan L. Burk and Mark A. Lemley, "Fence Posts or Sign Posts? Rethinking Patent Claim Construction," 157 *University of Pennsylvania Law Review* 1745 (2009).

13. E-mail from Hal Wegner (Feb. 2, 2009, 8:53:23 am PST) (on file with author). See also Kinetic Concepts Inc. v. Blue Sky Med. Group Inc. 554 F.3d 1010 (Fed. Cir. 2009).

14. See, e.g., Dawn-Marie Bay and Christopher A. Cotropia, "The Unreasonableness of the Patent Office's 'Broadest Reasonable Interpretation' Standard," 37 *American Intellectual Property Law Association Quarterly Journal* 1 (2009); Eric Brousseau and Christian Bessy, "Public and Private Institutions in the Governance of Intellectual Property Rights," in Birgitte Andersen, ed., *Intellectual Property Rights: Innovation, Governance, and the Institution* (Northampton, Mass., 2006), p. 260; Dan L. Burk and Mark A. Lemley, "Is Patent Law Technology-Specific?" 17 *Berkeley Technology Law Journal* 1191–1196 (2002); Rebecca S. Eisenberg, "Implementing Reform of the Patent System: Obvious to Whom? Evaluating Inventions from the Perspective of PHOSITA," 19 *Berkeley Technology Law Journal* 888 (2004). But see Merges and Nelson, "Complex Economies," p. 841 (arguing that legal principles and objective evidence often leave considerable room for discretion and discussing what policies should influence that discretion).

15. See, e.g., Judge James F. Holderman and Halley Guren, "The Patent Litigation Predicament in the U.S.," 2007 *University of Illinois Journal of Law, Technology & Policy* 107–108, 115–117 (2007); Kimberly A. Moore, "Markman Eight Years Later: Is Claim Construction More Predictable?" 9 *Lewis & Clark Law Review* 231 n.2 (2005); See also Donna M. Gitter, "Should the United States Designate Specialist Patent Trial Judges? An Empirical Analysis of H. R. 628 in Light of the English Experience and the Work of Professor Moore," 10 *Columbia Science & Technology Law Review* 173 (2009); Gregory D. Leibold, "In Juries We Do Not Trust: Appellate Review of Patent-Infringement Litigation," 67 *University of Colorado Law Review* 648 (1996).

16. See, e.g., University of Rochester v. G. D. Searle & Co. Inc., 375 F.3d 1309 (2004) (Rader, J., dissenting); Guang Ming Whitley, "Comment: A Patent Doctrine without Bounds: The 'Extended' Written Description Requirement," 71 *University of Chicago Law Review* 619 (2004); see also Holderman and Guren, "Litigation Predicament," pp. 109–110. One scholar argues that the system of peripheral claiming, with its need to identify categories, creates a circumstance in which patent claims are infinite in scope. He sees the resolution of the problem, however, in the proper application of the written description doctrine. See Jeffrey A. Lefstin, "The Formal Structure of Patent Law and the Limits of Enablement," 23 *Berkeley Technology Law Journal* 1212 (2008) (arguing in favor of a written description doctrine on the grounds that written description has "the

potential to resolve formal questions of claim scope in a way that enablement cannot").

17. See, e.g., Holderman and Guren, "Litigation Predicament," p. 112; Lichtman and Lemley, "Presumption of Validity," p. 46; Gideon Parchomovsky and R. Polk Wagner, "Patent Portfolios," 154 *University of Pennsylvania Law Review* 66 (2005).

18. Mark Lemley and Carl Shapiro also see uncertainty as inherent in the patent system. They analyze that uncertainty, however, as an efficiency-enhancing accommodation to the vast number of patents filed, the fact that most patents have little commercial value, and the fact that third parties do not have a meaningful opportunity to participate in the patent granting system. Mark A. Lemley and Carl Shapiro, "Probabilistic Patents," *J. Econ. Persp.* vol. 19, no 2 (2005), p. 95. Following the logic of their analysis, one might expect that uncertainty could be substantially eliminated in particular scenarios, for example, if we were willing to forgo efficiency, if the law provided for meaningful third-party participation, and/or if the ratio of valuable patents to all patents were higher. In contrast, the bargain aspect of patents suggests that uncertainty, by necessity, would exist in our patent system regardless.

19. See Mark A. Lemley, "Rational Ignorance at the Patent Office," 95 *Northwestern University Law Review* 1531 (2001); see also Christian Bessy and Eric Brousseau, "Technology Licensing Contracts: Features and Diversity," 18 *International Review of Law & Economics* 459 (1998); Brousseau and Bessy, "Public and Private Institutions," p. 251; F. Scott Kieff, "The Case for Registering Patents and the Law and Economics of Present Patent-Obtaining Rules," 45 *Boston College Law Review* 58 (2003); see also Kelly Casey Mullally, "Legal (Un)certainty, Legal Process, and Patent Law," 42 *Loyola of LA L. Rev.* 1109 (2010) (suggesting that uncertainty may not be a negative aspect of patent law given tension between accuracy and certainty and recommending different tradeoffs between the two for different doctrines).

20. Mark A. Lemley and Carl Shapiro, "Probabilistic Patents," p. 95.

21. For example, Dan Burk and Mark Lemley argue that courts should apply legal doctrines differently in different industries, arguing that "it makes sense to take economic policy and industry-specific variation into account explicitly in applying general patent rules to specific cases." See Dan L. Burk and Mark A. Lemley, "Policy Levers in Patent Law," 89 *Virginia Law Review* 1579 (2003). compare Merges and Nelson, "Complex Economies," pp. 840–841 (also suggesting that patent law principles and the objective evidence often leave considerable room for discretion on the part of patent judges and PTO examiners).

22. See, e.g., Jerome S. Bruner, Jacqueline J. Goodnow, and George A. Austin, *A Study of Thinking* (New Brunswick, N.J., 1986), p. 12.

23. This type of analysis is the province of the philosophy of "natural kinds." For a description of natural kinds philosophy, see Ronald de Sousa, "The Natural Shiftiness of Natural Kinds," *Canadian Journal of Philosophy,* vol. 14, no. 4 (1984), p. 562.

24. See Don Lincoln, *Understanding the Universe: From Quarks to the Cosmos* (Singapore, 2004), p. 234.

25. Tamar Yellin, *The Genizah at the House of Sheper* (New York, 2005), p. 211.

26. Burk and Lemley, "Fence Posts," p. 1745. But see Brousseau and Bessy, "Public and Private Institutions," p. 251 (arguing that intellectual property rights are incomplete in part because human language cannot completely grasp the very nature of knowledge that is partly embodied in human skills, organizational equipment, and routines).

27. See F. Max Müller, "My Predecessors," in *Last Essays* (London, 1901), p. 54.

28. See, e.g. J. Derrida, *Of Grammatology,* trans. F. P. Spivak, (Baltimore, Md., 1976), p. 6 ("Language itself is menaced in its very life, helpless, adrift in the threat of limitlessness, brought back to its own finitude at the very moment when its limits seem to disappear, when it ceases to be self-assured, contained, and guaranteed by the infinite signified which seemed to exceed it."); Alfred Sidgwick, *Elementary Logic* (London, 1941), pp. 192–194 (arguing that as a tool for reasoning, the "fundamental defect of language is its necessary indefiniteness . . . indefiniteness belongs to all *description*—to every word and while its function is to describe"); Rex A. Collings, "Unconstitutional Uncertainty—An Appraisal," 40 *Cornell Law Quarterly* 195 (1955) ("There is no sharp line between language which is uncertain and language which is certain. What is uncertain at one time may be certain at another.").

29. See, e.g., Richard Craswell, "Do Trade Customs Exist?" in Jody S. Kraus and Steven D. Walt, eds., *The Jurisprudential Foundations of Corporate and Commercial Law* (New York, 2000), pp. 132–133 (noting that many linguistic customs should not be conceived as bright-line rules that any competent language speaker will already have learned; even with ordinary language exchanges, much is still left to case-by-case balancing). See also Dan L. Burk and Mark A. Lemley, "Quantum Patent Mechanics," 9 *Lewis & Clark Law Review* 49 (2005) (noting that while much has been written on the exercise of interpreting legal texts such as statutes or contracts, "relatively little of this literature has been applied to understand the practice of patent claim interpretation"); Kristen Osenga, "Linguistics and Patent Claim Construction," 38 *Rutgers Law Journal* 70 (2006) (finding similarities between the practice of claim construction and interpretation of statutes and contracts); Alan Schwartz and Robert E. Scott, "Contract Theory and the Limits of Contract Law," 113 *Yale Law Journal* 570–573 (2003) (discussing the difficulties of linguistic interpretation in contracts).

30. For extensive discussion on this topic, see W. Brian Arthur, *The Nature of Technology: What It Is and How It Evolves* (New York, 2009).

31. Arthur argues that radar is a technological development of this type. Ibid., pp. 73–74.

32. Robin Feldman, *The Role of Science in Law* (Oxford, 2009), pp. 183–184 (discussing the difficulties of using language to describe innovations); see also Burk and Lemley, "Fence Posts," p. 1745.

33. See ibid., p. 92 (citing an unpublished manuscript of Margaret Jane Radin, "The Linguistic Turn in Patent Law," who argues that the relationship of patents to the objects they cover is not unique in comparison to statutes and contracts); Bessy and Brousseau, "Technology Licensing," p. 466 (arguing that because codification of anything that involves knowledge is often incomplete, patent holders try to make a patent unusable without the transmission of complementary resources).

34. See Jeanne C. Fromer, "Claiming Intellectual Property," 76 *University of Chicago Law Review* 731–735 (2009) (describing historic shifts from central to peripheral claiming and remnants of central claiming in patent law).

35. See Edmund W. Kitch, "The Nature and Function of the Patent System," 20 *Journal of Law & Economics* 268 (1977).

36. See, e.g., David Moroz, "Production of Scientific Knowledge and Radical Uncertainty: The Limits of the Normative Approach in Innovation Economics," 20 *European Journal of Law & Economics* 306 (2005) (citing the science philosopher Sir Karl Popper).

37. Compare Bessy and Brousseau, "Technology Licensing," p. 456 (noting that given radical uncertainty in technology and innovation markets, economic behavior modeling should be based on a bounded rationality model, not a substantive rationality model).

38. Bessy and Brousseau tantalizingly suggest something similar when they argue that patent holders have both an incentive and an opportunity to keep information secret during the patenting process. Such information, akin to trade secret knowledge, may relate to potential applications of the invention, know-how, or other knowledge. In their view, the patent system helps organize interactions among inventors, competitors, and users in which such information outside of the patent can be transmitted and the rights of use can be determined. See Christian Bessy and Eric Brousseau, "Brevet, Protection et Diffusion des Connaissances: Une Relecture Néo-institutionnelle des Propriétés de la Règle de Droit," 79 *Revue d'Economie Industrielle* 233–254 (1997) (no English translation exists); see also Bessy and Brousseau, "Technology Licensing," p. 466 (citing their French-language article, "Brevet, Protection et Diffusion des Connaissances," for the proposition that because codification of anything that involves

knowledge is often incomplete, patent holders try to make patents unusable without the transmission of complementary resources). The authors, however, suggest that public institutions have the ability to grant rights in a way that is either precise or vague. They argue that the doctrine of equivalence in patent law makes patent rights vague in contrast to the more precise rights granted in copyright. See Brousseau and Bessy, "Public and Private Institutions," pp. 243–277, 260.

39. See In re Hogan, 559 F.2d 606 (C.C.P.A. 1977); see also Merges and Nelson, "Complex Economies," p. 848.

40. In re Wands, 858 F.2d 737 (Fed. Cir. 1988).

41. See, e.g., United States v. Telectronics Inc., 857 F.2d 785 (Fed. Cir. 1988).

42. The case of Brenner v. Manson contains a wonderful exchange between the majority and the dissent. The majority argues passionately about the importance of the utility doctrine for limiting the boundaries of a patent:

> Until the process claim has been reduced to production of a product shown to be useful, the metes and bounds of that monopoly are not capable of precise delineation. It may engross a vast, unknown, and perhaps unknowable area. Such a patent may confer power to block off whole areas of scientific development without compensating benefit to the public.

Brenner v. Manson, 383 U.S. 534 (1966).

In its scoffing response, the dissent implicitly acknowledges the open-ended nature of the patent grant:

> I fail to see the relevance of these assertions . . . nor, in any event, does advance knowledge of a specific product use provide much safeguard on this score or fix "metes and bounds" precisely since a hundred more uses may be found after a patent is granted and greatly enhance its value.

Ibid., p. 537 (Harlan, J., dissenting).

43. See Merges and Nelson, "Complex Economies," p. 841.

44. Matthias Kamber, "Coming out of the Maze: Canada Grants the Harvard Mouse Patent," 35 George Washington International Law Review 762 (2003).

45. See U.S. Patent 4,736,866 (filed June 22, 1984).

46. Merges and Nelson, "Complex Economies," p. 841 (describing the oncomouse patent).

47. Ibid., p. 849.

48. See University of Rochester v. G. D. Searle & Co., 358 F.3d 918, 927–928 (Fed. Cir. 2004) (containing claims to an assay for searching for a type of compound that operated in a particular way and claims related to treatments using such compounds; the treatment claims were rejected because the patent holder did not identify even a single such compound); see also Shengfeng Chen, "Pathways to

Patents: Applying the Written Description Requirement Doctrine to Patents on Biological Pathways," 30 *Hastings Communications & Entertainment Law Journal* 571–572 (2008) (describing *Rochester v. Searle*).

49. See chapter 6 (discussing Schering Corp. v. Amgen Inc., 222 F.3d 1347 (Fed. Cir. 2000)).

50. See Lefstin, "Formal Structure of Patent Law," pp. 1169–1174 (explaining that all patent claims are essentially claims to a group).

51. See Burk and Lemley, "Fence Posts," p. 1760; Lefstin, "Formal Structure of Patent Law," pp. 1168, 1222; see also e-mail from Hal Wegner (Feb. 2, 2009, 8:53:23 a.m. PST) (on file with author).

52. See Burk and Lemley, "Fence Posts," pp. 1745–1747 (suggesting that claim construction may be inherently indeterminate and advocating a return to the pre-1870 central claiming system); Lefstin, "Formal Structure of Patent Law," pp. 1222–1223 (noting that the problems posed by the necessity to define a genus did not arise prior to the development of the peripheral claiming system in its modern form and comparing that system to early peripheral claiming practice, which required only claims defining the inventive principle).

53. Antitrust cases and briefs are particularly sloppy in implying that a patent confers exclusivity in the space defined by the patent. See, e.g., In re Independent Serv. Orgs. Antitrust Litig. (CSU, L.L.C. v. Xerox Corp.), 203 F.3d 1325 (Fed. Cir. 2000); Brief for Respondent, p. 24, Ill. Tool Works Inc. v. Independent Ink Inc., 547 U.S. 28 (2006) (No. 04–1329); see also Henry C. Su, "Intellectual Property Rights and Market Power," 877 *PLI Patents, Copyrights, Trademarks, & Literary Property Course Handbook Series* 144 n.22 (2006) (in which the commentator falls prey to the same improper implication in suggesting that "[h]istorically, patents and copyrights have garnered the most attention from the standpoint of antitrust law because they literally comprise a bundle of exclusive rights").

54. A similar hypothetical can be found in my article, "Patent and Antitrust: Differing Shades of Meaning," 13 *Virginia Journal of Law & Technology* 5, ¶¶26–3 (2008); see also Kitch, "Nature and Function," p. 269 (explaining that if an inventor patents a substance useful as a lubricant that is later discovered to be invaluable as a fuel additive, fuel additive use infringes the original patent even though the inventor never suspected the substance had those properties).

55. See Robin Feldman, "Rethinking Rights in Biospace," 79 *Southern California Law Review* 9–10 (2005).

56. 35 U.S.C. §101 ("or any new and useful improvement thereof"); see, e.g., Allegheny Drop Forge Co. v. Portec Inc., 541 F.2d 383 (3d Cir. 1976) ("A new use for an old process or product is patentable if the new use or application is itself not 'obvious' to one skilled in the art.").

57. Donald S. Chisum, *Chisum on Patents*, vol. 5, §16.02 (2010) ("Two patents may be valid when the second is an improvement on the first, in which event, if the second includes the first, neither of the two patentees can lawfully use the invention of the other without the other's consent." (quoting Cantrell v. Wallick, 117 U.S. 694 (1886))).

58. See "Same Blue Dye in M&Ms Linked to Reducing Spinal Injury," www.cnn.com, July 28, 2009 (accessed 8/4/10) (describing work in mice at the University of Rochester, demonstrating that the blue dye used in M&M candy appears to reduce damage caused by spinal-cord injuries when injected into the spinal cord).

59. See Feldman, "Patent and Antitrust," ¶¶23–26.

60. See Douglass C. North, *Institutions, Institutional Change and Economic Performance* (Cambridge, UK, 1990), p. 33; Bessy and Brousseau, "Brevet, Protection et Diffusion des Connaissances"; Moroz, "Production of Scientific Knowledge," p. 312.

61. See Bessy and Brousseau, "Brevet, Protection et Diffusion des Connaissances."

62. See Lemley and Shapiro, "Probabilistic Patents," pp. 85–87 (discussing aspects of the patent system that create uncertainty in litigation and the effects of resulting calculations).

63. See Ronald H. Coase, "The Problem of Social Cost," 3 *Journal of Law & Economics* 1–44 (1960) (analyzing a farmer and rancher in a hypothetical world of zero transaction costs); Ronald H. Coase, *The Firm, the Market, and the Law* (Chicago, Ill., 1988) (collecting and amplifying his earlier works).

64. See John J. Donohue III, "Opting for the British Rule, or If Posner and Shavell Can't Remember the Coase Theorem, Who Will?" 104 *Harvard Law Review* 1099 (1991). Theorists of new institutionalism have also offered perspectives on extrajudicial bargaining and governance structures; see North, *Institutions*, pp. 3–10, 33–35; Oliver E. Williamson, *The Economic Institutions of Capitalism: Firms, Markets, Relational Contracting* (New York, 1985); Bessy and Brousseau, "Technology Licensing," p. 459.

65. See Arthur L. Corbin and Joseph M. Perillo, "Mutual Assent—Meeting of the Minds," in *Corbin on Contracts*, vol. 1, chap. 4, §4.13 (St. Paul, Minn., 1993), pp. 634–636.

66. For descriptions of relational contract theory, see Bessy and Brousseau, "Technology Licensing," pp. 460–485; Jay M. Feinman, "Relational Contract Theory in Context," 94 *Northwestern University Law Review* 737 (2000); Elizabeth Mertz, "An Afterword: Tapping the Promise of Relational Contract Theory—'Real' Legal Language and a New Legal Realism," 94 *Northwestern University Law Review* 909 (2000). For early work in relational contract theory, see Charles L. Knapp, "Enforcing the Contract to Bargain," 44 *New York University Law Review*

673 (1969); Ian R. Macneil, "The Many Futures of Contracts," 47 *Southern California Law Review* 691 (1974).

67. See Mertz, "Tapping the Promise of Relational Contract Theory," p. 914.

68. For a more expansive exploration of the view of law described in this paragraph, see Feldman, *Role of Science,* pp. 79–95.

69. I have previously explored this vision of law in the context of understanding why importing scientific rules into legal doctrines so often fails. See ibid.

70. See ibid., pp. 90–94 (comparing patent law to constitutional law).

71. See Ian R. Macneil, "Values in Contract: Internal and External," 78 *Northwestern University Law Review* 389 (1983) (asserting that all conceptualizing is political).

72. See Feldman, *Role of Science,* pp. 195–196 (arguing that the misguided desire for perfection in law leads to fruitless attempts to have science solve law's problems and that, ultimately, the instinct to deconstruct everything loses power itself by leaving nothing).

73. See Kitch, "Nature and Function," p. 265.

74. See ibid., p. 271.

75. See ibid., p. 267.

76. See John F. Duffy, "Rethinking the Prospect Theory of Patents," 71 *University of Chicago Law Review* 439 (2004) (describing the controversy over Kitch's theories); Mark A. Lemley, "The Economics of Improvement in Intellectual Property Law," 75 *Texas Law Review* 1045–1046 (1997) (noting Kitch's significant effort); Roger L. Beck, "The Prospect Theory of the Patent System and Unproductive Competition," 5 *Research in Law & Economics* 194 (1983) (suggesting the theory's lack of foundation); Frederic M. Scherer, *Industrial Market Structure and Economic Performance* (Boston, Mass., 1980), p. 447 n.30 (suggesting descriptive inconsistencies).

77. See Merges and Nelson, "Complex Economies," p. 875 (comparing mineral claims to patents).

78. See Merges and Nelson, "Complex Economies," p. 842; Scherer, "Industrial Market Structure," p. 447.

79. For literature that analogizes fishing rights to property rights and details complex efforts to avoid overdevelopment and underdevelopment in even that more limited realm, see Anthony T. Charles, "Fishery Socioeconomics: A Survey," 64 *Land Economics* 279–280 (1988); Philip A. Neher, Ragnar Arnason, and Nina Mollett, eds., *Rights Based Fishing* (Dordrecht, NL, 1989).

80. See Lemley and Shapiro, "Probabilistic Patents," pp. 80–83 (characterizing patents as lottery tickets in which few pay off but those that do pay handsomely).

81. See Parchomovsky and Wagner, "Patent Portfolios," pp. 5 & n.3, 14–15. For an in-depth analysis of the value of patents, see John R. Allison, Mark A. Lemley,

Kimberly A. Moore, and R. Derek Trunkey, "Valuable Patents," 92 *Georgetown Law Journal* 435 (2004); John R. Allison and Thomas W. Sager, "Valuable Patents Redux: On the Enduring Merit of Using Patent Characteristics to Identify Valuable Patents," 85 *Texas Law Review* 1769 (2007).

82. See Brenner v. Manson, p. 536; see also In re Fisher, 421 F.3d 1376 (Fed. Cir. 2005).

83. See Michael Abramowicz, "The Danger of Underdeveloped Patent Prospects," 92 *Cornell Law Review* 1078 (2007); see also Wolfgang Leininger, "Escalation and Cooperation in Conflict Situations: The Dollar Auction Revisited," 33 *Journal of Conflict Resolution* 233 (1989); Duffy, "Rethinking Prospect Theory," pp. 442–444.

84. See Abramowicz, "Underdeveloped Patent Prospects," p. 1079; see also Duffy, "Rethinking Prospect Theory," pp. 444–446 (making the Demsetzian auction comparison); Harold Demsetz, "Why Regulate Utilities?" 11 *Journal of Law & Economics* 57–58, 63 (1968).

85. See Shaun Martin and Frank Partnoy, "Patents as Options," in F. Scott Kieff and Troy A. Paredes, eds., *Perspectives on Commercializing Innovation* (Cambridge, UK, 2011).

86. For a discussion of patent grants explicitly compared to real property rights, see Abramowicz, "Underdeveloped Patent Prospects," pp. 1066–1069; see also Duffy, "Rethinking Prospect Theory."

87. See John Gladstone Mills III, Donald C. Reiley III, and Robert C. Highley, *Patent Law Fundamentals*, part II, §6:3 (2010).

88. See Katherine J. Strandburg, "What Does the Public Get? Experimental Use and the Patent Bargain," 2004 *Wisconsin Law Review* 84–87; see also Madey v. Duke Univ., 307 F.3d 1351 (Fed. Cir. 2002). There is a statutory experimental use exemption, but it is limited to experimentation related to submission to public agencies. Peter Lee, "Contracting to Preserve Open Science: Consideration-Based Regulation in Patent Law," 58 *Emory Law Journal* 910–911 (2009); see also 35 U.S.C. §271(e).

89. Robin Feldman, "Coming to the Community," in Austin Sarat, Lawrence Douglas, and Martha Merrill Umphrey, eds., *Imagining New Legalities: Privacy and Its Possibilities in the 21st Century*, Amherst Series in Law, Jurisprudence, and Social Thought (Stanford, Calif., 2012).

90. For a discussion of the abuses in the 1600s that led to the enactment of the Statute of Monopolies, see Edward C. Walterscheid, "The Early Evolution of the United States Patent Law: Antecedents (Part 2)," 76 *Journal of the Patent & Trademark Office Society* 871–880 (1994); Adam Mossoff, "Rethinking the Development of Patents: An Intellectual History, 1550–1800," 52 *Hastings Law Journal* 1259–1276 (2001); Christine MacLeod, *Inventing the Industrial Revolution: The English Patent System, 1660–1800* (Cambridge, UK, 2002), pp. 15–19.

91. See generally Mark A. Lemley and Bhaven Sampat, "Examining Patent Examination," Working Paper (April 24, 2010) (describing the examination process and the interplay of initial rejections on the application process); see also ibid., p. 6 (noting that the majority of patent applications—86.5%—initially receive a nonfinal rejection).

92. Such groups include the Electronic Frontier Foundation, the Public Patent Foundation, the Center for Patent Innovation at New York Law School, and Article One Partners. See "Peer-to-Patent Project Begins Post-Issue Review," www .patentlyo.com, Jan. 26, 2009 (accessed 4/1/10). See also "EFF: The Patent Busting Project," www.w2.eff.org (accessed 4/1/10); "Public Patent Foundation," www.pubpat.org (accessed 4/1/10); "Center for Patent Innovations," www.nyls .edu (accessed 4/1/10); "Article One Partners," www.articleonepartners.com (accessed 4/1/10).

93. See "A Patent Validity Study: Semiconductor Memory Devices—Rambus," www.articleonepartners.com (accessed 4/1/10).

94. For additional discussion of the reexamination process, see chapter 2.

95. See SanDisk Corp. v. STMicroelectronics Inc., 480 F.3d 1372, 1381 (Fed. Cir. 2007). Third parties have a limited ability to challenge invalidity through an administrative *ex parte* request for reexamination based on new art submitted to the PTO. See James W. Beard, "A Better Carrot—Incentivizing Patent Reexamination," 1 *Hastings Science & Technology Law Journal* 173–176 (2009); 35 U.S.C. §§301–307.

96. See "EFF: The Patent Busting Project," www.w2.eff.org (accessed 4/1/10); "Protecting the Public Domain," www.pubpat.org (accessed 4/1/10); "Article One Partners: Frequently Asked Questions," www.articleonepartners.com (accessed 4/1/10).

97. See "EFF: The Patent Busting Project," www.w2.eff.org; "Protecting the Public Domain," www.pubpat.org; "Post Issue Peer-to-Patent," www.post-issue.org (accessed 4/1/10); "Article One: About Us," www.articleonepartners.com (accessed 4/1/10).

98. See "Troll Tracker Defamation Lawsuit: Trial Underway," www.patentlyo .com, Sept. 18, 2009 (accessed 4/1/10); Joe Mullin, "Patent Troll Tracker Defamation Case Goes to Trial," www.law.com, Sept. 16, 2009 (accessed 4/1/10); Joe Mullin, "In Patent Troll Tracker Trial, It's Frenkel on the Grill," www.law.com, Sept. 18, 2009 (accessed 4/1/10); see also Complaint, Invention Submission Corp. v. IP Watchdog Inc., No. 5:10-CV-74 (NPM/DEP) (N.D.N.Y. Jan. 21, 2010).

99. See Steve Lohr, "Now, an Invention Inventors Will Like," *New York Times,* Sept. 21, 2009, p. B1.

100. See ibid.

101. See Brenda Sandburg, "You May Not Have a Choice. Trolling for Dollars," *The Recorder,* July 30, 2001.

102. See James F. McDonough III, "The Myth of the Patent Troll: An Alternative View of the Function of Patent Dealers in an Idea Economy," 56 *Emory Law Journal* 199 (2006).

103. For example, Dan Burk and Mark Lemley have suggested that courts can use the malleability of patent doctrines as "levers" to adjust the level of rights to take account of differences between industries. They argue that patent rights should vary according to the industry and that the legislature lacks the dexterity to make such adjustments appropriately. See Burk and Lemley, "Policy Levers."

## 2. How Modern Patents Operate

1. For the statistics described in this paragraph and other interesting information about the patent examination process, see Bhaven Sampat and Mark A. Lemley, "Examining Patent Examination," *Stanford Public Law Working Paper No. 1485011* (2009).

2. The description in the text follows the facts of the *Eli Lilly* patent case, with the exception that the PTO allowed the patent claim, and the Federal Circuit then invalidated it. See Regents of the Univ. of Cal. v. Eli Lilly & Co., 119 F.3d 1559 (Fed. Cir. 1997).

3. See, e.g., In re Am. Acad. of Sci. Tech Ctr., 367 F.3d 1364 (Fed. Cir. 2004); In re Morris, 127 F.3d 1053–1054 (Fed. Cir. 1997); In re Zletz, 893 F.2d 321 (Fed. Cir. 1989); In re Yamamoto, 740 F.2d 1571–1572 (Fed. Cir. 1984). But see In re Buszard, 504 F.3d 1368 (Fed. Cir. 2007) (Prost, J., dissenting). For the purposes of the doctrine of equivalence, other authors have noted the dynamics of the timing and the requirements of equivalency. See Timothy R. Holbrook, "Equivalency and Patent Law's Possession Paradox," 23 *Harv. J. L. & Tech.* 1 (2009); Christopher Cotropia, "After-Arising Technologies and Tailoring Patent Scope," *N.Y.U. Ann. Surv. Am. L.* 151 (2005).

4. 35 U.S.C. §132(a); see also Agilent Technologies Inc. v. Affymetrix Inc., 567 F.3d 1379 (Fed. Cir. 2009).

5. The claims are technically included within the specification. See 35 U.S.C §112, ¶2.

6. See 37 C.F.R. §1.77.

7. See 35 U.S.C. §112, ¶1.

8. Donald S. Chisum, *Chisum on Patents,* vol. 3, §8.01 (2010).

9. U.S. Patent No. 5,205,473 (filed Mar. 19, 1992).

10. Robert P. Merges and Richard R. Nelson, "On the Complex Economies of Patent Scope," 90 *Columbia Law Review* 848–849 (1990) (suggesting that, given rules related to the burdens on the patent examiners during the course of patent prosecution, the job of narrowing the claims may be left to the courts in particular infringement suits).

11. Manual of Patent Examining Procedure §2164.02 (2008) (describing prophetic examples). Lack of a working example, however, may be considered, particularly in unpredictable or undeveloped arts. Ibid.

12. Patent applicants in the software and electronics arena are able to come much closer to claiming by function than applicants in the biotechnology arena. Compare Regents of the University of California v. Eli Lilly, 119 F. 3d 1559 p. 1557 (Fed. Cir. 1997). with Fonar Corp v. General Electric, 107 F. 3d 1543.

13. See "Hedy Lamarr," www.radio-electronics.com (accessed 8/13/10).

14. For a copy of the patent and a family member's account, see Chris Beaumont, "Secret Communication System: The Fascinating Story of the Lamarr/Antheil Spread-Spectrum Patent," www.ncafe.com/chris/pat2 (accessed 8/13/10).

15. See 35 U.S.C. §112, ¶1.

16. Chisum, *Chisum on Patents,* vol. 3, §7.05.

17. See In re Gleave, 560 F.3d 1334 (Fed. Cir. 2009).

18. See also Stuart Graham and Ted Sichelman, "Why Do Start-Ups Patent?" 23 *Berkeley Technology Law Journal* 1065 (2008) (arguing that, far from using patents offensively to stop others from making or selling their products, many companies view patents as necessary evils to shield them from infringement suits).

19. For perspectives on patents as a defensive mechanism to protect against the patents of others, see Mark A. Lemley, "Rational Ignorance at the Patent Office," 95 *Northwestern University Law Review* 1504–1505 (2001); Bronwyn Hall and Rosemarie Ziedonis, "The Patent Paradox Revisited: An Empirical Study of Patenting in the U.S. Semiconductor Industry, 1979–1995," 32 *RAND Journal of Economics* 110 (2001).

20. See 35 U.S.C. §271(d); see also Continental Paper Bag Co. v. Eastern Paper Bag Co., 210 U.S. 429 (1908); Kurt Saunders and Linda Levine, "Better, Faster, Cheaper—Later: What Happens When Technologies Are Suppressed," 11 *Michigan Telecommunications & Technology Law Review* 23 (2004).

21. The strategy, however, may face new constraints. The Supreme Court held in 2006 that a finding of infringement should not automatically lead to an injunction. Rather, in deciding whether to grant an injunction, a court must apply the traditional four equitable factors, including whether granting the injunction is in the public interest. In some cases, therefore, this analysis might allow an infringer to use the fact that the patent holder is suppressing the invention as a way to produce the invention, avoid an injunction, and pay damages instead. See eBay Inc. v. MercExchange, L.L.C., 547 U.S. 393–394 (2006) (injunction analysis after a finding of patent infringement must still use the traditional four equitable considerations, including whether the public interest would benefit by the grant of an injunction).

22. See Robin Feldman, "Patent and Antitrust: Differing Shades of Meaning," 13 *Virginia Journal of Law & Technology* 5, ¶¶44–52 (2008).

23. See Merges and Nelson, "Complex Economies," p. 862.

24. "U.S. Patent Statistics Summary Table, Calendar Years 1963 to 2009," www .uspto.gov, Apr. 20, 2010 (accessed 5/5/10) (showing that the PTO received 482,871 patent applications in 2009).

25. See Pal v. Department of Commerce, 301 Fed. Appx. 987–988 (Fed. Cir. 2008) (nonprecedential opinion), cert. denied, 129 S. Ct. 1648 (2009).

26. See ibid., p. 986.

27. Ibid. Although the assertion was not addressed by the Federal Circuit, the specialist claimed that similarly situated employees who had error rates as high as 45–50% were not rated unacceptable. See Brief of Petitioner Asokkumar Pal, p. 4, Pal v. Department of Commerce, 301 Fed. Appx. 984 (Fed. Cir. 2008) (No. 2008–3213), 2008 WL 3833925.

One might ask how the error rate compares to other types of administrative agency decisions, if any of those decisions might arguably be comparable to the grant of a patent. That comparison, however, might demonstrate only that other forms of rights are subject to error in the process of granting in a manner that leaves room for subsequent maneuvering as to the extent of those rights.

28. "United States Patent and Trademark Office, Performance and Accountability Report—Fiscal Year 2009," www.uspto.gov (accessed 5/5/10) (citing the average total pendency time for patents in 2009 as 34.6 months).

29. See 35 U.S.C. §122. But see Manual of Patent Examining Procedure §1122 (2008).

30. See Mark A. Lemley and Kimberley A. Moore, "Ending Abuse of Patent Continuations," 84 *Boston University Law Review* 63 (2004) (noting that patent owners also have the incentive to prolong and keep their patent rights malleable by filing continuation applications); see also Robert M. Asher, "Post Issuance Strategies for Patentee and Third Parties," www.sunsteinlaw.com (accessed 5/5/10) (discussing Lemley and Moore).

31. See 35 U.S.C. §132; 35 U.S.C. §251.

32. See Benjamin Sovacool, "Placing a Glove on the Invisible Hand: How Intellectual Property Rights May Impede Innovation in Energy Research and Development," 18 *Albany Law Journal of Science & Technology* 416 (2008) (noting that the patent term was changed from seventeen years from the date of issue to twenty years from the date of filing to address the concerns about an endemic of submarine patents); Marie Wilson, "TRIPS Agreement Implications for ASEAN Protection of Computer Technology," 4 *Annual Survey of International & Comparative Law* 33 (1997) (mandatory publication of patent applications reduces the problem of submarine patents).

33. See Kingsdown Med. Consultants Ltd. v. Hollister Inc., 863 F.2d 874 (Fed. Cir. 1988); see also Christian E. Mammen, "Controlling the 'Plague': Reforming the Doctrine of Inequitable Conduct," 24 *Berkeley Technology Law Journal* 1331 (2009) (discussing Kingsdown Med. Consultants Ltd. V. Hollister Inc.).

34. See Jeanne C. Fromer, "Claiming Intellectual Property," 76 *University of Chicago Law Review* 721 (2009).

35. See generally Michael Risch, "The Failure of Public Notice in Patent Prosecution," 21 *Harvard Journal of Law & Technology* 179 (2007).

36. See Greg Aharonian, "Greg Aharonian Discussed the WSJ's 'Idiotic Article on Patent Tr-lls,'" www.patentlyo.com, Aug. 25, 2008 (accessed 5/5/10) (noting the need for a discussion of the comparison of these).

37. It is within the court's discretion to increase damages up to three times the actual amount based on the egregiousness of the infringer's conduct. 35 U.S.C. §284; Electro Scientific Indus. Inc. v. Gen. Scanning Inc., 247 F.3d 1353 (Fed. Cir. 2001).

38. In re Seagate Tech., LLC, 497 F.3d 1360 (Fed. Cir. 2007).

39. For a discussion of the relationship between patents and products in the context of antitrust analysis, see Feldman, "Patent and Antitrust," ¶¶41–69.

40. See, e.g., U.S. Patent Application 11/614,278 (filed Dec. 21, 2006).

41. See U.S. Patent No. 6,219,694 (filed May 29, 1998).

42. See The CAMBIA BiOS Initiative, *Biological Innovation for Open Society: Implementation Phase 2006–2008*, p. 7, www.patentlens.net (accessed 8/20/10).

43. See MedImmune Inc. v. Genentech Inc., 549 U.S. 127 (2007).

44. See Carl Shapiro, "Antitrust Limits to Patent Settlements," 34 *RAND Journal of Economics* 394 (2003).

45. See Kimberly A. Moore, "Forum Shopping in Patent Cases: Does Geographic Choice Affect Innovation?" 79 *North Carolina Law Review* 897 (2001).

46. Moore, "Forum Shopping," p. 898.

47. Ibid., p. 900 ("explaining that a patent holder may believe that a fast jurisdiction will give the infringer less time to scour the earth looking for invalidating prior art and less time to mount a defense in general").

48. Stuart Weinberg, "Caught in the Crossfire," *The Wall Street Journal*, Aug. 11, 2008, p. R6.

49. See ibid.

50. See Gideon Parchomovsky and R. Polk Wagner, "Patent Portfolios," 154 *University of Pennsylvania Law Review* 5, 14–15 (2005).

51. See Graham and Sichelman, "Why Do Start-Ups Patent?" p. 1066 (describing the interactions in the hard drive industry).

52. See Francis Bidault, *Technology Pricing: From Principles to Strategy* (New York, 1989), p. 91.

53. See Stuart Graham, Robert P. Merges, Pam Samuelson, and Ted Sichelman, "High Technology Entrepreneurs and the Patent System: Results of the 2008 Berkeley Patent Survey," 24 *Berkeley Technology Law Journal* 1255 (2009) (presenting empirical results showing that, although software entrepreneurs see patents as less important for competitive success than conventional wisdom might suggest, an impetus for at least some of the patenting activities by these entrepreneurs was that funding sources thought patents would be important to the company's success); Clarissa Long, "Patent Signals," 69 *University of Chicago Law Review* 625 (2002) (patents have value as a signaling device to investors).

54. See Univ. of Rochester v. G. D. Searle & Co., 358 F.3d 916 (Fed. Cir. 2004).

55. See Univ. of Rochester v. G. D. Searle & Co., 375 F.3d 1303 (Fed. Cir. 2004) (denial of en banc consisting of five separate dissenting and concurring opinions).

56. Univ. of Rochester v. G. D. Searle, 358 F.3d 916 (Fed. Cir. 2004).

57. One could argue that the pharmaceutical company filed composition of matter claims because that is the only invention they had. Although that is certainly possible, creativity in claims reach exists for all types of innovations, including those involving composition of matter. See, e.g., "Broadening Claim Language in Gene Patents," www.patentlens.com (accessed 5/25/10) (explaining different forms of claim language used to broaden the scope beyond that disclosed in the specification); U.S. Patent No. 5,747,327 (filed July 26, 1995) (claiming any nucleotide sequence that hybridizes to the disclosed sequence); U.S. Patent No. 7,268,271 (filed July 19, 2002) (claiming all nucleotide sequences that encode a disclosed amino acid).

58. See, e.g., FTC v. Rambus Inc., 522 F.3d 456 (D.C. Cir. 2008), cert. denied, 129 S.Ct. 1318 (2009); Hon Hai Precision Indus. Co. v. Molex Inc., No. 08 C 5582, 2009 U.S. Dist. LEXIS 9165 (N.D. Ill. Feb. 9, 2009).

59. See Thomas G. Field Jr., "Pre-Litigation Hardball after Dominant Semiconductor," www.ipfrontline.com, May 15, 2008 (accessed 5/5/2010) (describing this effect in the context of the copyright case, Cardtoons, L.C. v. Major League Baseball Players Ass'n, 95 F.3d 959 (10th Cir. 1996)).

60. Campbell Pet Co. v. Miale, 542 F.3d 879 (Fed. Cir. 2008).

61. See ibid., p. 886.

62. See, e.g., Hon Hai v. Molex, p. *3.

63. See GP Indus. Inc. v. Eran Indus. Inc., 500 F.3d 1369 (Fed. Cir. 2007).

64. Ibid., p. 1372.

65. See ibid., p. 1374.

66. See ibid.

67. See 35 U.S.C. §§302–318; see also generally James W. Beard, "A Better Carrot—Incentivizing Patent Reexamination," 1 *Hastings Science & Technology Law Journal* 173–176 (2009).

68. See 35 U.S.C. §302.

69. See 35 U.S.C. §§303–304.

70. See 35 U.S.C. §§302–307; 35 U.S.C. §§307–318.

71. 35 U.S.C. §303.

72. See U.S. Patent and Trademark Office, "Office Action in *Ex Parte* Reexamination," Patent No. 5,843,780 (Mar. 30, 2007) (rejecting all claims of the '780 patent); U.S. Patent and Trademark Office, "Office Action in *Ex Parte* Reexamination," Patent No. 6,200,806 (Mar. 30, 2007) (rejecting all claims of the '806 patent); U.S. Patent and Trademark Office, "Office Action in *Ex Parte* Reexamination," Patent No. 7,029,913 (Mar. 30, 2007) (rejecting all claims of the '913 patent); see also Karen Kaplan, "Patents for Human Stem Cells Invalidated," *Los Angeles Times,* Apr. 3, 2007, p. 18; Kristen Philipkoski, "Patent Office Invalidates Wisconsin Embryonic Stem Cell Patents," www.wired.com, Apr. 3, 2007 (accessed 5/25/10).

73. See U.S. Patent and Trademark Office, "Notice of Intent to Issue *Ex Parte* Reexamination Certificate: Reasons for Allowance/Confirmation," Patent No. 6,200,806 (Mar. 3, 2008) (withdrawing objections to the validity of the '806 patent on the basis of the patentee's amendments); U.S. Patent and Trademark Office, "Notice of Intent to Issue *Ex Parte* Reexamination Certificate: Reasons for Allowance/Confirmation," Patent No. 5,843,780 (Mar. 3, 2008) (withdrawing objections to the validity of the '780 patent on the basis of the patentee's amendments); Found. for Taxpayer and Consumer Rights v. Wis. Alumni Research Foundation, No. 2010–001854 (B.P.A.I. Apr. 28, 2010) (reversing the examiner's confirmation of patentability of U.S. Patent No. 7,029,913).

74. Lawrence M. Sung and Jeff E. Schwartz, *Patent Law Handbook,* §3:35 (Eagan, Minn., 2009); see also 35 U.S.C. §251.

75. See Sung and Schwartz, *Patent Law Handbook,* §3:35; Revolution Eyewear Inc. v. Aspex Eyewear Inc., 563 F.3d 1366–1367 (Fed. Cir. 2009).

76. See "Intellectual Ventures," www.intellectualventures.com (accessed 4/7/2010).

77. Thomas Ewing and Robin Feldman, "The Giants among Us," *Stanford Technology Law Journal* (forthcoming Winter 2012).

78. See ibid.

79. See ibid.

80. See ibid.

81. See 35 U.S.C. §154(b); see also Wyeth v. Kappos, 591 F.3d 1364 (Fed. Cir. 2010).

82. See Dennis Crouch, "Extending Patent Terms," www.patentlyo.com, Feb. 19, 2009 (accessed 5/4/10).

83. See C. Edward Polk, Courtenay C. Brinckerhoff, and Harold C. Wegner, "PTA Strategies: Wyeth, RCE's and the PCT," www.grayonclaims.com, Nov. 19, 2009 (accessed 5/4/10).

84. For descriptions of the negotiations and their resolution, see Matthew Aslett, "Microsoft Blinks First on Interoperability with Red Hat," www.blogs.the 451group.com, Feb. 16, 2009 (accessed 4/4/2010); Ryan Paul, "Red Hat Virtualization Deal a Major Change for Microsoft," www.arstechnica.com, Feb. 17, 2009 (accessed 4/4/2010); Matt Asay, "Microsoft, Red Hat to Interoperate Patent-Free," www.news.cnet.com, Feb. 16, 2009 (accessed 4/4/2010).

85. Chiron Corp. v. Genentech Inc. 363 F.3d 1247 (Fed. Cir. 2004).

86. Ibid., p. 1252.

87. Ibid., p. 1250.

88. Ibid., p. 1252.

89. Ibid.

90. See, e.g., In re Ruschig, 379 F.2d 990 (C.C.P.A. 1967). In Re Ruschig has the following history: an inventor filed a patent on a substance encompassing a group, listing a few examples but not the one eventually at issue. The patent examiner noted an application from another inventor on a similar invention and suggested adding a claim to create an interference between the two. The examiner eventually rejected both as covered by the prior art and was reversed by the C.C.P.A., the predecessor to the Federal Circuit. In the meantime, the parties filed related patents with claims for using the substance to treat diabetes, which themselves become the subject of litigation that related to the original question of whether the substance encompassing the group, as listed in the original application, could be interpreted to sufficiently disclose the example that proved to be the one in the group that the other company had used in its product and invention. The court ruled that the disclosure was insufficient.

91. See New Medium Techs. LLC v. Barco N. V., No. 05 C 5629, 2007 U.S. Dist. LEXIS 47644 (N.D. Ill. July 2, 2007).

92. See New Medium LLC v. Barco N. V., 582 F. Supp. 2d 994–995 (N.D. Ill. 2008).

93. See ibid.

94. Bilski v. Kappos, 130 S. Ct. 3218 (2010).

95. See Michael Crichton, "Patenting Life," The New York Times, Feb. 13, 2007, p. A23; Genomic Research and Accessibility Act, H.R. 977, 110th Congress (2007) (bill sponsored by Rep. Xavier Becerra to prohibit the patenting of human genetic material); Ass'n for Molecular Pathology v. United States PTO, No. 09 Civ. 4515, 2010 U.S. Dist. LEXIS 35418 (S.D.N.Y. Apr. 2, 2010) (finding that Myriad Genetics' BRCA1 and BRCA2 gene patents do not qualify as patentable subject matter under 35 U.S.C. §101).

96. Robert H. Mnookin and Lewis Kornhauser, "Bargaining in the Shadow of the Law: The Case of Divorce," 88 Yale Law Journal 950 (1979).

97. See ibid., pp. 952, 996–997.

98. See ibid., p. 978.

99. I am grateful to Tom Ewing for providing this interesting metaphor.

100. The details in the preceding text are described in an unpublished trial court opinion, Aspex Eyewear Inc. v. Clariti Eyewear Inc., No. 07 Civ. 2373, 2008 U.S. Dist. LEXIS 99433 (S.D.N.Y. Nov. 26, 2008).

101. Failure to follow through on an assertion of patent infringement can be costly to a patent holder given that the later suit may be barred. See, e.g., New Medium v. Barco, 612 F. Supp. 2d 968–969 (holding that the delay of six years barred the suit despite the patent holder's claim to have been engaging in licensing negotiations with the accused infringer and noting that a plaintiff cannot make an unreasonable delay reasonable by continuously harassing the defendant with letters requesting payment).

102. For a good procedural history of the 1999 and 2002 cases, see Revolution Eyewear Inc. v. Aspex Eyewear Inc., 563 F.3d 1363–1364 (Fed. Cir. 2009).

103. See ibid. (citing Aspex Eyewear Inc. v. Revolution Eyewear Inc., No. 99-CV-1263, 2001 U.S. Dist. LEXIS 25831, pp. *1–2 (C.D. Cal. June 4, 2001), aff'd, 42 Fed. Appx. 436 (Fed. Cir. 2002).

104. See ibid. (noting that the lawsuit was filed in 1999 and ended with a summary judgment motion on June 4, 2001, which was summarily affirmed in 2002); U.S. Patent No. RE37,545 (filed Oct. 21, 1998). A reissuance is a voluntary return by the patentee to the patent office within two years to broaden the scope of the patent application to include subject matter that was erroneously omitted from the original patent but is supported by the disclosure.

105. See Revolution v. Aspex, 563 F.3d 1363 (describing the reissue).

106. See ibid.

107. See ibid. Prior to the original 1999 litigation, Revolution had filed for its own patent, an application that was later continued and separated into different patents before issuance. One of those patents served as the basis for Revolution's 2002 lawsuit. Another, which did not issue until 2003 due to continuations, formed the basis of a later suit between the parties. For a description of Revolution's patents and their relationship, see Revolution Eyewear Inc. v. Aspex Eyewear Inc., No. 03-05965, 2004 U.S. Dist. LEXIS 31065, p. *17 (C.D. Cal. Aug. 12, 2004) (unpublished order construing claims of U.S. Patent No. 6,550,913, describing the relationship between the '858 patent and the '913 patent, which formed the basis of the 2003 lawsuit); see also Revolution v. Aspex, 563 F.3d 1363–1364 (describing the 2002 lawsuit involving the '858 patent).

108. See Revolution v. Aspex, 563 F.3d 1363 (describing the counterclaim); U.S. Patent No. RE37,545 (showing date of reissuance). Revolution is certainly not the only company to seek reissuance to counter the effects of a disappointing claim construction. For example, in its press release announcing a reissued patent, one company commented: "This new patent removes the limitation recently im-

posed by the Court of Appeals." See Brady v. Perfect Wall, p. 362; see also Dennis Crouch, "Reissue Claim Is Improperly Broadened If 'Broader in Any Respect,'" www.patentlyo.com, Aug. 17, 2008 (accessed 5/5/10). The timing for such a tactic, however, is critical. See Brady v. Perfect Wall, p. 364 (affirming the district court's invalidation of the reissued patent for enlarging the scope of the claims beyond the two-year statutory limitation).

109. See Revolution v. Aspex, 563 F.3d 1363–1364.

110. See Revolution v. Aspex, 2004 U.S. Dist. LEXIS 31065, p. *18.

111. See Revolution v. Aspex, 563 F.3d 1363–1364.

## 3. Implications of the Bargain Aspect for Current Debates

1. The United States adheres to several multinational treaties that refer to moral rights in the context of copyright and performing rights for singers and actors, including the Berne Convention, the WIPO Copyright Treaty, and the WIPO Performances and Phonograms Treaty. See Berne Convention for the Protection of Literary and Artistic Works, Sept. 9, 1886, as revised at Stockholm on July 14, 1967, 828 U.N.T.S. 222; World Intellectual Property Organization Copyright Treaty, Dec. 20, 1996, S. Treaty Doc. No. 105–17, 2186 U.N.T.S. 121; World Intellectual Property Organization Performances and Phonograms Treaty, Dec. 20, 1996, S. Treaty Doc. No. 105–17, 2186 U.N.T.S. 203.

2. Adam Mossoff, "Who Cares What Thomas Jefferson Thought about Patents? Reevaluating the Patent 'Privilege' in Historical Context," 92 *Cornell Law Review* 953 (2007).

3. Graham v. John Deere Co. of Kan. City, 383 U.S. 9 (1966).

4. For a more extensive discussion of various forms of moral philosophy, see Robin Feldman, "Consumption Taxes and the Theory of General and Individual Taxation," 21 *Virginia Tax Review* 303–314 (2002) (explaining consequentialism and nonconsequentialism in the context of the philosophical roots of modern tax theory). The section also explains other commonly used and sometimes distorted terms in modern legal discourse, including teleological, deontological, and rights-based theories. See ibid., pp. 304 n.16, 311 n.47; see also Amartya Sen and Bernard Williams, *Utilitarianism and Beyond* (Cambridge, UK, 1982), pp. 3–5; Samuel Scheffler, *The Rejection of Consequentialism* (Oxford, 1982), p. 1.

5. See Scheffler, *Rejection of Consequentialism*, pp. 4–5.

6. See Feldman, "Consumption Taxes," p. 304 n.15.

7. See ibid.

8. See William K. Frankena, *Ethics* (Englewood Cliffs, NJ, 1973), p. 15; see also Paul J. Heald and Suzanna Sherry, "Implied Limits on the Legislative Power: The Intellectual Property Clause as an Absolute Constraint on Congress," 200 *University of*

*Illinois Law Review* 1119 (2000); Timothy R. Holbrook, "The Treaty Power and the Patent Clause: Are There Limits on the United States' Ability to Harmonize?" 22 *Cardozo Arts & Entertainment Law Journal* 1 (2004).

9. See ibid., pp. 15–16.

10. See Daniel N. Shaviro, "Inequality, Wealth, and Endowment," 53 *Tax Law Review* 413 (2000).

11. See, e.g., T. M. Scanlon, "Preference and Urgency," 72 *The Journal of Philosophy* 658, 663–664 (1975) (arguing that objective criteria should be used for measuring well-being so that society will not be hijacked by those who have unusually expensive tastes or who attach inordinate importance to minor concerns); see also Ronald Dworkin, *Taking Rights Seriously* (Cambridge, Mass., 1977), p. 234 (describing and criticizing modern utilitarianism).

12. See Mossoff, "Who Cares," p. 476 (criticizing certain modern forms of utilitarianism).

13. See U.S. Const., art. I, §8.

14. See Feldman, "Consumption Taxes," p. 312 (comparing consequentialism and nonconsequentialism and explaining that nonconsequentialism is not merely utilitarianism with the key rights as the desired state of affairs); Robert Nozick, *Anarchy, State, and Utopia* (New York, 1974), pp. 28–29 (explaining that protection of rights is more than merely "utilitarianism of rights").

15. See, e.g., U.S. Patent No. 5,741,957 (filed June 5, 1995); U.S. Patent No. 7,138,562 (filed July 18, 2001).

16. See, e.g., Robert P. Merges and Richard R. Nelson, "On the Complex Economies of Patent Scope," 90 *Columbia Law Review* 844 (1990).

17. Cf. Mark A. Lemley and Carl Shapiro, "Probabilistic Patents," *J. Econ. Persp.* Vol. 19, no 2 (2005), p. 95; Mark A. Lemley, "Rational Ignorance at the Patent Office," 95 *Northwestern University Law Review* 1531 (2001).

18. See James M. Buchanan and Gordon Tullock, *The Calculus of Consent: Logical Foundations of Constitutional Democracy* (Ann Arbor, Michigan, 1965), p. 11–15.

19. 35 U.S.C. §154;

20. See 35 U.S.C. §156;

21. See Frank H. Alpert, "An Analysis of Patent Length: Encouraging Innovation by Shortening Patent Protection," 11 *Journal of Macromarketing* 42 (1991) (providing examples of brands that have become synonymous with their class of product).

22. See David M. Fritch, "Should 'The Purple Pill' by Any Other Drug Company Still Be as Purple? The Changing Face of Trade Dress Protection for Pharmaceutical Manufacturers," 47 *IDEA: The Intellectual Property Law Review* 188 (2006).

23. See Qualitex Co. v. Jacobson Prods. Co. Inc., 514 U.S. 164–165 (1995) (explaining that although product characteristics such as shape and color may be protected

as trade dress, such protection is not available if the shape is a functional aspect of the product because such trademark protection would extend the patent protection indefinitely); see also TrafFix Devices v. Mktg. Displays, 532 U.S. 23 (2001) (finding that where features are claimed in a patent, there is a particularly strong presumption that the features are functional and therefore not subject to trade dress protection). For further discussion on the interaction between patent and trademark law, see Moshe H. Bonder, "Patent & Lanham Acts: Serving Two Legitimate Purposes or Providing an Indefinite Monopoly," 15 *Albany Law Journal of Science & Technology* 1 (2004).

24. See, e.g., Peter N. Golder and Gerard J. Tellis, "Pioneer Advantage: Marketing Logic or Marketing Legend," 30 *Journal of Marketing Research* 158 (1993); Alpert, "Patent Length," pp. 41–42.

25. See discussion in chapter 4.

26. See, e.g., Christian Bessy and Eric Brousseau, "Technology Licensing Contracts: Features and Diversity," 18 *International Review of Law & Economics* 456 (1998).

27. See Robert C. Ellickson, "Riding Herd on Coase's Cattle," 105 *Harvard Law Review* 1141 (1992); see also Merges and Nelson, "Complex Economies," p. 876 (noting that elaborations of Coase's work show that the initial distribution of property rights can make a difference in the equilibrium level of output of the bargaining parties).

28. See the introduction. See also Robin Feldman, *The Role of Science in Law* (Oxford, 2009), p. 3 (discussing the lack of enduring structures in law); H. L. A. Hart, *The Concept of Law* (2d ed. Oxford, 1994), p. 135 (presenting his concept of the "open texture" of law and arguing that although the life of the law consists largely of guidance from determinate rules, at the margin and in the fields left open by precedent, courts perform a rule-producing function that is the same as what is central to administrative bodies); cf. Aristotle, *The Nicomachean Ethics, Book V, Ch. X*, (J. L. Achrell and J. O. Urmon, eds.; David Ross, trans.) (New York, 1998) (discussing the view that general rules cannot decide particular cases and that although general rules reach out to the specific, only practical reason can arrive at the correct results in difficult cases). But compare Ronald Dworkin, *Taking Rights Seriously* (Cambridge, Mass. 1977), pp. 16, 14–45 (criticizing H. L. A. Hart on the grounds that Hart's open texture suggests that judges do as they wish, an approach that appears neither descriptively accurate nor normatively desirable), with Hart, p. 259 (acknowledging some validity in Dworkin's criticisms but arguing that what is valid in the critique can be accommodated without serious consequences for the theory as a whole, on the grounds that the more difficult questions remain relatively open).

29. See Paul McDougall, "How to Avoid the Patent Trap," *InformationWeek*, Oct. 30, 2006, p. 23 ("Before 1990, only one patent damage award larger than $100 million

had been awarded; in the past five years there have been at least 10 judgments and settlements of that size and at least four that topped $500 million. . . .").

30. See, e.g., Sinead Carew, "Microsoft Hit with $1.52 Billion Patent Damage Verdict," www.reuters.com, Feb. 23, 2007 (accessed 7/15/10); Centocor Ortho Biotech Inc. v. Abbott Labs., 669 F. Supp. 2d 756 (E.D. Tex. 2009) ($1.67 billion award).

31. 35 U.S.C. §284.

32. See Panduit Corp. v. Stahlin Bros. Fibre Works Inc., 575 F.2d 1152 (6th Cir. 1978).

33. See e.g., ibid. This is the predominate but not the exclusive framework used by the Federal Circuit to analyze lost profits. See also Gyromat Corp. v. Champion Spark Plug Co., 735 F.2d 549 (Fed Cir 1984).

34. See Panduit Corp. v. Stahlin Bros., pp. 1157–1158; 35 U.S.C. §284. For examples of such cases, see e.g., SmithKline Diagnostics Inc. v. Helena Labs. Corp., 926 F.2d 1164 (Fed. Cir. 1991); Trell v. Marlee Elecs. Corp., 912 F.2d 1445 (Fed. Cir. 1990); Hanson v. Alpine Valley Ski Area Inc., 718 F.2d 1078 (Fed. Cir. 1983).

35. Riles v. Shell Exploration & Prod. Co., 298 F.3d 1311 (Fed. Cir. 2002).

36. Georgia-Pac. Corp. v. U.S. Plywood Corp., 318 F. Supp. 1120 (S.D.N.Y. 1970) *modified sub nom. Georgia-Pac. Corp. v. U.S. Plywood-Champion Papers Inc.,* 446 F.2d 295 (2d Cir. 1971).

37. Fromson v. Western Litho Plate & Supply Co., 853 F.2d 1574 (Fed. Cir. 1988).

38. Daralyn J. Durie and Mark A. Lemley, "A Structured Approach to Calculating Reasonable Royalties," 14 *Lewis & Clark Law Review* 627 (2010); Lucent Techs. Inc. v. Gateway Inc., 580 F.3d 1336 (Fed. Cir. 2009) ("Creating a licensing agreement for patented technology is, at best, an inexact science."); *H.R. 1260: The Patent Reform Act of 2009: Hearing before the House Judiciary Committee,* 111th Congress (2009) (statement of Rep. Conyers, Chairman, House Committee on the Judiciary).

39. NTP Inc. v. Research In Motion Ltd., 418 F.3d 1282 (Fed. Cir. 2005); Research In Motion Ltd. v. NTP Inc., 546 U.S. 1157 (2006) (U.S. Supreme Court certiorari denied).

40. "Settlement Reached in BlackBerry Patent Case: Research In Motion Pays NTP $612.5 Million; Devices to Stay On," www.msnbc.com, Mar. 3, 2006 (accessed (7/14/2010).

41. See *Patent Reform in the Courts and Congress: Hearing before the Senate Committee on the Judiciary,* 111th Congress, 1st Session (Mar. 10, 2009) (testimony of Mark A. Lemley, professor, Stanford Law School).

42. Some scholarship has attributed the problem to the application of concepts from lost profits damages calculation to reasonable royalty damages calculation, such as the "entire market value rule." See Mark A. Lemley, "Distinguishing Lost Profits from Reasonable Royalties," 51 *William & Mary Law Review* 655

(2009). This "entire market value rule" allows the owner of a component invention to capture the entire value of a larger infringing product that unlawfully incorporates its invention. See ibid., p. 659.

43. See Mark A. Lemley and Carl Shapiro, "Patent Holdup and Royalty Stacking," 85 *Texas Law Review* 1991 (2007).

44. See, e.g., Patent Reform Act of 2009, S. 515, S. 610, H.R. 1260, 111th Congress (2009); Patent Reform Act of 2007, H.R. 1908, S. 1145, 110th Congress (2007) (the bills broadly resemble the proposed Patent Reform Act of 2005); Patent Reform Act 2005, H.R. 2795, 109th Congress (2005); see also David W. Opderbeck, "Patent Damages Reform and the Shape of Patent Law," 89 *Boston University Law Review* 135–36 (2009).

45. Compare Patent Reform Act of 2007, H.R. 1908, S. 1145, 110th Congress (2007) (requiring that damages recoverable as a reasonable royalty should be based on the economic value attributable to the patent's specific contribution over the prior art), with Patent Reform Act of 2009, S. 515, S. 610, H.R. 1260, 111th Congress (2009) (requiring that a court identify the methodologies and factors relevant to the determination of damages in writing and with particularity and that courts and juries consider only those methodologies relevant to making such determination). The final patent reform legislation signed into law in 2011 contained no provisions relating to calculating damages. See Leahy-Smith America Invents Act, Pub.L. 1229-29 (Sept. 16, 2011).

46. See IP Innovation L.L.C. v. Red Hat Inc., No. 2:07-cv-447, 2010 U.S. Dist. LEXIS 28372 (E.D. Tex. Mar. 2, 2010) (Rader, J., sitting by designation); see also Zusha Elinson, "Big Tech Shouts 'Yippee!' Patent Bar Chattering as Rader Heads to Texas," *The Recorder,* Mar. 15, 2010.

47. Cornell Univ. v. Hewlett-Packard Co., 609 F. Supp. 2d 279 (N.D.N.Y 2009) (Rader, J., sitting by designation).

48. i4i Ltd. P'ship v. Microsoft Corp., 598 F.3d 831 (Fed. Cir. 2010) (upholding lower court expert testimony, as well as a judge's decision to add $40 million to the original $200 verdict).

## 4. Where Do Processes of Nature End and Processes of Human Inventions Begin?

1. Diamond v. Chakrabarty, 447 U.S. 309 (1980) (citing legislative language). For example, the following courts use the quote to suggest that patentable subject matter is quite broad and that everything under the sun made by human beings is eligible for patent protection: State St. Bank & Trust Co. v. Signature Fin. Group, 149 F.3d 1373 (Fed. Cir. 1998), abrogated by In re Bilski, 545 F.3d 943 (Fed. Cir. 2008) (en banc), aff'd sub nom. Bilski v. Kappos, 130 S. Ct. 3218 (2010); AT&T

Corp. v. Excel Communs., 172 F.3d 1355 (Fed. Cir. 1999), abrogated by In re Bilski, 545 F.3d 943; Ex parte Allen, 2 U.S.P.Q.2D 1427 (B.P.A.I. 1987); Ex parte Hibberd, 227 U.S.P.Q. 444 (B.P.A.I. 1985).

2. See S. Rep. No. 82–1979 (1952), p. 5, reprinted in 1952 U.S.C.C.A.N. 2399; H.R. Rep. No. 82–1923 (1952), p. 6, reprinted in 1952 U.S.C.C.A.N. 2399 (language in square brackets added); see also In re Bilski, p. 1000 (Mayer, J., dissenting) (noting that although the quote is used to suggest that Congress intended anything under the sun to be patentable, the legislative history says no such thing).

3. See William C. Robinson, *The Law of Patents for Useful Inventions,* vol. 1 (Boston, Mass., 1890), p. 101 n.2 (discussing an 1862 case related to methods of eye surgery, Morton v. New York Eye Infirmary, 17 F. Cas. 879 (C.C.S.D.N.Y. 1862) (No. 9,865)).

4. Categories of proper subject matter are described in the Patent Act as including machines, compositions of matter, manufactures, and processes. 35 U.S.C. §101. Categories excluded from proper subject matter are described in the courts as laws of nature, natural phenomena, mathematical formulas, mental steps, and abstract ideas. Gottschalk v. Benson, 409 U.S. 67 (1972).

5. U.S. Const. art. 1, §8, cl. 8.

6. See Graham v. John Deere Co. of Kan. City, 383 U.S. 5 (1966) (discussing the constitutional language and noting that the clause is both a grant of power and a limitation).

7. A number of authors, however, argue in favor of the general proposition that the constitutional clause on the whole or other parts can be read as a limitation. See, e.g., Dotan Oliar, "Making Sense of the Intellectual Property Clause: Promotion of Progress as a Limitation on Congress's Intellectual Property Power," 94 *Georgetown Law Journal* 1771 (2006); Alan L. Durham, "'Useful Arts' in the Information Age," 1999 *Brigham Young University Law Review* 1424–1430 (1999); Cynthia M. Ho, "Who Deserves the Patent Pot of Gold?: An Inquiry into the Proper Inventorship of Patient-Based Discoveries," 7 *DePaul Journal of Health Care Law* 240–242.

8. Feist Publ'n Inc. v. Rural Tel. Serv. Co. Inc., 499 U.S. 347 (1991) (ruling that telephone numbers do not meet the constitutional requirements for copyright protection).

9. See O'Reilly v. Morse, 56 U.S. (15 How.) 116 (1853) (finding "the discovery of a principle in natural philosophy or physical science" is not patentable."); Le Roy v. Tatham 55 U.S. (14 How.) 174–175 (1852) (dicta in case concerning lead pipe).

10. Le Roy v. Tatham, pp. 174–175.

11. Funk Bros. Seed Co. v. Kalo Inoculant Co., 333 U.S. 130 (1948); see also Diamond v. Diehr, 450 U.S. 187–188 (1981) (noting that the invention is patentable because it applies laws of nature to a specific application); Mackay Radio & Tel. Co. v.

Radio Corp. of America, 306 U.S. 94 (1939) ("While a scientific truth, or the mathematical expression of it, is not [a] patentable invention, a novel and useful structure created with the aid of knowledge of scientific truth may be."); In re Alappat 33 F.3d 1542–1543 (Fed. Cir. 1994) (arguing that when an abstract concept has no claimed practical application, it is not patentable); Robinson, *Law of Patents*, p. 116 (noting that an unapplied idea is not an invention).

12. Ex parte Bilski and Warsaw, No. 2002–2257, 2006 Pat. App. LEXIS 51, pp. *12–13 (B.P.A.I. Sept. 26, 2006) (citing Ex parte Lundgren, 76 U.S.P.Q.2D 1393–1394 (2005); and Durham, "Useful Arts," pp. 1431–1437).

13. See Brunswick Corp. v. U.S., 34 Fed. Cl. 584 (1995). See also Manual of Patent Examination Procedure §2138.05 (2008).

14. See, e.g., Diamond v. Chakrabarty, p. 309 (noting that laws of nature, physical phenomena, and abstract ideas are "manifestations of . . . nature, free to all men and reserved exclusively to none" (citing Funk Bros. Seed v. Kalo Inoculant, p. 130)); Gottschalk v. Benson, p. 67 (same); Le Roy v. Tatham, p. 175 (same).

15. Ariad Pharms. Inc. v. Eli Lilly & Co., 598 F.3d 1353 (Fed. Cir. 2010) (en banc). See also PharmaStem Therapeutics Inc. v. Viacell Inc., 491 F.3d 1363–1364 (Fed. Cir. 2007); Robinson, *Law of Patents*, p. 101 n.2.

16. See Robinson, *Law of Patents*, p. 105 & n.2.

17. See ibid., p. 104 n.1 (describing the English case, Edgebury v. Stephens, 2 Salk. 447 (1691), for the proposition that "whether learned by travel or by study it is the same thing").

18. See Gottschalk v. Benson, p. 67 ("Phenomena of nature, though just discovered, mental processes, and abstract intellectual concepts are not patentable, as they are the basic tools of scientific and technological work.").

19. Funk Bros. Seed v. Kalo Inoculant, p. 130 (citation omitted) (quoted in Diamond v. Chakrabarty, p. 309).

20. O'Reilly v. Morse, p. 113.

21. In Lab. Corp. of Am. Holdings v. Metabolite Labs Inc., 548 U.S. 124 (2006), discussed in detail later, Lab. Corp. argued that the lower court, the Federal Circuit, had essentially held "that a doctor infringes the Patent merely by looking at a test result and *thinking* in his or her mind that there is an 'association of homocysteine levels with vitamin deficiencies,'" whereas "a valid process patent must claim something more than thinking about a natural phenomenon or law of nature." Brief for Petitioner, pp. 13, 22–23, Lab. Corp. v. Metabolite, 548 U.S. 124 (No. 04–607), 2005 WL 3543099 (quoting Metabolite Labs. Inc. v. Lab. Corp. of Am. Holdings, 370 F.3d 1354 (Fed. Cir. 2004)). Compare Plaintiffs' Memorandum of Law in Support of Motion for Summary Judgment, pp. 33–35, Ass'n for Molecular Pathology v. United States PTO, 94 U.S.P.Q.2D (BNA) 1683 (S.D.N.Y. 2010) (No. 09 Civ. 4515), 2009 WL 3269113 (arguing that patents should

not be granted in subject matter in a way that would impinge on First Amendment freedoms of thought and knowledge).

22. See, e.g., Stanley v. Georgia, 394 U.S. 566 (1969) (in discussing the First Amendment, "Whatever the power of the state to control public dissemination of ideas inimical to the public morality, it cannot constitutionally premise legislation on the desirability of controlling a person's private thoughts."); Griswold v. Connecticut, 381 U.S. 482 (1965) ("The right of freedom of speech and press includes not only the right to utter or to print, but . . . freedom of inquiry, freedom of thought. . . .") (citation omitted); Ashcroft v. Free Speech Coalition, 535 U.S. 253 (2002) ("First Amendment freedoms are most in danger when the government seeks to control thought or to justify its laws for that impermissible end. The right to think is the beginning of freedom, and speech must be protected from the government because speech is the beginning of thought.").

23. See, e.g., Michael Risch, "Everything Is Patentable," 75 *Tennessee Law Review* 591 (2008); see also Brief of Amicus Curiae of 22 Law and Business Professors in Support of Appellants, pp. 21–25, In re Bilski, 545 F.3d 943 (No. 2007–1130), 2008 WL 1842281.

24. Ariad v. Lilly, 598 F.3d 1336.

25. See ibid., p. 1358.

26. See Robin Feldman, "The Inventor's Contribution," 2005 *UCLA Journal of Law & Technology* 6, ¶¶24–34 (2005) (discussing the written description requirement as a safeguard against overreaching by inventors in the context of Regents of Univ. of Cal. v. Eli Lilly & Co., 119 F.3d 1559 (Fed. Cir. 1997) and Enzo Biochem. Inc. v. Gen-Probe Inc., 296 F.3d 1316 (Fed. Cir. 2002)).

27. See Lab. Corp. v. Metabolite, 548 U.S. 124 (2006).

28. See ibid., p. 129 (quoting the claim language).

29. See Michael Meehan, "The Handiwork of Nature: Patentable Subject Matter and Laboratory Corporation v. Metabolite Labs," 16 *Albany Law Journal of Science & Technology* 317 (2006).

30. See Brief for the American Medical Association et al., Lab. Corp. v. Metabolite, 548 U.S. 124 (No. 04–607), 2005 WL 3597812.

31. See Brief for Amici Curiae Perlegen Sciences Inc. and Mohr, Davidow Ventures in Support of Respondents, p. 11, Lab. Corp. v. Metabolite, 548 U.S. 124 (No. 04–607), 2006 WL 303908.

32. See Philip McGarrigle and Vern Norviel, "Laws of Nature and the Business of Biotechnology," 24 *Santa Clara Computer & High Technology Law Journal* 302–303 (2008) (describing the types of claims that one might expect to survive scrutiny given the patents granted).

33. See In re Prater, 415 F.2d. 1378, 1402 n.21 (1968), modified on rehearing, 415 F.2d. 1393 (1969); see also Diamond v. Diehr, pp. 198–199 (Stevens, J., dissenting) (describing *Prater*).

34. See Brief for the United States as Amicus Curiae, p. 19, Lab. Corp. v. Metabolite, 548 U.S. 124 (No. 04–607), 2005 WL 2072283.

35. See Lab. Corp. v. Metabolite, pp. 135–138 (Breyer, J., dissenting).

36. William Shakespeare, *Hamlet,* act 2, scene 2.

37. See Vincent Chiappetta, "Patentability of Computer Software Instruction as an 'Article of Manufacture': Software as Such as the Right Stuff," 17 *John Marshall Journal of Computer & Information Law* 106–107 (1998); David L. Bohan, "Note: Computer Programs: Abstract Ideas or Patentable Subject Matter?" 29 *Suffolk University Law Review* 817 (1995); see also Diamond v. Diehr, pp. 194–195 (Stevens, J., dissenting).

38. Thomas H. Cormen, Charles E. Leiserson, Ronald L. Rivest, and Clifford Stein, *Introduction to Algorithms* (Cambridge, Mass., 2003), p. 5.

39. Gottschalk v. Benson, 409 U.S. 63 (1972).

40. See ibid., p. 65.

41. BCD stands for binary-coded decimal.

42. See Gottschalk v. Benson, p. 65.

43. See ibid., pp. 69, 72 (noting that, if upheld, "the patent would wholly pre-empt the mathematical formula and in practical effect would be a patent on the algorithm itself").

44. See ibid., p. 64.

45. See ibid., p. 70 (emphasis added).

46. See ibid., p. 71.

47. Parker v. Flook, 437 U.S. 584 (1978).

48. See Karim Nice and Charles W. Bryant, "How Catalytic Converters Work," www.howstuffworks.com (accessed 6/11/10).

49. See Parker v. Flook, p. 594.

50. See ibid.

51. See ibid.

52. See Cormen et al., *Introduction to Algorithms,* p. 5.

53. See ibid., pp. 5, 9.

54. See ibid., pp. 10–11.

55. See Diamond v. Diehr, pp. 185–187 (using all three terms); Gottschalk v. Benson, pp. 71–72 (using the terms "mathematical formula" and "algorithm").

56. In re Alappat, 33 F.3d 1543 (Fed. Cir. 1994).

57. See Diamond v. Diehr, 450 U.S. 175 (1981). The description of the invention in the following text is taken from the case on pp. 177–179.

58. See ibid., p. 177.

59. Ibid., p. 187.

60. Ibid., pp. 192, 188 (describing the need to determine patentable subject matter by looking at the claims as a whole).

61. See ibid., p. 193.

62. See Diamond v. Diehr, p. 209 (Stevens, J., dissenting).

63. See In re Maucorps, 609 F.2d 481 (C.C.P.A. 1979).

64. See In re Meyer, 688 F.2d 789 (C.C.P.A. 1982).

65. See Hotel Security Checking Co. v. Lorraine Co., 160 F. 467 (2d Cir. 1908).

66. See State St. Bank & Trust Co. v. Signature Fin. Group Inc., 149 F 3d 1368 (Fed. Cir. 1998).

67. Compare In re Bilski, 545 F.3d 989 (Fed. Cir. 2008) (en banc) (Newman, J., dissenting), aff'd sub nom. Bilski v. Kappos, 130 S. Ct. 3218 (2010); Risch, "Everything Is Patentable," p. 610; with In re Bilski, pp. 998–1001 (Mayer, J., dissenting); see also Malla Pollack, "The Multiple Unconstitutionality of Business Method Patents: Common Sense, Congressional Consideration, and Constitutional History," 28 *Rutgers Computer & Technology Law Journal* 90 (2002); Rochelle C. Dreyfuss, "Are Business Method Patents Bad for Business?" 16 *Santa Clara Computer & High Technology Law Journal* 265–266 (2000). But see Durham, "Useful Arts," p. 1437 (describing the historic materials but noting that, in the end, such historical information takes us only so far).

68. See In re Bilski, p. 1004 (Mayer, J., dissenting) (listing the patents described in the following sentence in the text).

69. U.S. Patent No. 5,851,117 (filed Apr. 23, 1997).

70. U.S. Patent No. 5,862,223 (filed July 24, 1996).

71. U.S. Patent No. 6,119,099 (filed Mar. 5, 1999).

72. U.S. Patent No. 7,255,277 (filed Apr. 6, 2006).

73. U.S. Patent No. 6,329,919 (filed Aug. 14, 1999).

74. Gottschalk v. Benson, pp. 69–70.

75. Diamond v. Diehr, p. 181.

76. See Gottschalk v. Benson, p. 71 (explaining the following: "It is argued that a process patent must either be tied to a particular machine or apparatus or must operate to change articles or materials to a 'different state or thing.' We do not hold that no process patent could ever qualify if it did not meet the requirements of our prior precedents.").

77. In re Alappat, p. 1541.

78. See Jed Lengyel, Mark Reichert, Bruce R. Donald, and Donald P. Greenberg, "Real-Time Robot Motion Planning Using Rasterizing Computer Graphics Hardware," *Proceedings of the 17th Annual Conference on Computer Graphics and Interactive Techniques* (Dallas, Tex., 1990), pp. 327–335; U.S. Patent No. 4,688,167 (filed Sept. 27, 1984).

79. In re Alappat, p. 1544.

80. State St. v. Signature Fin., p. 1373. The "useful, concrete, and tangible" test replaced an earlier muddle known as the Freeman-Walter-Abele test, which had been in place for sixteen years. The Freeman-Walter-Abele test is a two-part

test that asks whether a claim recites an algorithm and, if so, whether the algorithm is applied to a process step or physical element. See In re Freeman, 573 F.2d 1237 (C.C.P.A. 1978); In re Walter, 618 F.2d 758 (C.C.P.A. 1980); In re Abele, 684 F.2d 902 (C.C.P.A. 1982). The Freeman-Walter-Abele test was explicitly rejected in *Bilski,* although the test had rarely been used after *Alappat* and *State Street.* See In re Bilski, 545 F.3d 959. Other tests the courts have developed and discarded include the "technological arts test," which requires a nexus between the claimed invention and the technological arts. *Bilski* stated that the terms "technology" and "technology arts" were too vague to provide the test with sufficient contours. See ibid., p. 959.

81. See 35 U.S.C. §101 (relating to a "new and useful process"); Donald S. Chisum, *Chisum on Patents,* vol. 1, §§1.01, 4.01 (2010) (interpreting usefulness as a separate requirement from utility). But see Manual of Patent Examination Procedure §2107 (2008) (suggesting that the two requirements are identical and that a patent application that fails one will fail the other).

82. Ass'n for Molecular Pathology v. U.S. Patent & Trademark Office, 702 F. Supp. 2d 219 (S.D.N.Y. 2010), as amended (Apr. 5, 2010) (citing *Application of Bergy,* 596 F.2d 960 (C.C.P.A. 1979)).

83. State St. v. Signature Fin., p. 1373.

84. See In re Alappat, p. 1561.

85. In re Bilski, 545 F.3d 959–960.

86. Matthew D. Show, "A Dreadful Prognosis: Patentability of Diagnostic and Personalized Medical Procedures in the Wake of *In re Bilski,*" 2 *Hastings Science & Technology Law Journal* 316 (2010); see also U.S. Patent Application 08/833,892 (filed Apr. 10, 1997).

87. See In re Bilski, p. 953 (citing Diamond v. Diehr, p. 187).

88. See In re Bilski, p. 954 (citing Gottschalk v. Benson, p. 70; Diamond v. Diehr, p. 192).

89. See In re Bilski, p. 957 (citing Diamond v. Diehr, pp. 191–192).

90. See In re Bilski, p. 962 (citing Gottschalk v. Benson, p. 70).

91. For a slightly different analysis see Stefania Fusco's "Is In re Bilski a *Déjà Vu?*" *Stanford Technology Law Review* P1 (reiterating Judge Newman and Judge Rader's point that much of today's innovation is not always directly linked to a physical object and that in many of today's new inventions, determining whether the nature of an invention is physical or nonphysical is not a simple matter).

92. In re Bilski, p. 957.

93. Robin Feldman and Deborah Furth, "The Intellectual Property Landscape for iPS Cells," 3 *Stanford Journal of Law, Science & Policy* 16 (2010).

94. See Prometheus Labs Inc. v. Mayo Collaborative Servs., 581 F.3d 1336 (Fed. Cir. 2009).

95. See U.S. Patent No. 6,680,302, Fig. 3 and Examples I, II, and III (filed Dec. 27, 2001).

96. See Prometheus v. Mayo, p. 1343. Although the patent holder could have argued that data representing the drug metabolite (i.e., a physical object) was transformed into a result that had therapeutic meaning, having a true physical transformation was seen as being a "slam dunk" as far as post-*Bilski* patent eligibility was concerned. Numerous amicus briefs from stakeholders in the area of personalized medicine also argued that the metabolism of drugs constituted a physical transformation.

97. Prometheus v. Mayo, p. 1346.

98. In re Alappat, pp. 1557–1558.

99. See ibid., p. 1544.

100. See, e.g., U.S. Patent and Trademark Office, "Office Action," Application No. 11/338,957 (Mar. 3, 2010), pp. 4–6.

101. See In re Grams, 888 F.2d 835 (Fed. Cir. 1989).

102. See Prometheus Labs Inc. v. Mayo Collaborative Servs., 628 F.3d 1347, 1358 (Fed. Cir. 2010) (on remand) (discussing *In re Grams).*

103. Ibid.

104. See Robin Feldman, "Whose Body Is It Anyway? Human Cells and the Strange Effects of Property and Intellectual Property Law," [hereinafter "Whose Body Is It Anyway"] 63 *Stanford. L. Rev.* 1377 (2011).

105. See In re Bilski, pp. 952–953, 957.

106. Bilski v. Kappos, 130 S. Ct. 3218 (2010).

107. Ibid., p. 3226.

108. Ibid., p. 3231 (full citation to *State Street* and additional case citation omitted).

109. Ibid.

110. Mayo Collaborative Servs. v. Prometheus Labs Inc., 130 S. Ct. 3543 (2010)

111. Prometheus Labs Inc. v. Mayo Collaborative Servs., 628 F.3d 1347 (Fed. Cir. 2010).

112. Ibid., p. 1355.

113. Metabolite v. Lab. Corp., 370 F.3d 1358–1359.

114. Ariad v. Lilly, p. 1336.

115. See ibid., pp. 1340–1341 (describing claims "encompassing the use of all substances that achieve the desired result of reducing the binding of NF-[K]B to NF-[K]B recognition sites").

116. "Aspirin: Questions and Answers," www.fda.gov (accessed 6/19/10).

117. In re Comiskey, 499 F.3d 1365 (Fed. Cir. 2007).

118. See ibid., pp. 1368–1370.

119. See ibid., p. 1378.

120. Classen Immunotherapies Inc. v. Biogen IDEC, 304 Fed. Appx. 866 (Fed. Cir. 2008).

121. See Classen Immunotherapies Inc. v. Biogen IDEC, No. WDQ-04-2607, 2006 U.S. Dist. LEXIS 98106, pp. *13–15 (D. Md. Aug. 16, 2006) (discussing the content

of U.S. Patent No. 6,520,139, U.S. Patent No. 6,638,739, and U.S. Patent No. 5,723,283).

122. See Classen v. Biogen, 304 Fed. Appx. 866 (Fed. Cir. 2008).

123. One scholar has suggested that even *LabCorp* could have survived as patentable subject matter if the claims drafter had chosen a narrower description. See Patricia Dyck, "Post-Bilski Personalized Medicine: At Home on the Range" (forthcoming) (manuscript on file with author) (presenting an empirical survey of the most frequently claimed biomarkers in personalized medicine and discussing problems in allowing claims for sets of biomarkers that are small and not limited to the diagnosis of a specific disease state or condition).

124. I have discussed some of the misconceptions described here in the context of patenting genes. See Feldman, "Whose Body Is It Anyway?" 1400–1402.

125. One could easily argue that all math is invented. It is a human-made method of imposing order and structure on the natural world. For an interesting and accessible discussion of Wittgenstein's view that all mathematics is a human invention and various responses to that argument, see Ludwig Wittgenstein, *Wittgenstein's Philosophy of Mathematics* §3.1, http://plato.stanford.edu/entries/wittgenstein-mathematics.

126. Diamond v. Diehr, p. 191 (citation omitted).

127. See, e.g., In re Bilski, p. 957 (noting that mere field-of-use limitations are generally insufficient to render an otherwise ineligible process claim patent eligible).

128. Bilski v. Kappos, p. 3231.

## 5. The Interaction of Patents with Contracts and Antitrust

1. For a more detailed history of patent misuse from its inception to modern case law see Robin Feldman, "The Insufficiency of Antitrust Analysis for Patent Misuse," 55 *Hastings Law Journal* 399 (2003); see also Robin Feldman, "Patent and Antitrust: Differing Shades of Meaning," 13 *Virginia Journal of Law & Technology* 5 (2008).

2. See Feldman, "Patent and Antitrust," ¶¶1, 8–9 (describing the dilemma and noting that antitrust law does not forbid monopoly, only monopolization, and that patent law does not grant monopoly, only the possibility of obtaining a monopoly in the relevant market).

3. See Henry v. A. B. Dick Co., 224 U.S. 29–30 (1912) (commenting in dicta that in a patent infringement case, the general rule is absolute freedom in relation to the terms imposed on users, while in a suit to recover contract damages, one could defend on grounds that the contract was against public policies such as the antitrust laws), overruled on other grounds by Motion Picture Patents Co. v. Universal Film Mfg., Co., 243 U.S. 514–18 (1917); Strait v. National Harrow Co.,

51 F. 820 (C.C.D.N.Y. 1892) (arguing that if a patent holder sued for breach of contract, a court could examine the nature of the agreement, while in a suit for patent infringement, a court could not).

4. See Fritz Machlup, *An Economic Review of the Patent System, Study of the Subcommittee on Patents, Trademarks, and Copyrights of the Committee on the Judiciary, United States Senate, 85th Cong., 2d Sess., Study No. 15* (Washington, D.C., 1958), p. 11 n.56 (citing Hearings before the Senate Committee on Patents on S. 2303 and S. 2491, pt. 3, p. 1318 (1942)); see also United States v. Gen. Elec. Co., 272 U.S. 476 (1926) (upholding price-fixing agreement in the context of a patent license).

5. See Carbice Corp. of Am. v. Am. Patents Dev. Corp., 283 U.S. 27 (1931); Int'l Salt Co. v. United States, 332 U.S. 392 (1947); Mercoid Corp. v. Mid-Continent Inv. Co., 320 U.S. 661 (1944); United States v. Masonite, p. 265 ; Morton Salt Co. v. G. S. Suppiger Co., 314 U.S. 488 (1942), overruled on other grounds by Ill. Tool Works Inc. v. Indep. Ink Inc., 547 U.S. 28 (2006).

6. See Gideon Parchomovsky and R. Polk Wagner, "Patent Portfolios," 154 *University of Pennsylvania Law Review* 5 & n.3, 14–15 (2005).

7. See Windsurfing Int'l. Inc. v. AMF Inc., 782 F.2d 1001 (Fed. Cir. 1986) (emphasis added).

8. See ibid., pp. 1001–1002.

9. See Blonder-Tongue Lab. v. Univ. of Ill. Found., 402 U.S. 313 (1971); see also Robert J. Hoerner, "The Decline (and Fall?) of the Patent Misuse Doctrine in the Federal Circuit," 69 *Antitrust Law Journal* 672–673 (2002) (noting that the citation of *Blonder-Tongue* after the words "with anticompetitive effect" could be regarded as misleading); Patricia A. Martone and Richard M. Feustel Jr., "The Patent Misuse Defense—Does It Still Have Viability?" 708 *PLI Patents, Copyrights, Trademarks, and Literary Property Course Handbook Series* 250 (2002) (noting that the antitrust-type findings required in *Windsurfing* are not required by Supreme Court precedent).

10. See Windsurfing v. AMF, p. 1001.

11. See ibid., pp. 1001–1002.

12. See Senza-Gel Corp. v. Seiffhart, 803 F.2d 665 n.5 (Fed. Cir. 1986) (full internal citation omitted). For a modern scholarly perspective questioning the logic of the patent misuse doctrine, see Cotter, Thomas F., "Four Questionable Rationales for the Patent Misuse Doctrine," Minnesota Legal Studies Research Paper No. 10–30 (2010).

13. For a detailed description of the path of the 1988 act, see Kenneth J. Burchfiel, "Patent Misuse and Antitrust Reform: 'Blessed Be the Tie?' " 4 *Harvard Journal of Law & Technology* 2 n.9 (1991). See also Feldman, "Insufficiency," pp. 418–421.

14. The final language of the 1988 act is codified as 35 U.S.C. §271(d)(5).

15. See Mallinckrodt v. Medipart Inc., 976 F.2d 706 (Fed. Cir. 1992).

16. See ibid.

17. See, e.g., Feldman, "Insufficiency," pp. 447–449 (discussing patent misuse implications of reach-through royalties); Princo Corp. v. ITC, 563 F.3d 1301 (Fed. Cir. 2009) (the Federal Circuit Panel decision now being reviewed en banc has allegations of patent misuse based on using a standard agreement involving one patented technology to suppress a potentially competing product).

18. Quanta Computer Inc. v. LG Elecs. Inc., 553 U.S. 617, 128 S.Ct. 2109 (2008). For a detailed history of patent misuse and a criticism of its application in *Quanta* see Herbert Hovenkamp, "Post-Sale Restrictions & Competitive Harms: The First Sale Doctrine," 66 *N.Y.U. Ann. Surv. Am. L.* 487 (2011).

19. See Donald S. Chisum, *Chisum on Patents*, vol. 6, §19.04[3][h] (2010).

20. See Am. Cotton-Tie Co. v. Simmons, 106 U.S. 89 (1882); "Note: Patent Use Restrictions," 75 *Harvard Law Review* 606 (1962). For a discussion tracing the first-sale doctrine through Supreme Court and lower court decisions, see Robin Feldman, "The Open Source Biotechnology Movement: Is It Patent Misuse?" 6 *Minnesota Journal of Law, Science & Technology* 147–153 (2004).

21. See Brief Amicus Curiae of Computer & Communications Industry Ass'n in Support of Petitioners, pp. 4–5, Quanta v. LG Elecs., 553 U.S. 617 (No. 06–937), 2007 WL 3407026 (arguing that without the exhaustion doctrine markets and competition could be harmed by those who try to control patents and products after they have been sold).

22. See Mallinckrodt v. Medipart, p. 708 (discussing early Supreme Court cases including Adams v. Burke, 84 U.S. 453 (1874); Bloomer v. McQuewan, 55 U.S. 539 (1852); and Mitchell v. Hawley, 83 U.S. 544 (1973)). See also Erin J. D. Austin, "Note: Reconciling the Patent Exhaustion and Conditional Sale Doctrines in Light of Quanta Computer v. LG Electronics," 30 *Cardozo Law Review* 2968 & n.133; See, e.g., Richard H. Stern, "The Unobserved Demise of the Exhaustion Doctrine in US Patent Law: Mallinckrodt v. Medipart," 15 *European Intellectual Property Review* 461 (1993); Mark R. Patterson, "Contractual Expansion of the Scope of Patent Infringement through Field-of-Use Licensing," 49 *William & Mary Law Review* 167 (2007); Harold C. Wegner, "Post-Quanta, Post-Sale Patentee Controls," 7 *John Marshall Review of Intellectual Property Law* 688.

23. Quanta v. LG Elecs., p. 2113.

24. Ibid.

25. See MedImmune Inc. v. Genentech Inc., 549 U.S. 118 (2007). See, e.g., Microsoft Corp. v. AT&T Corp., 550 U.S. 437 (2007) (limiting extraterritorial reach of patents); KSR Int'l Co. v. Teleflex Inc., 550 U.S. 398 (2007) (raising the bar for demonstrating that an invention is nonobvious); eBay Inc. v. MercExchange, L.L.C., 547 U.S. 388 (2006) (rejecting the rule that patent infringement should always lead to an injunction); Merck KGaA v. Integra LifeSciences I Ltd., 545 U.S. 193

(2005) (expanding the research exemption to infringement for research related to government submissions).

26. Quanta v. LG Elecs., p. 2122 n.7.

27. For examples of single-party behavior using leveraging to block nascent technology and protect existing market power see Robin Feldman, "Defensive Leveraging in Antitrust," 87 *Georgetown Law Journal* 2079 (1999).

28. See, e.g., Zenith Radio Corp. v. Hazeltine Research Inc., 395 U.S. 100 (1969) (finding no patent misuse in a breach of contract case); Brulotte v. Thys (379 U.S. 29 (1965) (invalidating licensing contract on grounds of misuse).

29. See MedImmune v. Genentech, pp. 134–135 (Thomas, J., dissenting).

30. See U.S. Const., art. III, §2, cl. 1 (providing that federal courts are not permitted to hear cases that do not present an actual controversy). For a discussion of the case and controversy requirement and an exploration of how the lower courts have applied *MedImmune* since its passage see David I. Levine and Charles E. Belle, "Declaratory Relief after MedImmune," 14 *Lewis & Clark Law Review* 491 (2010). For an extensive exploration of the history of case law leading to *MedImmune* and its implications for common law, implied-licensee estoppel and explicit contractual provisions see Alfred C. Server and Peter Singleton, "Licensee Patent Validity Challenges following *MedImmune:* Implications for Patent Licensing" (forthcoming) (manuscript on file with author).

31. See Levine and Belle, "After *MedImmune*," p. 493.

32. MedImmune Inc. v. Genentech Inc., 549 U.S. 118 (2007).

33. MedImmune v. Genentech, 427 F.3d 961 (Fed. Cir. 2005); see also Gen-Probe Inc. v. Vysis Inc., 359 F.3d 1376 (Fed. Cir. 2004).

34. See ibid. (noting that infringement may have resulted in MedImmune's being enjoined from selling Synagis, which accounted for 80% of its sales revenue since 1999).

35. See ibid., p. 137.

36. See ibid., pp. 129–131.

37. See ibid., p. 129; see also, e.g., Terrace v. Thompson, 263 U.S. 197 (1923); Steffel v. Thompson, 415 U.S. 459 (1974); ibid., p. 480 (Rehnquist, J., concurring).

38. See MedImmune v. Genentech, p. 130 (citing Keener Oil & Gas Co. v. Consolidated Gas Utils. Corp., 190 F.2d 985 (10th Cir. 1951); Am. Machine & Metals Inc. v. De Bothezat Impeller Co., 166 F.2d 535 (2d Cir. 1948); Hess v. Country Club Park, 213 Cal. 613 (1931); and Washington-Detroit Theatre Co. v. Moore, 249 Mich. 673 (1930)).

39. See MedImmune v. Genentech, p. 132 (citing Frederic Woodward, *The Law of Quasi Contracts* (Boston, Mass., 1913), p. 218) (cited in Altvater v. Freeman, 319 U.S. 365 (1943).

40. See MedImmune v. Genentech, p. 129.

41. See, e.g., Server and Singleton, "Licensee Patent Validity."

42. See, e.g., Wilder v. Adams, 29 F. Cas. 1217–1218 (C.C.D. Mass. 1846) (describing the concept in both contract-law and property-law terms).

43. See ibid., p. 1217 (cited in Kinsman v. Parkhurst, 59 U.S. (18 How.) 289 (1856)).

44. See Wilder v. Adams, p. 1217.

45. See William C. Rooklidge, "Licensee Validity Challenges and the Obligation to Pay Accrued Royalties: *Lear v. Adkins* Revisited (Part I)" 68 *Journal of the Patent & Trademark Office Society* 511 (1986).

46. See Server and Singleton, "Licensee Patent Validity," p. 29.

47. See, e.g., H. Tibbe & Son Mfg. Co. v. Heineken, 37 F. 686 (1889); Kinsman v. Parkhurst, 59 U.S. 289; see also Server and Singleton, "Licensee Patent Validity," pp. 21–52 (describing the case history of licensee estoppel).

48. See MacGregor v. Westinghouse Elec. & Mfg. Co., 329 U.S. 402 (1947).

49. See Sola Elec. v. Jefferson Elec., p. 173 (finding that a license holder was not estopped by virtue of his license from "challeng[ing] a price-fixing clause in the agreement by showing that the patent is invalid, and that the price restriction is accordingly unlawful because not protected by the patent monopoly").

50. Lear Inc. v. Adkins, 395 U.S. 653 (1969).

51. Ibid., p. 664.

52. See ibid., 671 (repudiating Automatic Radio v. Hazeltine, 339 U.S. 827 (1950)); ibid., pp. 675–676 (reversing the California Supreme Court decision).

53. Ibid., p. 670.

54. See Server and Singleton, "Licensee Patent Validity," pp. 81–157 (describing the potential argument in depth).

55. See William C. Rooklidge, "Licensee Validity Challenges and the Obligation to Pay Accrued Royalties: *Lear v. Adkins* Revisited (Part I)," 68 *Journal of the Patent & Trademark Office Society* 527–528 (1986); see also Brief for the American Bar Association as Amicus Curiae Supporting Respondents, p. 5, MedImmune v. Genentech, 549 U.S. 118 (No. 05–608), 2006 WL 2091230.

56. See Server and Singleton, "Licensee Patent Validity," pp. 158–160; Brief for the United States as Amicus Curiae Supporting Petitioner, pp. 29–30, MedImmune v. Genentech, 549 U.S. 118 (No. 05–608), 2006 WL 1327303.

57. See ibid., pp. 134–135 (describing the patent holder's failed argument).

58. Lear v. Adkins, p. 673.

59. See, e.g., Panther Pumps & Equipment Co. Inc. v. Hydrocraft Inc., 468 F.2d 225 (7th Cir. 1972); Bendix Corp. v. Balax Inc., 471 F.2d 149 (7th Cir. 1972); Blohm & Voss v. Prudential-Grace Lines Inc., 346 F. Supp. 1116 (D. Md. 1972), reversed on other grounds in 489 F.2d 231 (4th Cir. 1973); Congoleum Indus. Inc. v. Armstrong Cork Co., 366 F. Supp. 220 (E.D. Pennsylvania 1973).

60. See Christian Chadd Taylor, "No-Challenge Termination Clauses: Incorporating Innovation Policy and Risk Allocation into Patent Licensing Law," 69 *Indiana*

*Law Journal* 236 (1993); see also Server and Singleton, "Licensee Patent Validity," p. 171.

61. See, e.g., Massillion-Cleveland-Akron Sign Co. v. Golden State Adver. Co., 444 F.2d 425 (9th Cir. 1971) (holding a no-challenge provision unenforceable in light of *Lear*); Kraly v. Nat'l Distillers & Chemical Corp., 319 F. Supp 1349 (N.D. Ill. 1970) (dismissing an infringement action with prejudice when the parties entered into a settlement that included a no-challenge clause).

62. See MedImmune v. Genentech, p. 145 (Thomas, J., dissenting).

63. See Quanta v. LG Elecs., p. 2122 n.7.

64. I originally chose this title for a panel that I organized for the American Association of Law Schools Annual Conference in January 2011. Some of the papers from that panel appear in the *Hastings Science & Technology Law Journal*. 3 *Hastings Science & Technology Law Journal* (forthcoming).

65. See Jessie Cheng, "An Antitrust Analysis of Product Hopping in the Pharmaceutical Industry," 108 *Columbia Law Review* 1476 n.30 (2008); see also Henry G. Grabowski and John M. Vernon, "Brand Loyalty, Entry, and Price Competition in Pharmaceuticals after the 1984 Drug Act," 35 *Journal of Law & Economics* 335–336 (1992); Answer, Affirmative Defenses, and Counterclaims, p. 23, Bayer Schering Pharma AG v. Sandoz Inc., Nos. 08 Civ. 03710, 08 Civ. 08112 (S.D.N.Y. July 11, 2008), 2008 WL 4486682.

66. See Medicare Prescription Drug, Improvement, and Modernization Act of 2003, Pub. L. No. 108–173, §1101, 117 Stat. 2071 (2003) (codified as amended at 21 U.S.C. §355 (j)).

67. Press release, Henry A. Waxman, "Representative Henry A. Waxman on the Delay of Approval of Generic Drugs," www.citizen.org, Nov. 20, 2001 (accessed 8/9/10).

68. See Catherine J. K. Sandoval, "Pharmaceutical Reverse Payment Settlements: Presumptions, Procedural Burdens, and Covenants Not to Sue Generic Drug Manufacturers," 26 *Santa Clara Computer & High Technology Law Journal* 141 (2010); Matthew Avery, "Note: Continuing Abuse of the Hatch-Waxman Act by Pharmaceutical Patent Holders and the Failure of the 2003 Amendments," 60 *Hastings Law Journal* 171 (2008).

69. See Avery, "Continuing Abuse," pp. 175–176; Holly Soehnge, "The Drug Price Competition and Patent Term Restoration Act of 1984: Fine-Tuning the Balance between the Interests of Pioneer and Generic Drug Manufacturers," 58 *Food and Drug Law Journal* 54 (2003). See also 21 U.S.C. §355(j)(2)(A)(ii)–(iv).

70. See Avery, "Continuing Abuse," p. 176 (the Hatch-Waxman Act created an experimental-use exception to patent infringement, which provided that a "generic manufacturer may obtain a supply of a patented drug product during the life of the patent and conduct tests using that product if the purpose of those tests is to submit an application to FDA for approval").

71. See 21 U.S.C. §355(b)(2)(A)(iv).

72. See U.S. Department of Health and Human Services, Food and Drug Administration, Center for Drug Evaluation and Research, Office of Pharmaceutical Science, Office of Generic Drugs, "Orange Book: Approved Drug Products with Therapeutic Equivalence Evaluations," www.fda.gov (accessed 8/9/10).

73. See Federal Trade Commission, "Analysis to Aid Public Comment: In the Matter of Bristol-Myers Squibb Company," www.ftc.gov (accessed 8/9/10) ("The FDA has repeatedly stated that its role in patent listings is solely ministerial and that it lacks the resources and expertise to scrutinize patent information in the Orange Book." Moreover, "[a]s long as the patent remains listed, the brand-name company can continue to benefit from the availability of an automatic 30-month stay of FDA approval of ANDAs, by initiating a patent suit against generic applicants.").

74. 21 U.S.C. §355.

75. 35 U.S.C. §271.

76. See C. Scott Hemphill, "An Aggregate Approach to Antitrust: Using New Data and Rulemaking to Preserve Drug Competition," 109 *Columbia Law Review* 639 n.40 (2009) (noting that more than thirty articles and book chapters address the issue).

    Reverse payments have also been the subject of several legislative proposals in Congress, although none has been successful at this point. See, e.g., Protecting Consumer Access to Generic Drugs, H.R. 1706, 111th Congress (2009); Preserve Access to Affordable Generics Act, S. 3582, 109th Congress (2006); Drug Competition Act of 2002, S. 754, 107th Congress (2001).

77. See Hemphill, "Aggregate Approach to Antitrust," p. 638.

78. See ibid., pp. 638–639.

79. See Duncan Bucknell, "US Court of Appeal Invalidates Lipitor Patent due to Improper Claim Dependency," Aug. 17, 2006, www.mondaq.com (accessed 8/9/10) (noting the March 2010 expiration of the '893 patent); press release, Pfizer Inc., "U.S. Patent and Trademark Office Accepts Pfizer's Reissue Application on Lipitor Enantiomer Patent," www.pfizer.com, Jan. 6, 2009 (accessed 8/9/10) (noting the June 2011 expiration of the '995 patent).

80. See Pfizer Inc. v. Ranbaxy Labs., 457 F.3d 1290, 1292 (Fed. Cir. 2006).

81. See press release, Pfizer Inc., "Pfizer and Ranbaxy Settle Lipitor Patent Litigation Worldwide," www.pfizer.com, June 18, 2008 (accessed 8/9/10).

82. See Hemphill, "Aggregate Approach to Antitrust," p. 639 n.39 (citing "Pfizer Sues to Protect Lipitor, Caduet Process Patents," *Drug Industry Daily,* Mar. 27, 2008, and Complaint, pp. 1, 5–6, Pfizer Inc. v. Ranbaxy Labs., No. 08–164 (D. Del. Mar. 24, 2008) (suing for declaratory judgment of validity and infringement as to patents '511 and '740, both expiring in July 2016)).

83. See e.g., In re Tamoxifen Citrate Antitrust Litig., 466 F.3d 187, 212 (2d Cir. 2006); In re Cardizem CD Antitrust Litig., 332 F.3d 896 (6th Cir. 2003); In re Schering

Plough Corp., No. 9297 (F.T.C. Dec. 18, 2003), rev'd, 402 F.3d 1056 (11th Cir. 2005); Valley Drug Co. v. Geneva Pharmaceuticals Inc., 344 F.3d 1294 (11th Cir. 2003); In re Ciprofloxacin Hydrochloride Antitrust Litig., 544 F.3d 1323 (Fed. Cir. 2008).

84. See Valley Drug Co. v. Geneva Pharmaceuticals Inc., 344 F.3d 1294 (11th Cir. 2003); In re Schering Plough Corp., 402 F.3d 1056 (11th Cir. 2005); In re Tamoxifen Citrate Antitrust Litig., 466 F.3d 187, 212 (2d Cir. 2006); In re Ciprofloxacin Hydrochloride Antitrust Litig., 544 F.3d 1323 (Fed. Cir. 2008). But see In re Cardizem CD Antitrust Litig., 332 F.3d 896 (6th Cir. 2003).

85. For the details of the allegations see Answer, Affirmative Defenses, and Counterclaims, Bayer Schering Pharma AG v. Sandoz Inc., Nos. 08 Civ. 03710, 08 Civ. 08112 (S.D.N.Y. July 11, 2008), 2008 WL 4486682; see also Feldman, "Patent and Antitrust," ¶¶55–63 (describing the Yasmin example).

86. See ibid., pp. 29–30.

87. See ibid., p. 23.

88. See ibid.

89. See ibid.

90. See ibid., p. 24. Sandoz brought counterclaims under sections 1 and 2 of the Sherman Act, alleging that Bayer was unfairly trying to extend its monopoly. However, these counterclaims were dismissed due to market-definition issues. Bayer Schera Pharma AG v. Sandoz Inc., Nos. 08 Civ. 03710, 08 Civ. 08112, 2010 WL 1222012 (S.D.N.Y. Mar. 29, 2010).

91. See Answer, Affirmative Defenses, and Counterclaims, Bayer v. Sandoz, p. 30.

92. See Feldman, "Patent and Antitrust," ¶62.

93. See ibid.

94. See Class Action Complaint, Exhibit 1, La. Wholesale Drug Co. v. Sanofi-Aventis, 2009 U.S. Dist. LEXIS 77206 (S.D.N.Y. Aug. 28, 2009) (No. 07 Civ. 7343), 2007 U.S. Dist. Ct. Pleadings 500553.

95. See La. Wholesale Drug Co. v. Sanofi-Aventis, No. 07 Civ. 7343, 2009 U.S. Dist. LEXIS 77206, p. 1 (S.D.N.Y. Aug. 28, 2009).

96. See ibid., pp. 17–20.

97. Although Noerr-Pennington doctrine is typically associated with antitrust, its constitutional aspects have been applied in other contexts. See Citizens United v. FEC, 130 S. Ct. 907 (2010).

98. See Kaiser Found. Health Plan Inc. v. Abbott Labs. Inc., 552 F.3d 1044 (9th Cir. 2009).

99. Eastern R.R. Presidents Conference v. Noerr Motor Freight Inc., 365 U.S. 127 (1961).

100. See ibid.; see also United Mine Workers v. Pennington, 381 U.S. 657 (1965).

101. See Cal. Motor Transp. Co. v. Trucking Unlimited, 404 U.S. 510 (1972).

102. See Eastern R.R. v. Noerr, p. 144.

103. See City of Columbia v. Omni Outdoor Advertising, 499 U.S. 380 (1991).

104. Prof'l Real Estate Investors v. Columbia Pictures Indus., 508 U.S. 49 (1993).

105. See ibid., pp. 60–61. See also ibid., p. 58 (characterizing the Court's discussion in *Cal. Motor Transport* of the difficulty in evaluating whether a claim is baseless as endorsing an objective standard); Cal. Motor Transport v. Trucking Unlimited, p. 513.

106. See Prof'l Real Estate v. Columbia, p. 60 ("First, the lawsuit must be objectively baseless in the sense that no reasonable litigant could realistically expect success on the merits.").

107. C. R. Bard Inc. v. M3 Sys., 157 F.3d 1369 (Fed. Cir. 1998).

108. See Handgards Inc. v. Ethicon Inc., 601 F.2d 996 (9th Cir. 1979); Loctite Corp. v. Ultraseal Ltd., 781 F.2d 876 (Fed. Cir. 1985), overruled on other grounds by Nobelpharma AB v. Implant Innovations, 141 F.3d 1059 (Fed. Cir. 1998); Honeywell Int'l Inc. v. Universal Avionics Sys. Corp., 343 F. Supp. 2d 323 (D. Del. 2004).

109. USS-POSCO Indus. v. Contra Costa County Bldg. & Constr. Trades Council, 31 F.3d 810–811 (9th Cir. 1994) (citing Cal. Motor Transport. v. Trucking Unlimited, 404 U.S. 508).

110. See Cal. Motor Transport v. Trucking Unlimited, p. 513.

111. See Primetime 24 Joint Venture v. NBC, 219 F.3d 100–101 (2d Cir. 2000); Livingston Downs Racing Ass'n v. Jefferson Downs Corp., 192 F. Supp. 2d 538–539 (M.D. La. 2001).

112. Kaiser Found. Health Plan Inc. v. Abbott Labs. Inc., 552 F.3d 1033 (9th Cir. 2009).

113. See ibid., p. 1046.

114. See Nobelpharma AB v. Implant Innovations, 141 F.3d 1059 (Fed. Cir. 1998).

115. See C. R. Bard v. M3 Sys., p. 1369.

116. See Nobelpharma AB v. Implant Innovations, pp. 1067–1068.

117. See B. D. Daniel, "Walker Process Proof: The Proper Prescription," 41 *Rutgers Law Journal* 105 (2009).

118. Norbert M. Maier, Pilar Franco, and Wolfgang Lindner, "Separation of Enantiomers: Needs, Challenges, Perspectives," 906 *Journal of Chromatography* 3–33 (2001).

119. See Cheng, "Antitrust Analysis of Product Hopping," p. 1490.

120. See Schering Corp. v. Geneva Pharm., 339 F.3d 1373 (Fed. Cir. 2003) (holding that the metabolite of the drug Claritin was inherently produced by the drug itself and therefore not separately patentable); see also Dan L. Burk and Mark A. Lemley, "Inherency," 47 *William & Mary Law Review* 371 (2005) (expressing approval of the *Schering v. Geneva* analysis); Robin Feldman, "The Inventor's Contribution," 2005 *UCLA Journal of Law & Technology* 6 (2005) (agreeing with the result of *Schering v. Geneva* while disagreeing with the logic).

121. Jonathan J. Darrow, "The Patentability of Enantiomers: Implications for the Pharmaceutical Industry," 2007 *Stanford Technology Law Review* 2 (2007) (examining obviousness issues in the patentability of enantiomer under tests prior to the Supreme Court decision in KSR International Co. v. Teflex Inc., 550 U.S. 398 (2007)); Sweet, "Patentability of Chiral Drugs Post-KSR" (concluding that in a post-KSR prosecution climate, pharmaceutical houses are left to argue either that the results obtained using the single enantiomer are unexpectedly better than those obtained with the racemic compound or that the synthesis of the enantiomer was very challenging).

122. For example, a simple search of claims with the phrase "enantiomer thereof" yields 655 hits. See "Patent Searching Database," www.freepatentsonline.com (accessed 8/9/10).

123. See Harris, "Thwarting Generics."

124. Grill von Markus, "Vorsicht, Pharma—Wie die Industrie Ärzte manipuliert und Patienten täuscht," *Der Stern*, Aug. 14, 2007, available at www.stern.de (accessed 8/9/10).

125. See Cheng, "Antitrust Analysis of Product Hopping," p. 1514; "Over-the-Counter Drug Coverage Changes Marketing Strategies," *Drug Week*, Dec. 26, 2003, p. 401.

126. See First Amended Complaint and Demand for Jury Trial, pp. 36–37, Walgreen Co. v. AstraZeneca Pharm. L.P., 534 F. Supp. 2d. 146 (D.D.C. 2008) (No. 06–2084), 2006 WL 4527449 (asserting that once Prilosec became available over the counter, most managed-care organizations declined coverage for the generic version of Prilosec).

127. Walgreen Co. v. AstraZeneca Pharm. L.P., 534 F. Supp. 2d 146 (D.D.C. 2008).

128. See ibid., pp. 150–151 (comparing the case to *U.S. v. Microsoft* and *Abbott v. Teva)*; see also Abbott Labs. v. Teva Pharms. USA Inc., 432 F. Supp. 2d 408 (D. Del. 2006); United States v. Microsoft Corp., 253 F.3d 50 (D.C. Cir. 2001). For an exploration of defensive leveraging behavior, see Robin Feldman, "Defensive Leveraging in Antitrust," 87 *Georgetown Law Journal* 2079 (1999).

129. See Walgreen v. AstraZeneca, p. 151.

130. See ibid.

131. See, e.g. Michael Waldholz, "Prescriptions: Patients Need to View Drug Ads with Some Healthy Skepticism," *The Wall Street Journal*, July 11, 2002, p. D6; Cheng, "Antitrust Analysis of Product Hopping," pp. 1479–1480, 1488; see also Eric L. Cramer and Daniel Berger, "Superiority of Direct Proof of Monopoly Power and Anticompetitive Effects in Antitrust Cases Involving Delayed Entry of Generic Drugs," 39 *University of San Francisco Law Review* 119 (2004); James J. Wheaton, "Generic Competition and Pharmaceutical Innovation: The Drug Price Competition and Patent Term Restoration Act of 1984," 34 *Catholic University Law Review* 437 (1986).

132. Although the court mentions the expertise of physicians in the context of wise advisors to the patient, the analysis does not fully account for the time and training limitations on the average physician's ability to interpret results. See Walgreen v. AstraZeneca, p. 152.

133. Phillip E. Areeda and Herbert Hovenkamp, *Antitrust Law: An Analysis of Antitrust Principles and Their Application,* vol. 3, pt. 2, ch. 7, ¶704a (New York, 2007).

134. For extensive details of the scheme see Second Amended Answer, Affirmative Defenses, and Counterclaims, Abbott Labs. v. Teva Pharm. USA Inc., 432 F. Supp. 2d 408 (D. Del. 2006) (No. 02–1512), 2005 WL 6155984; see also Abbott v. Teva, 432 F. Supp. 2d 408. For a discussion of the case and its implications see Steve D. Shadowen, Keith B. Leffler, and Joseph T. Lukens, "Anticompetitive Product Changes in the Pharmaceutical Industry," 41 *Rutgers Law Review* 1 (2009); Stacey L. Dogan and Mark A. Lemley, "Antitrust Law and Regulatory Gaming," 87 *Texas Law Review* 685 (2009); Cheng, "Antitrust Analysis of Product Hopping."

135. Abbott Labs. v. Novopharm Ltd., Nos. 00 C 2141, 00 C 5094, 01 C 1914, 2002 U.S. Dist. LEXIS 4659 (N.D. Ill. Mar. 20, 2002).

136. Abbott v. Teva, 432 F. Supp. 2d 416 (D. Del. 2006).

137. See Second Amended Answer, Affirmative Defenses, and Counterclaims, ¶99, Abbott Labs. v. Teva Pharm. USA Inc., 432 F. Supp. 2d 408 (D. Del. 2006) (No. 02–1512), 2005 WL 6155984; see also Dogan and Lemley, "Antitrust Law and Regulatory Gaming," p. 712.

138. See ibid., Shadowen, Leffler, and Lukens, "Anticompetitive Product Changes," p. 75 (citing Trial Exhibit 317R, p. 24, Teva Pharm. Inc. v. Abbott Labs., No. 02–1512 (D. Del) (admitted on Nov. 17, 2008).

139. See Shadowen, Leffler, and Lukens, "Anticompetitive Product Changes," pp. 75–76.

140. See Abbott v. Teva, 432 F. Supp. 2d 408 (D. Del. 2006) (denying Abbott's motion to dismiss prior to trial).

## 6. Beyond the State of the Art

1. An earlier version of this chapter was published as an article, Robin Cooper Feldman, "Rethinking Rights in Biospace," 79 *S. Cal. L. Rev.* 1 (2005). It is included here with the permission of the *Southern California Law Review.*

2. Diamond v. Chakrabarty, 447 U.S. 303 (1980) (interpreting section 101 of the Patent Act, which lists patentable subject matter).

3. For example, Burk and Lemley advocate that, when determining inventors' rights, the invention should not reach unknown qualities because the inventors cannot show they are in possession of the invention if they do not recognize it.

However, when determining the rights of others, Burk and Lemley argue that a prior invention should reach unknown qualities (and anticipate future patents) because the public was already receiving the benefit of that invention. Dan L. Burk and Mark A. Lemley, "Inherency," 47 *William & Mary Law Review* 394–395 (2005).

4. In prior publications I have described the solution presented here as particularly appropriate in the uncertain arts. The bargain aspect of patents, however, suggests that the issues related to the lack of definite boundaries at the time of the patent grant are likely to play out in all fields.

5. Diamond v. Chakrabarty, p. 305.

6. Ibid.; John M. Conley and Roberte Makowski, "Back to the Future: Rethinking the Product of Nature Doctrine as a Barrier to Biotechnology Patents (Part II)," 85 *Journal of the Patent & Trademark Office Society* 371–372 (2003).

7. See Diamond v. Chakrabarty, pp. 305–306.

8. Ibid., p. 306.

9. See ibid., p. 307.

10. 35 U.S.C. §101.

11. Ibid.

12. See Diamond v. Chakrabarty, p. 308 (describing expansiveness of the terms) and p. 306 (describing the inventions as "laboratory created micro-organisms").

13. See ibid., p. 313.

14. See Commissioner of Patents and Trademarks, "Policy Statement on Patentability of Animals," 1077 *Official Gazette of the United States Patent and Trademark Office for Patents* 24 (1987), reprinted in Donald S. Chisum, *Chisum on Patents*, vol. 9, 24 app. (2010).

15. See ibid.

16. For a detailed description of the history and of modern controversies surrounding patenting genes see Robin Feldman, "Whose Body Is It Anyway? Human Cells and the Strange Effects of Property and Intellectual Property Law," 63 *Stanford. L. Rev.* 1377 (2010).

17. See, e.g., Chisum, *Chisum on Patents*, vol. 1, §1.02 (separating patentable subject matter into products and processes).

18. See 35 U.S.C. §101.

19. See Chisum, *Chisum on Patents*, vol. 3, §8.05.

20. See 35 U.S.C. §101 (describing patentable subject matter as "new and useful" inventions).

21. See, e.g., Schering Corp. v. Gilbert, 153 F.2d. 432 (2d Cir. 1946); Maurer v. Dickerson, 113 F. 874 (3d Cir. 1902); PTO, "Utility Examination Guidelines," p. 1095; See also Amgen Inc. v. Chugai Pharm. Co., 927 F.2d 1213 (Fed. Cir. 1991); In re Angstadt, 537 F.2d 503 (C.C.P.A. 1976).

22. See O'Reilly v. Morse, 56 U.S. (15 How) 113 (1853); Winner, "Enablement," pp. 610–611.

23. See Karl Drlica, *Understanding DNA and Gene Cloning: A Guide for the Curious* (Hoboken, N.J., 1997), p. 3.

24. See ibid., p. 5, figs. 1–2.

25. See ibid., pp. 2–3.

26. See Stephen A. Merrill, Richard C. Levin, and Mark B. Myers, eds., *A Patent System for the 21st Century* (Washington, D.C., 2005), p. 93; Kelly M. Jolley, "Reviews in Health Law: Patenting Technology Instead of Identity," 32 *Journal of Law Medicine & Ethics* 524 (2004). See also Amgen v. Chugai, p. 1206.

27. See Amgen v. Chugai, p. 1206.

28. Rebecca S. Eisenberg, "Reaching through the Genome," in John V. Duca and Mine K. Yucel, eds., *Science and Cents: Proceedings of the 2002 Conference on Exploring the Economics of Biotechnology* (2003), p. 106.

29. See ibid.

30. See W. Wayt Gibbs, "The Unseen Genome: Gems among the Junk," *Scientific American,* Nov. 2003, p. 48.

31. See ibid.

32. See, e.g., ibid.; Sabine Schmitt and Renato Paro, "Gene Regulation: A Reason for Reading Nonsense," 429 *Nature* 510 (2004); Misia Landau, "Junk DNA Yields New Kind of Gene," *Focus: "News from Harvard Medical, Dental and Public Health Schools,"* www.focus.hms.harvard.edu, June 4, 2004 (accessed 4/15/10).

33. C. Claiborne Ray, "Q & A: DNA Junk or Not?" *The New York Times,* Mar. 4, 2003, p. F2 (describing the effects of changes in two sections of junk DNA).

34. Ribonucleic acid (RNA) is synthesized by transcription of DNA or by copying of RNA. The three types of cellular RNA—mRNA, rRNA, and tRNA—play different roles in protein synthesis. See Harvey Lodish et al., *Molecular Cell Biology* (New York, 2000), p. G-15.

35. See Gibbs, "Unseen Genome," p. 48.

36. See Bruce Alberts et al., *Molecular Biology of the Cell* (New York, 2002), pp. 1375–1376.

37. Each cell contains all of an individual's genes, but only certain genes will be activated in each cell.

38. For example, in Noelle v. Lederman, the Federal Circuit stated the following: "[B]ased on our past precedent, as long as an applicant has disclosed a 'fully characterized antigen,' either by its structure, formula, chemical name, or physical properties, or by depositing the protein in a public depository, the applicant can then claim an antibody by its binding affinity to that described antigen." Noelle v. Lederman, 355 F.3d 1349 (Fed. Cir. 2004) (denying patent because the applicant failed to describe not only the antibody but also the antigen to

which it binds). See also United States Patent and Trademark Office, *Written Description Training Materials* (2008), pp. 45–46, available at http://www.uspto .gov/web/menu/written.pdf (accessed 4/15/10).

39. Alberts et al., *Molecular Biology*, p. 1376.

40. An exception to this rule is a means-plus-function claim.

41. See, e.g., Noelle v. Lederman, p. 1349.

42. Jennifer L. Davis, "Comment: The Test of Primary Cloning: A New Approach to the Written Description Requirement in Biotechnological Patents," 20 *Santa Clara Computer & High Technology Law Journal* 478 (2004). See also Enzo Biochem Inc. v. Gen-Probe Inc., 296 F.3d 1324–1325 (Fed. Cir. 2002).

43. See Eli Benjamini, Richard Coico, and Geoffrey Sunshine, *Immunology* (Hoboken, N.J., 2000), pp. 65–79.

44. See ibid., pp. 51–52.

45. Schering Corp. v. Amgen Inc., 222 F.3d 1347 (Fed. Cir. 2000).

46. See ibid., p. 1349.

47. See ibid., p. 1352.

48. See ibid.

49. See ibid.

50. For the purposes of this book I refer to the time of the invention. One could further consider, however, whether the proper moment for measuring the time of the invention is the moment of creation or the moment of the patent application.

51. Ibid., p. 1321.

52. See ibid.

53. See ibid.

54. Ibid.

55. See ibid.

56. See U.S. Patent No. 5,547,933 (filed June 7, 1995).

57. Amgen v. Hoechst II, p. 1321.

58. Ibid., p. 1322.

59. Amgen Inc. v. Hoechst Marion Roussel Inc., 126 F. Supp. 2d 85 (D. Mass. 2001) [hereinafter Amgen v. Hoechst I].

60. Ibid., p. 95.

61. See Amgen v. Hoechst II, p. 1328.

62. See ibid., p. 1329.

63. See ibid., p. 1331 (regarding written description); ibid., p. 1335 (regarding enablement).

64. See ibid., p. 1335 (quoting Amgen v. Hoechst I, p. 160) (internal citation omitted). See also ibid., pp. 1338–1339 (reiterating that the lower court applied the proper logic by upholding the patent based on both written description and enablement).

65. See Schering v. Amgen, p. 1353.

66. See ibid., p. 1349. For example, in response to a viral infection, the body may secrete interferons that bind to receptors on noninfected neighboring cells, inducing those cells to produce proteins that increase the resistance to the infection. See Alberts et al., *Molecular Biology,* p. 884.

67. See Schering v. Amgen, p. 1349.

68. See Alberts et al., *Molecular Biology,* pp. 1284, 1300–1301.

69. See Schering v. Amgen, p. 1350. The patent holder successfully isolated the gene that codes for an interferon, creating recombinant molecules that contained the genes and could be transferred to host cells to continue producing the desired interferon. The patent claimed recombinant molecules that contain the gene and genetically engineered microorganisms that contain such molecules. See ibid., pp. 1350–1351.

70. See ibid., pp. 1349, 1352. See also Shahla Al-Hasso, "Interferons: An Overview," *U.S. Pharmacist,* www.uspharmacist.com (accessed 10/21/07) (on file with author).

71. See ibid. See also Schering v. Amgen, p. 1352.

72. See Schering v. Amgen, p. 1352.

73. See ibid., pp. 1353–1354.

74. See ibid., p. 1349.

75. See ibid., p. 1353 (finding that the term in the patent could not enlarge the patent's scope to include technology arising after its filing).

76. Phillip B. Philbin and Carmen E. Griffin, "Intellectual Property Law," 58 *SMU Law Review* 986 (2005).

77. See, e.g., Schering v. Amgen, p. 1351 (referring to the "pre-trial Markman hearing"). See also Markman v. Westview Instruments Inc., 517 U.S. 378 (1996). For a detailed description of the widely varying district court procedural rules for Markman hearings see Janice M. Mueller, *An Introduction to Patent Law* (New York, 2003), pp. 232–234.

78. See, e.g., Key Pharms. v. Hercon Labs. Corp., 161 F.3d 713 (Fed. Cir. 1998). See also Cybor Corp. v. FAS Techs. Inc., 138 F.3d 1456 (Fed. Cir. 1998) (en banc) (establishing de novo appellate review for claim construction).

79. Ibid., p. 1353.

80. Ibid.

81. See, e.g., Bell Atl. Network Servs. Inc. v. Covad Communs. Group Inc., 262 F.3d 1268 (Fed. Cir. 2001).

82. See Schering v. Amgen, p. 1353.

83. Ibid., p. 1352 (internal citation omitted).

84. See ibid., p. 1353 (finding that the patentee expressly limited the meaning of the term "IFN-a" to define only the leukocyte interferon described in the original application).

85. At the time of the amendment scientists already knew that IFN-a itself had subtypes beyond what had been known at the time of the invention. Even the *Nature* article cited in the amendment mentions subtypes of IFN-a interferons. See ibid., pp. 1352–1353.

86. Chiron v. Genentech, p. 1247.

87. See ibid., p. 1250.

88. See Alberts et al., *Molecular Biology*, pp. 1375–1376.

89. See Donald Voet, Judith G. Voet, and Charlotte W. Pratt, *Fundamentals of Biochemistry* (Hoboken, N.J., 2008), pp. 95, G-2.

90. See Alberts et al., *Molecular Biology*, p. 1358.

91. See ibid.

92. See ibid.

93. See, e.g., Chiron v. Genentech, p. 1252.

94. See Voet, Voet, and Pratt, *Biochemistry*, p. 213.

95. See Alberts et al., *Molecular Biology*, p. 476.

96. See ibid.

97. See ibid.

98. See Chiron v. Genentech, pp. 1250–1251.

99. Ibid., p. 1251.

100. Ibid., p. 1250.

101. Ibid.

102. Ibid.

103. Ibid.

104. Ibid., p. 1251.

105. See ibid., pp. 1251–1252.

106. See ibid.

107. See ibid.

108. Ibid.

109. See ibid. Although the case did not discuss this aspect of the claim, presumably the claim was intended to reach all antibodies that bind to Her2 regardless of their binding location or method of interaction with Her2.

110. See ibid., p. 1252.

111. See ibid., p. 1251.

112. See generally Mueller, *Patent Law*, pp. 296–329.

113. 35 U.S.C. §112.

114. See, e.g., Grant v. Raymond, 31 U.S. 247 (1832) (noting that description ensures that, after the privilege expires, the public receives the benefit for which the privilege was granted).

115. See Evans v. Eaton, 20 U.S. 433–434 (1822).

116. For a description of the evolving role of 112, see Robin Feldman, "The Inventor's Contribution," 2005 *UCLA Journal of Law & Technology* 6 (2005).

117. Regents v. Eli Lilly, p. 1559.

118. See Univ. of Rochester v. G. D. Searle & Co., 358 F.3d 921–922 (Fed. Cir. 2004), reh'g and reh'g en banc denied, 375 F.3d 1303 (Fed. Cir. 2004) (Rader, J. dissenting) (describing the *Lilly* case), cert. denied, 125 S. Ct. 629 (2004).

119. See ibid., p. 922 n.5; ibid., p. 926.

120. See, e.g., Chiron v. Genentech, p. 1255.

121. See Feldman, "Inventor's Contribution," ¶7.

122. See Chiron v. Genentech, p. 1251.

123. Ibid., p. 1252 (framing the case as an appeal from determinations concerning written description and enablement).

124. In re Hogan, 559 F.2d 595 (C.C.P.A. 1977).

125. Plant Genetic Sys., N.V. v. DeKalb Genetics Corp., 315 F.3d 1335 (Fed. Cir. 2003).

126. See In re Hogan, p. 595.

127. Ibid., p. 597.

128. See 35 U.S.C. §132(a).

129. In re Hogan, p. 600.

130. See ibid., pp. 600–601.

131. See ibid., p. 606.

132. Plant Genetic Sys. v. DeKalb Genetics, pp. 1340–1341.

133. Ibid., p. 1340.

134. See ibid.

135. See Chiron v. Genentech, pp. 1256–1257.

136. See ibid., p. 1255 (finding that the patent holder could not have described antibodies beyond the state of the art at the time of the invention).

137. Moba, B. V. v. Diamond Automation Inc., 325 F.3d 1322–1327 (Fed. Cir. 2003) (Rader, J., concurring); Enzo Biochem Inc. v. Gen-Probe Inc., 323 F.3d 976–983 (Fed. Cir. 2002) (Rader, J., dissenting).

138. See Univ. of Rochester v. G. D. Searle, 375 F.3d 1307–1314 (Fed. Cir. 2004) (Rader, J., dissenting).

139. Moba v. Diamond, p. 1323.

140. See 35 U.S.C. §102.

141. See Chisum, *Chisum on Patents*, vol. 1, §3.02[1].

142. See Helifix Ltd. v. Blok-Lok Ltd., 208 F.3d 1347 (Fed. Cir. 2000).

143. Similarly, although the test for anticipation requires a single reference and should not combine prior references, a court may look at additional references to interpret what a person of ordinary skill in the art would understand. See Telemac Cellular Corp. v. Topp Telecom Inc., 247 F.3d 1328 (Fed. Cir. 2001). Understandably, courts have experienced some difficulty in distinguishing between the use of extrinsic evidence to explain a piece of prior art, which is permissible, and combining two pieces of prior art, which is not. See Chisum, *Chisum on Patents*, vol. 1, §3.02[1][d] n.26 (citing discussion of this dilemma in

Fenton Golf Trust v. Cobra Golf Inc., No. 97 C 247, 1998 U.S. Dist. LEXIS 8452, p. *1 (N.D. Ill. 1998)).

144. See, e.g., Schering v. Geneva, p. 1377; Brassica Protection Products LLC v. Sunrise Farms (In re Cruciferous Sprout Litig.), 301 F.3d 1349 (Fed. Cir. 2002) [hereinafter In re Cruciferous]; MEHL/Biophile Int'l Corp. v. Milgraum, 192 F.3d 1365 (Fed. Cir. 1999). See also Chisum, *Chisum on Patents*, vol. 1, §3.03[2][c].

145. Schering Corp. v. Geneva Pharms. Inc., 339 F.3d 1373 (Fed. Cir. 2003).

146. See ibid., p. 1375.

147. Ibid.

148. See ibid., pp. 1375–1376.

149. See ibid., p. 1375.

150. See, e.g., Jean O. Lanjouw, "A New Global Patent Regime for Diseases: U.S. and International Legal Issues," 16 *Harvard Journal of Law & Technology* 94–95 (2002) (defining the term); Robert M. Schulman, "A Review of Significant 2003 Federal Circuit Decisions Affecting Chemical, Pharmaceutical, and Biotech Inventions," *Journal of Proprietary Rights*, vol. 16, no. 3 (2004).

151. See Schering v. Geneva, pp. 1375–1376.

152. See ibid., p. 1376.

153. See ibid.

154. See ibid., p. 1377.

155. See ibid.

156. See ibid.

157. In re Cruciferous, 301 F.3d 1351–1352 (Fed. Cir. 2002).

158. See ibid., p. 1345.

159. See ibid.

160. See ibid.

161. See ibid.

162. Ibid., pp. 1345–1346; ibid., p. 1350.

163. See ibid., p. 1351.

164. See ibid., p. 1349.

165. See ibid., pp. 1349–1350.

166. Ibid., p. 1351.

167. See ibid., p. 1350.

168. Ibid., p. 1350 (internal citations omitted).

169. See ATD Corp. v. Lydall Inc., 159 F.3d 545 (Fed. Cir. 1998); Glaxo Inc. v. Novopharm Ltd., 52 F.3d 1047 (Fed. Cir. 1995); Continental Can Co. v. Monsanto Co., 948 F.2d 1268–1269 (Fed. Cir. 1991). See also Chisum, *Chisum on Patents*, vol. 1, §3.03[2][c] (noting that Federal Circuit opinions have oscillated on the question of whether a person of ordinary skill in the art must recognize the existence of an inherent feature of prior art). Compare In re Seaborg, 328 F.2d 998–999

(C.C.P.A. 1964) (finding lack of anticipation because the claimed product, if produced in the prior art process, was produced in such miniscule amounts and under such conditions that its presence was undetectable).

170. See In re Cruciferous, pp. 1351–1352.

171. See Schering v. Geneva, p. 1380.

172. Elan Pharms. I, 304 F.3d 1221 (Fed. Cir. 2002).

173. See ibid., p. 1228.

174. Elan Pharms. Inc. v. Mayo Found. for Med. Educ. & Research, 314 F.3d 1299 (Fed. Cir. 2002) (en banc) [hereinafter Elan Pharms. II].

175. Elan Pharms. Inc. v. Mayo Found. for Med. Educ. & Research, 346 F.3d 1051 (Fed. Cir. 2003) (replacement opinion) [hereinafter Elan Pharms. III].

176. See Elan Pharms. I, p. 1228.

177. See Elan Pharms. III, p. 1054. This holding fits logically with enablement's traditional role of ensuring that an inventor adequately teaches those skilled in the art how to practice the invention. If a patent reference, for example, serves to bring something into the prior art so that future inventors cannot claim it, then that reference must actually teach those skilled in the art how to accomplish the invention. See ibid., pp. 1056–1057.

178. See, e.g., Amgen v. Hoechst II, p. 1313.

179. Compare Schering v. Amgen, p. 1347.

180. Schering v. Chiron, p. 1247.

181. See Derzko, "Hatch-Waxman Scheme," p. 221 (noting that the court's holding in *Geneva* will eliminate some types of metabolite claims and that, to the extent that metabolite claims constitute evergreening, the case will dampen incentives for certain forms of evergreening).

182. See Feldman, "Inventor's Contribution," ¶¶119–125.

183. See Burk and Lemley, *"Inherency,"* p. 374 (arguing that confusion in inherency law is unnecessary given that the facts of inherency cases offer a simple way to understand them).

184. Ibid., p. 388.

185. Ibid. (outlining a proposed public-benefit test).

186. For example, the rule forbids patenting a metabolite formed in the process of ingesting an earlier drug but allows patenting a by-product formed in the process of producing an earlier invention where the by-product was discarded as a waste product. Compare ibid., pp. 380–381 (describing Schering v. Geneva), with ibid., pp. 375–376 (describing Tilghman v. Proctor, 102 U.S. 707 (1880)), and ibid., p. 382 (describing Edison Electric Light Co. v. Novelty Incandescent Lamp Co., 167 F. 977 (3d Cir. 1909)). Thus, the rule brings into harmony some difficult cases.

187. See Schering v. Geneva, pp. 1375–1376.

188. See Schering Corp. v. Geneva Pharms. Inc., 348 F.3d 993 (Fed. Cir. 2003) (Newman, J., dissenting).

189. Compare ibid., p. 994 (objecting to the rule that prior art can anticipate even as to unknown elements and asking whether the panel intends to disallow the patenting of any newly discovered product found in an organism).

190. See Burk and Lemley, *"Inherency,"* p. 394 (noting that the "result, while seemingly odd in its asymmetry, makes sense as a policy matter").

191. See Rasmussen v. Smithkline Beecham Corp., 413 F.3d 1325 (Fed. Cir 2005) (citing Application of Hafner, 410 F.2d 1404 (C.C.P.A. 1969); see also Burk and Lemley, *"Inherency,"* p. 385.

192. See Amgen v. Hoechst II, p. 1313.

193. See In re Hogan, p. 595.

194. See Schering v. Amgen, p. 1353.

195. See Plant Genetic Sys. v. DeKalb Genetics, p. 1335 (holding that a patent holder can reach things that could not have been contemplated in the art at the time of the invention but not things desired but difficult to obtain).

196. See earlier discussion describing the court's holding in *Chiron* and noting its failure to follow *Hoechst*.

197. See Elan Pharms. III, p. 1054.

198. For those interested in seeing a discussion of this approach in the context of the doctrine of equivalents see Robin Feldman, "Rethinking Rights in Biospace," 79 *Southern California Law Review* 41–43 (2005).

199. See Feldman, "Inventor's Contribution," ¶¶119–125 (arguing that disclosure may include things not directly expressed but known in the art at the time).

# Acknowledgments

I wish to thank Matt Avery, Margreth Barrett, Jyh-Kwang (Matt) Chen, Susan Creighton, Tom Ewing, Rick Frenkel, William Garfinkel, Shubha Ghosh, Selwyn Goldberg, Charles Tait Graves, Sarah Harrington, Scott Hemphill, Herbert Hovenkamp, Esther Kepplinger, Catherine Kirkman, Joel Kirschbaum, Chuck Knapp, Evan Lee, Jeff Lefstin, Ethan Leib, Mark Lemley, Chris Mammen, Adam Mossoff, Gary Nolan, Vern Norviel, Augie Rakow, Anie Roche, Fred Server, Darien Shanske, Eric Wesenberg, George Wilman, and Alan Yu for taking the time to provide comments and insights. I am also grateful to the participants in the Ninth and Tenth Annual Intellectual Property Scholars Conference for their comments. Additionally, I wish to thank those practitioners who were kind enough to share their experiences but did not wish to be named. I also extend my thanks to Harold Wegner and Dennis Crouch, whose blogs and listservs are a constant source of information and interesting perspectives.

In addition, I am grateful to Tom Abeles, Michael Adelsheim, Ian Anderson, James Beard, Tom Boardman, Gabor Brasnjo, Dana Drusinsky, Tanya Dubar, Matthew Elliott, Deborah Furth, Igor Hiller, Cheryl Lee Johnson, Lawrence Kang, Jason Kanter, Sarah Lange, Sean McGilvray, James Nachtwey, William Newsom, Mike Olds, Adam Powell, Pilar Stillwater, Peter Touschner, and Jeanne Yang for their research assistance. I also thank Melissa Dean, who followed in her brother's footsteps in providing research assistance for me. I am grateful beyond measure to Brittany Yang not only for carrying out her excellent research but also for supervising the research team and assembling the manuscript. Her work was beyond compare. I am also greatly indebted to Patricia Dyck, whose research and insights significantly shaped the chapter on subject matter patentability. I am indebted to U. C.

Hastings Public Services Librarian Linda Weir for her insights and research support and to Stephen Lothrop, Lesley King, and Divina Morgan for their patience and manuscript assistance. I also wish to thank the Chip Robertson Fund for financial support of the project, as well as Production Editor Melody Negron for her ever-patient work and Nanette McGuinness for spectacular proofreading. Finally, I am grateful to Harvard University Press Senior Editor Elizabeth Knoll for her encouragement and her faith in the project.

Portions of Chapter 6 were published as an article, Robin Cooper Feldman, "Rethinking Rights in Biospace," 79 S. Cal. L. Rev. 1 (2005). This material is incorporated here with the permission of the Southern California Law Review.

# Index